The Management
of People in Mergers
and Acquisitions

The Management of People in Mergers and Acquisitions

Teresa A. Daniel
and Gary S. Metcalf

QUORUM BOOKS
Westport, Connecticut • London

Library of Congress Cataloging-in-Publication Data

Daniel, Teresa A., 1957–
    The management of people in mergers and acquisitions / Teresa A. Daniel, Gary S. Metcalf.
        p.   cm.
    Includes bibliographical references and index.
    ISBN 1–56720–369–8 (alk. paper)
    1. Consolidation and merger of corporations—Management.   2. Organizational change.   I. Metcalf, Gary S., 1957–   II. Title.
    HD58.8D344   2001
    658.3—dc21   00–062776

British Library Cataloguing in Publication Data is available.

Library of Congress Catalog Card Number: 00–062776
ISBN: 1–56720–369–8

First published in 2001

Quorum Books, 88 Post Road West, Westport, CT 06881
An imprint of Greenwood Publishing Group, Inc.
www.quorumbooks.com

Printed in the United States of America

The paper used in this book complies with the Permanent Paper Standard issued by the National Information Standards Organization (Z39.48–1984).

10 9 8 7 6 5 4 3 2 1

Contents

Acknowledgments

Any real learning involves the experiences of other people, in addition to our own. We'd like to thank each and every one of the employees and professional colleagues with whom we've struggled through times of angst and transition—who have helped us make sense of what were oftentimes periods of confusion and turmoil while they occurred. We hope that what this book gives back is not only a way to make sense of the chaos, but the possibility of doing future deals better.

Special thanks go to Rick Wall and Stuart Webb for their input and review of specific sections. And a very special thanks to Martha Ann Daniel (our children's grandmother) who helped make the time possible to write this book.

Introduction

This book began as a very practical handbook for human resources professionals involved in merger or acquisition activity. But as it evolved, we found a need to ground our ideas in a slightly more theoretical context—to provide a rationale for why we were making the specific recommendations that we do. The practical and specific recommendations are based on our experiences of what has not worked, as well as what seems to have been much more successful. They are also based on a good deal of digging and contemplation about *why* things have worked or not. But the essence of the book has not been lost—it is still intended to provide direct and useful information for those involved in mergers or acquisitions, or similar magnitudes of organizational change.

The first chapter provides an overview of recent merger and acquisition activity and some of the issues this presents. The next three chapters (2–4) provide the theoretical base for our positions about the importance of the human side of these deals. Some readers may choose to skip directly to Chapter 5, to begin with the more practical aspects. (Those readers who automatically toss anything longer than a three-line e-mail note can just go straight to Chapter 14, which summarizes the key concepts without the detail of accomplishing them. You can always come back to the earlier chapters as time and interest allow.) The appendices provide a series of checklists for use in implementing many of the very specific recommendations made throughout the book.

Chapters 5–11 provide increasing levels of detail about the process of mergers and acquisitions and about the very practical issues involved in them. The focus is on human resources as the key manager of the human side of such deals, and therefore many of the "how-to" suggestions are in the form of communications, compensation, benefits plans, and the like. More general areas of interest to a broader range of executives and managers are also covered, including a notion of leadership that goes well beyond those in traditional positions of power and authority. In the end, it is the way that all of these come together and, more importantly, the underlying values and beliefs that they represent which will make a difference.

As noted, Chapter 14 is a summary of the key points of the book. These are the practices we have found to make a difference in the human side of the equation. Of course, no amount of focus on human issues can overcome a deal simply done badly. If a deal maker has gotten him- or herself emotionally involved in a bidding war and run the price of the deal beyond what can be recouped, no amount of effort by the employees involved will compensate for this. (And typically, the first thing to happen in such deals is deeper employee cuts in order to try to gain dramatic early cost savings.)

The final chapter is a story of a rather long history of mergers and acquisitions. As shown, despite the recent attention that such deals have attracted, they are not all that new. In fact, this century has begun not all that differently from the last in this respect; and in some companies, growth through mergers and acquisitions has been an ongoing activity since the beginning of the 1900s.

The key question is whether we've learned anything of real value in all that time—anything that can help improve the success of the deals or the fate of the people impacted by them—or ideally, of course, both. The way that deals are still done would suggest not. But from our experiences, there should be hope, if only in the potential. Putting what we've learned into practice is the challenge. We hope the tools and ideas outlined in this book provide some answers for the opportunities that will undoubtedly occur as you work through the complexities that any major organizational changes will surely present.

The Management
of People in Mergers
and Acquisitions

Chapter 1

Why Merge if Most Deals Fail?

The goals of this book are to provide human resources (HR) professionals with practical help in surviving a merger or acquisition and to help the organizations involved achieve the results they intend when striking the deals. As will be shown, there's a great deal to be learned about bringing organizations together. Working as a HR practitioner through a company's growth cycle is an exciting proposition, though it can be an intense, complex, and somewhat daunting time as well.

Cowritten by an HR and legal practitioner and an organizational development (OD) professional for HR people such as yourself, the goal of this book is to provide an advance framework for the issues you will likely face. It is also intended to offer suggestions and alternative solutions for helping you and your organization through the myriad of complexities that these sorts of business combinations typically create.

Even while we're writing this, the landscape of merger and acquisition (M&A) activity is changing—just as it is for many other aspects of business. The rules of thumb in one market or industry may sound entirely foreign to those who work in another. Preparation that may take small armies of attorneys and months of work for a company with decades of history may be completed between small teams over a day or two if the acquisition target is a small start-up company. Contrast, for example, the acquisition activities of Cisco with the merger of Exxon and Mobil. Between 1993 and 1999, Cisco completed at least 43 acquisitions worth over $20 billion. These involved both growth and expansion strategies—to acquire needed talent and to expand into new areas of converging technology. In many cases, the deals themselves were made in no more than a few days and completed in a month or two. So far, Cisco has maintained a "no layoff" policy for acquired companies and has experienced only about a 2% turnover of those employees.[1]

Exxon's merger with Mobil alone was valued at about $81 billion and created (at least for the moment) the largest corporation in the world with an estimated market value of $250 billion.[2, 3] But despite its continued dominance in world energy, the petroleum industry is in its "mature" years. Mergers and acquisitions here are not about growth—they're about competing for increased market share and decreasing competition and searching for new levels of efficiency. (Reportedly, a statement was made some years ago at a high-level oil industry meeting that "none of us is going to make any money until some of us get out of the business.")

The Exxon–Mobil deal took 11 months to pass Federal Trade Commission (FTC) scrutiny after it was officially announced, and it has been speculated that it could take five years to complete integration. Together, both companies employed teams of lawyers from at least eight different law firms to review corporate, tax, and employment law issues, as well as U.S. and European antitrust provisions. They created more than 31 million pages and 1,000 CD-ROMs of documents initially and another 240,000 pages of responses to federal follow-up questions.[4, 5]

As opposed to a "no layoff" policy, the companies initially speculated that they would terminate 9,000 employees. Following federal antitrust review, the latest estimate is 16,000 employees to be terminated, and over 2,400 service stations and at least one refinery to be sold.[6]

As dramatically different as these two examples would appear to be, there are still some fundamental steps that are involved in most transactions and basic issues that need to be addressed. Part of the goal of this book is to give you an overview of the steps of a merger or acquisition, the usual issues that arise, and the essential information you'll need for beginning the HR part of the process. But a second goal is to raise some of the human issues that you'll face which, although not always understood as part of the process, may impact whether or not the deal is a success in the end.

It's helpful to understand at the outset that there are many forms that M&A deals can take. An alliance may be as simple as a licensing agreement for a product, service, or trademark or as complex as a merger of two independent entities. In between, there are strategic partnerships or joint ventures and outright acquisitions of a company for stock or cash (or a combination of both). Each arrangement carries with it its own set of complexities and requirements. But all require incorporating people and practices from previous settings into new ones, often involving changes in very basic assumptions and understandings.

In reality, mergers and acquisitions, and other forms of alliances and joint ventures, are only the latest approaches to organizational change. They represent something of a "plug and play," modularized approach to growth, as opposed to a more traditional approach of internally driven growth and development. So while the broader issue is ongoing organizational change, we'll focus our discussions primarily on mergers and acquisitions, as these are the types of partnerships that most change the basic structure of the organizations involved, and most affect the employees who make up the organizations.

All deals are done with some goal in mind. Sometimes this is clearly stated, and sometimes the real goal seems to be masked beneath the activity itself. But the primary goal of most mergers and acquisitions has to do, ultimately, with increasing the value of the company. And interestingly, as will be shown, this central goal has been achieved in less than half of all M&A transactions.[7]

SOME HISTORY ON RECENT DEAL MAKING

During the past decade, M&A activity has steadily increased as measured both by the total number of deals and by the value of those transactions. In 1998, some 20,448 transactions were completed worth a total of $2 *trillion* dollars. In 1999, M&A activity topped $3 trillion. KKR's buyout of RJR Nabisco in 1988, at $25 billion, set a record that wasn't topped until 1997 by MCI WorldCom's deal for MCI Communications, at $37 billion. Then in 1999, Sprint Corp. completed a $115 billion merger with MCI WorldCom, Vodafone AirTouch is currently up to $125 billion in their bid for Mannesmann AG,[8] and both deals are eclipsed by America Online's merger with Time Warner, initially valued at over $156 billion.[9]

The average merger or acquisition deal, of course, is far less than these extremes. But the average deal (excluding those valued at less than $50 million) has now risen to $1 billion.[10]

In contrast to this explosion in M&A activity, though, is the fact that few of these transactions have lived up to their promises. In fact, according to one study, 83% failed to increase shareholder value, and 53% actually reduced it.[11] And this is not just a recent phenomenon. Several studies over the past 75 years have concluded that *less than half of mergers and acquisitions actually produced their expected value.* In many cases, value was actually destroyed, and the company's performance after the deal was significantly below what it had been before the deal.[12]

WHY MERGE IF SO MANY DEALS FAIL?

Companies have many reasons supporting their decision to merge with or acquire a new firm. The two most prevalent reasons cited are to accelerate growth or to expand or protect current market share. Other reasons given are to acquire new technology or a new business segment, to reduce competition, to increase efficiency, to acquire intellectual or physical capital, to ensure predictability of raw materials needed for production, or to achieve a global presence. And in the language of "make or buy" decisions (do something internally or acquire it from the outside), few companies have the time or the expertise to "grow their own" everything and still keep up with the pace of change and competition.

In fact, the trend for many of the dominant Internet-related companies seems to be to avoid their own research and development costs by simply allowing entrepreneurs and venture capitalists in Silicon Valley to create new technologies, then acquire the ones that prove to be of worth.[13] But buying cutting edge expertise comes at a premium. When IBM acquired Lotus for $3.5 billion, the accounting value was only $230 million.[14] And in 1997, Cisco was cited as paying the equivalent of *$2 million per employee* in its acquisitions in order to gain the talent it needed.[15]

The amount of money involved in these deals, combined with the risk, might lead one to believe that mergers and acquisitions are done only according to strict business analysis or necessity. But many factors seem to be involved.

Competition and market factors are often cited as leaving no choice. The drive is for ever-greater efficiencies and economies of scale. Companies that survive are the ones that outlast or eliminate competitors, increase market share and customer bases, and minimize overhead costs.

As industries mature, the drive for efficiencies increases. What were new innovations that could be sold at a premium quickly become commodities where price is the only crucial factor. Quality and performance become so similar that they are taken for granted, and customers simply look for the best deals. This happened quickly in the computer hardware industry where "off-brands" were considered of questionable quality early on but where now the great majority rely on very similar internal components, and few noticeable differences in reliability exist. As a result, price competition increased and profit margins decreased. Only the continuing leaps in speed and memory drive personal computer (PC) sales, with some innovation in size and weight of laptops, and some customization, such as units built specifically for Internet connection rather than stand-alone computing. But a handful of major computer manufacturers is all that seems necessary, at present, to meet sales demands.

Computer software, on the other hand, has continued to maintain larger profit margins. We have not yet arrived at a static number of applications or software programs produced by an excessive number of companies. While Microsoft has established extreme dominance in basic operating systems for PCs, and there are only a few choices for applications such as word processing and spreadsheets, there seems to be no limit yet to the number of games and other programs that can still be developed. And the true growth, of course, lies in Internet applications, which at this point remains a wide open universe.

In addition to traditional market forces of supply and demand and economies of scale, broader political and economic changes have also driven a long-term trend toward consolidation. These include the growth of free trade and new markets that have opened, deregulation of industries such as power and telecommunications, and the effects of technology on the management of global business.[16]

But whatever apparent external forces might be driving changes, never underestimate the importance of ego as a factor. Sometimes it is management's irrational exuberance about the strategic importance of the deal or simply enthusiasm built up during the excitement of the negotiations, which can be both sexy and seductive. In some cases, it is simply that even experienced acquirers sometimes get too "attached" and "emotional" about a deal or fall in love with the *idea* of the deal.

And occasionally, there is the lure of wealth. Part of the incentive, as well as the means, behind this immense growth is the rise in the stock value of corporations. More than half of all M&A deals are now stock transactions rather than financed with cash. In turn, the stock market seems to be rewarding corporations for size. And transactions based solely on exchanges of stock tend to be much looser about valuations of assets.

By using the increase in stock value to leverage growth and acquisitions, companies get rewarded with even greater stock value. Based on recent initial public offerings (IPOs), shares can treble or quintuple overnight from the opening offering price, making the blocks of stock options owned by key executives worth small (or not so small) fortunes. (This is not as true in Europe, especially in countries such as France, where stock options are viewed and taxed quite differently than in the United States.)

Add to all this the current accounting standards favoring stock mergers, plus the potential gain for the investment bankers that work out the details. When combined with the fear by executives and boards of directors that it's "eat or be eaten," it's easier to understand why so much of the incentive behind these deals is focused on short-term results rather than long-term survival of the organization.

Not every merger or acquisition is touched by Midas, though. In fact, during the first nine months of 1999, the stock of acquiring companies actually *dropped* an average of 0.25% following the announcement of a deal.[17] In some notable examples, shares of Qwest Communications International lost 24% of their value the day following the announcement of a planned acquisition of U.S. West Inc. and Frontier Corp.[18] Burlington Northern Sante Fe Corp. announced a planned merger with Canadian National Railway and saw its stock value drop 13% as a result.[19] And shares of Pharmacia fell from over $53 a share to under $37 on news of its planned takeover of Monsanto.[20]

As noted above, things don't necessarily get better with time. AT&T purchased NCR for $7.4 billion in stock and spun it off to shareholders four years later in a deal valued at $3.4 billion. Novell bought Word-Perfect for $1.4 billion and sold it to Corel for $124 million. Smithkline Beecham paid $2.3 billion for Diversified Pharmaceutical Services and got $700 million in cash and $300 million in tax benefits when it was sold. And Quaker Oats bought Snapple for $1.7 billion and sold it less than three years later for $300 million.[21]

There are many pressures pushing the recent waves of mergers of acquisitions: market forces, competitive threats, power issues, political decisions, and sometimes simply the momentum of the number of deals being made. And as demonstrated, despite the momentum, there are no guarantees of success, and many risks are involved. So what are some of the pitfalls to avoid, and what might increase the chances for success? These are the issues to which we turn.

SOME REASONS FOR FAILURE

Deals fail for many obvious, and sometimes not so obvious, reasons. A common cause of failure is simply that the acquiring company pays too much for the business. A good example is Quaker Oats' acquisition of Snapple. Some industry analysts estimated that the $1.7 billion purchase price was as much as $1 billion too high. The stock price of both companies declined the day the deal was announced. Problems with implementation and a downturn in the market for New Age drinks quickly led to performance difficulties.[22] In short, there appears to be no way that Snapple's performance could live up to its purchase price.

Aside from paying too much, other frequent causes for failure are that the business is not a good strategic fit or that the company did not perform adequate due diligence to learn of potential problem areas in advance. In some cases blame for these kinds of problems lies with the investment bankers involved. Their fees tend to track the skyrocketing prices of the deals themselves, and they have little direct incentive to stop a bad deal, even if they recognize it as such. The top three investment banking firms in 1999 each advised on over $1 *trillion* in mergers and acquisitions, and investment banks overall made $3.23 billion in fees.[23] (In several of the more notable cases of lost value mentioned above, the same investment banking firm helped complete both the acquisition and divestiture of the problem company.)[24]

But this blame can fall equally to the executives and board members involved. Two of the most common arguments for ignoring the due diligence and financial numbers are when people believe that it is the "last deal of its kind" or that "if we don't acquire it, our competition will." Deals motivated primarily from fear are not likely to have been thought through in the same way that more strategic opportunities would have.

But some of the most crucial factors in the success or failure of mergers and acquisitions may be only beginning to be recognized. They are intangible and not typically captured in the balance sheets or other data examined by financial analysts. They often come up only after the fact when efforts at integration may feel more like cultural wars. These are the human side of organizations. And despite recent attempts to measure and quantify some of these factors, through efforts such as human capital or intellectual capital calculations, they remain much more subjective than objective.

Baruch Lev, Professor of Accounting and Finance at New York University, spells this out more clearly than most. As he explains, current accounting practices are still based on a 500-year-old system of recording transactions, then matching revenues against expenses.[25] This creates a number of problems. First, the balance sheet numbers produced by traditional accounting measures represent only 10% to 15% of the total value any given company in the Standard & Poor's 500. And tangible assets (buildings, equipment, cash, etc.) make up only about 37% of the value.

Value can no longer be measured by transactions. (As pointed out, valuation of a company is now primarily based on *anticipation* by analysts.) Nor do transactions measure the value of intangible assets, in general.

Lev breaks intangible assets into four general areas. First are ideas and product innovations, such as come from research and development (R&D) functions. Second is the value of brand names, which allow for premium pricing. Third are "structural assets"—essentially ways of doing business that set a company apart from competitors. And last he refers to "monopolies" or "franchises," meaning a competitive advantage in given areas or markets that would make it difficult for others to enter or compete.

Addressing these issues in the context of M&A transactions begins with answering a very critical question: "Just what is it we're buying?" Traditionally, this seemed to be very clear. What were purchased or joined were companies' assets—their facilities, raw materials in stock, equipment, and other means of production, distribution channels, and so on. Everything else that seemed to count for anything was captured in a leftover category known as "goodwill," which encompassed things such as brand recognition and ongoing relationships with strategic customers. But as business itself becomes a less "tangible" process, the question becomes even more relevant—just what is it that is considered of value to the deal?

In more mature industries, the traditional answers still seem to apply (or at least are assumed to apply, based on the nature of the deals). Exxon and Mobil expect to be able to run their combined operations with some 16,000 fewer employees than were present at the time the deal was struck and generate savings approaching $4 billion in the process. There is no apparent expectation that the deal will generate new breakthrough technologies, or even radical innovations. The goal is to achieve greater market share and efficiency in production and distribution. The people, in this case, are part of the means of production, and therefore calculated as an expense rather than an asset on the balance sheets.

Contrast this with Cisco, or other high-tech players, where facilities and equipment are the least of what is being purchased. The most tangible assets of value in these industries are things such as lines of software code or memory chip designs, and the assets of real interest are the talent of the employees involved and their ability to generate and execute new ideas. This changes not only the concept of valuation, but also the process of the transaction itself.

Cisco cites a five-point strategy for acquisitions: (1) the target company's vision; (2) its short-term success with customers; (3) its long-term strategy; (4) the "chemistry" between the target company's employees and Cisco's own; and (5) the geographic proximity between the companies.[26] While the cost of the transaction is important, Cisco is apparently more interested in how things work after the deal is done than in the numbers alone. To that effect, Cisco goes to great effort in making sure that acquired employees are integrated into the company fully from Day One and is, at the moment of this writing, working to hire additional HR professionals with M&A experience.

Intel seems to follow very similar protocols. In 1998 alone, Intel completed 130 investments (some of these partnerships rather than controlling interests) in companies worth $3.5 billion.[27] Like Cisco, most of these deals were done quickly, with formal due diligence often happening *after* the deal was struck. And, partly because of the pace, intuition played at least as great a role as analysis.

So we're left at this point with a picture of two extremes. The older model involves months of laborious analysis and scrutiny by regulatory agencies, wiping out small forests with production of documents. Aging facilities, environmental liabilities, and pensions and medical plans for generations of employees must all be accounted for. The apparent goal is typically increased efficiency on all levels, but the real goal may simply be appeasing financial analysts in order to maintain investment capital.

The new model involves a whole range of partnerships and alliances, completed in days and involving only small teams and minimal oversight. Many of the deals are done with startup companies employing relatively small numbers of highly skilled employees and virtually no history or liabilities to be scrutinized.

Between these extremes are almost every imaginable combination. Each brings with it its own issues and complexities. Each also has some goal in mind, which may or may not be the one presented for public consumption.

So what makes so many of these deals fail? Lots of things, as noted—wrong price, poor strategic fit, bad timing in industry cycles, and probably many more. But the ones of most interest to you as an HR professional, and the ones that seem to be growing in recognition, have to do with the human side of organizations.

THE HUMAN SIDE OF THE EQUATION

The focus of this book is the heart of what actually makes a company work or not—the human efforts that either get things done or do not, at all levels of an organization. This is not to be so naïve as to imply that human issues are the *only* important ones. Treating people well and having motivated employees will not, by itself, overcome a deal done badly. Employees may work themselves to the bone and still not be able to generate enough business or cash to pay exorbitant debts in a down-turned market. But if employees are not engaged in the success of the organization, there is little else that will overcome this—and with increasing emphasis as value hinges more and more on things such as talent, creativity, and customer service.

The critical question for M&A transactions remains, in our minds, "What is being bought?" (i.e., What is it about this deal that will create value?).

The critical question for you, as an HR professional, is more specifically, "Where do the people fit in this deal?" From the organization's view, are most employees simply a part of the means of production, or a part of the "excess overhead" that must be reduced to increase efficiency? Of those who do remain (and organizations, by definition, seem to require at least some people), are they easily replaceable at minimal cost and effort, or do they play key roles without which the organization could not function? The answers to such questions should help begin to shape your expectations about the role that you need to play in these transactions. But given the nature and history of these deals, it doesn't mean that traditional decision makers will necessarily understand the value that you can potentially add to the end results.

Human issues often begin at the top, with key decision makers themselves. Regardless of the numbers or the strategic intent, there are always personal ramifications of the decisions that are made. Decisions to merge with or acquire another company may signal a change in future direction, which may seem to make or break certain careers. In some cases, the senior management team is simply unprepared for managing either the size or the technical aspects of the new company—but feel they dare not admit this.

It is not only at senior levels that the human issues matter, though. Communication problems frequently arise to create conflict and anxiety during a merger effort. Employees are often unclear about their accountabilities. If they do not fully support a new management style, it can lead to a failed effort. Even the up-front integration work is frequently viewed as a distraction from the company's "real work," which is a perspective that can lead to disaster.

If you understand that human issues of all kinds are the root cause of many of the failed deals and transactions that simply do not capitalize on their potential, then you can manage your transaction successfully by considering the issues, alternatives, and recommended strategies in this book.

SO, WHY MERGE IF SO MANY DEALS FAIL?

The bottom-line answer is, "for many reasons." But the most important, currently, seems to be because a merger or acquisition creates real potential for explosive growth and enhanced profitability *if* the transaction is done right. And being done right includes an appreciation of the people involved and the part they play in the success or failure of the venture. Regardless of the organization's view of employees, the way in which *people* issues are handled always has an impact on the ultimate outcomes, whether obvious or not.

Armed with the information contained in this book, you can help to set the context and climate for employee satisfaction and motivation following your company's transaction. Your knowledge and awareness of the potential *human* issues that commonly arise, coupled with the application of these strategies, will help to ensure the success of your company's future mergers and acquisitions.

NOTES

1. Henry Goldblatt, "Cisco's Secrets," *Fortune*, November 8, 1999.
2. David Koenig, "Exxon Mobil Expects Bigger Job Cuts," Associated Press, December 17, 1999.
3. Anonymous, "$79 Billion Exxon/Mobil Merger," *International Law Review* (January 1999).
4. Ibid.
5. Virginia Stone Mackin, "Monday Morning," *Washington Post*, December 20, 1999.

6. Koenig, "Exxon Mobil Expects Bigger Job Cuts."

7. Based on a KPMG International study of 700 M&A transactions between 1996 and 1998, as reported in Nikhil Deogun, "Deals & Deal Makers: Merger Wave Spurs More Stock Wipeouts—Acquirers Shares Drop on Average," *Wall Street Journal*, November 29, 1999.

8. Steven Lipin, "As Hostile Takeovers Spread, Few Companies Can Avoid Them," *Wall Street Journal*, November 22, 1999.

9. Thomas E. Weber, Martin Peers, and Nick Wingfield, "Two Titans in a Strategic Bind Bet on a Futurisic Megadeal," *Wall Street Journal*, January 11, 2000.

10. Lipin, "As Hostile Takeovers Spread, Few Companies Can Avoid Them."

11. Deogun, "Deals & Deal Makers."

12. For a good summary of these studies see Dennis C. Mueller, "Mergers: Theory and Evidence," in G. Mussati (ed.), *Mergers, Markets and Public Policy* (Kluwer Academic Publishers, 1995).

13. Eric Schonfeld, "Born to Be Bought," *Fortune*, November 8, 1999.

14. Leif Edvinsson and Michael S. Malone, *Intellectual Capital: Realizing Your Company's True Value by Finding Its Hidden Roots* (HarperBusiness, 1997).

15. B. Wysocki, "Why an Acquisition? It's Often the People," *Wall Street Journal*, October 6, 1997.

16. Tim Smart, "Increasingly Size Counts: Falling Prices in a World of Plenty Drive Mergers Such as Exxon-Mobil," *Washington Post*, December 4, 1998.

17. Based on research by J. P. Morgan and Co., as reported in Deogun, "Deals & Deal Makers."

18. Deogun, "Deals & Deal Makers."

19. Daniel Machalaba and Christopher J. Chipello, "Big Rail Merger Gets a Cool Reaction: Analysts Say More Deals May Follow," *Wall Street Journal*, December 21, 1999.

20. Robert Langreth, "Pharmacia Says Linking Drug Units Validates Merger with Monsanto," *Wall Street Journal* December 23, 1999.

21. Nikhil Deogun and Steve Lipin, "Deals and Deal Makers: Cautionary Tales: When Big Deals Turn Bad—Some Hot Mergers Can Come Undone for Many Reasons," *Wall Street Journal*, December 8, 1999.

22. Robert G. Eccles, Kersten L. Lanes, and Thomas C. Wilson, "Are You Paying Too Much for That Acquisition?" *Harvard Business Review* (July–August 1999), p. 137.

23. Nikhil Deogun, "Big Deal Advisers Make the Most of Big Deals," *Wall Street Journal*, January 3, 2000.

24. Langreth, "Pharmacia Says Linking Drug Units Validates Merger with Monsanto."

25. Alan M. Webber, "New Math for a New Economy," *Fast Company* (January–February 2000).

26. Goldblatt, "Cisco's Secrets."

27. Katharine Mieszkowski, Profile of Avram Miller in *Fast Company* (December 1999).

Chapter 2

Structure, Function, and Purpose
of Organizations

A business begins as an idea, as a way to produce and sell products and/or services. Business organizations become the realization of these ideas and the means for accomplishing the objectives. The ways in which all this comes about, from the formulation of the initial idea to the people involved in implementing it to the ways in which a company first defines itself, play a role in the unique identity and culture that develops within that organization.

MODELS OF EFFICIENCY

But there are also very basic characteristics that are common to businesses. In the simplest terms, they become mechanisms for the production and delivery of goods and services. They take materials and turn them into products, and use skills to deliver services. A generic way to model this process is illustrated in Figure 2.1.

Figure 2.1 could represent the turning of iron ore into steel, the production of components into automobiles, or the writing of software code. In each case the elements involved would be different (e.g., for the writing of software code, the raw materials would be knowledge and ideas), but the basic process would remain intact. A merger or acquisition attempts to join the components of different organizations, with their own histories and cultures and ways of operating, into single entities that can efficiently accomplish these kinds of processes.

In many ways, this model represents a very machine-like view of business but one that still underlies most organizational thinking. An inventor discovered a way to harness or channel some force in nature (e.g.,

Figure 2.1
Basic Model of Production

the production of gasoline from crude oil) which was then converted to practical applications (e.g., the internal combustion engine) that could be sold to consumers—in this case by adding wheels and seats to make an automobile. Fundamentally, though, it is no different than the software programmer who is looking for the next "killer app" for a video game or Internet site.

Optimization of this model is a matter of efficiency. Henry Ford, of course, is credited with moving the process of automobile production to a whole new level of efficiency through the use of mass production assembly lines with clear divisions of labor. But what Ford offered to consumers was product availability rather than choice. Consumers got what he produced—take it or leave it.

This early mass production model also focused on a particular type of efficiency, that of *economies of scale*. As long as demand exceeded supply, profitability was primarily a matter of productivity—of how fast units could be gotten out the door. A certain percentage of defects were to be expected when moving at this pace, but they were simply factored in as a cost of business. It was easier to catch them at the end of the line than to slow the production process. This was a model built on growth and optimism with no limits to resources or opportunities. It was typical of the American automobile industry until competition forced changes. (There are those who might argue that it also looks surprisingly like the process used in developing Microsoft's Windows operating systems, whose first versions are routinely shipped with thousands of known defects.)

But in the automobile industry and many other manufacturing processes, competition did force changes. As markets became established, creating a steady supply of demand, more and more companies got into those businesses. The more competition, the less market share for each company and the greater the pressure on efficiency. As industries mature and competition heats up, increased costs of production can't necessarily be passed along. If a competitor can produce a similar enough product at less cost, they are likely to attract customers.

These kinds of changes led to a new type of efficiency, focused on quality. In the automobile industry specifically, Japanese manufacturers used principles developed by such thinkers as Deming and Juran to in-

Figure 2.2
Simple Model of Quality Improvement

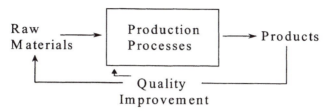

crease the reliability of their cars while simultaneously decreasing the cost of making them. Part of the theory was that it is much more efficient in the long run to decrease wasted materials and wasted efforts in the processes themselves than to ignore them and fix problems at the end.

The essence of this model is shown in Figure 2.2, in which feedback loops are added, indicating some method of detecting information about the products or services produced and using this information to change the processes themselves.

Figure 2.2 is characteristic of an organization involved in quality improvement efforts such as Total Quality Management (TQM) or Continuous Quality Improvement (CQI). (This model, of course, might be replicated thousands of times within a complex manufacturing process representing many individual activities along the way.)

Employee initiative and involvement are critical components of most quality improvement efforts. In many cases these center around the use of workplace teams which ideally are self-managing. The theory is that those closest to the work are most apt to be the ones who know the most about it and are therefore most likely to spot problems or inefficiencies the earliest. Waiting for customers to become aware of problems or defects and complain about them only worked as long as there was demand but no choice.

Before a problem requires a response, it has to pass a certain threshold of awareness—it has to appear on the "organizational radar," if you will. If the problem does not cause a significant upset in a supervisor's own duties, it's much easier to ignore it than to address it. (Doing something about it just means creating more work for the supervisor.) Granted, ignoring problems is not the way that things are *supposed* to work, but in the real world, it's often what happens. And the leaner organizations become, the more significant problems have to be in order to be noticed, as a rule. Giving ownership of functions directly to employee work teams is intended to increase their concerns for their operations and thereby increase product quality and decrease waste and defects.

Another major shift in organizational focus, of course, was to that of being "customer-driven." This moved the orientation from one of internal efficiency in an organization or function to an external orientation of meeting needs or desires. Rather than being "science-driven" in terms of producing the highest quality product that could be developed, this was a "market-driven" process that responded, essentially, "Who cares how good it is if no one wants to buy it?" As an overlay to the trend toward decentralization, this trend suggested that every organizational function had both suppliers (meaning that it was someone's customer) and customers of its own, even if within the same organization.

The current business model, of course, is based on *speed*. For some Internet applications, getting an idea implemented before anyone else seems to outweigh all other priorities (at least for now). And generally, speed requires a focus on simplicity rather than on perfection in quality or meeting of customer demands.[1] Others seem to operate from what looks like a very traditional process of detailed planning and division of labor—or even a scientific approach to testing ideas—prior to implementation, but run at fiber optic speed (for example, three weeks maximum between initial concept and launch).[2]

The commonality of all these models is an emphasis on process efficiency. For purposes of getting large quantities of products out the door of a factory, using an assembly line with clear divisions of labor is much more efficient than having large numbers of individual craftsmen each producing whole, finished products. While this model is modified somewhat by the use of work teams, there is still a fairly narrow range of tasks shared by the team, resulting in a division of labor more specific to the team level than the individual. Customer-driven processes generate a different target in terms of specifications and expectations, requiring a focus on external rather than internal demands. And speed-driven processes require that ideas be generated and implemented with as little hesitation as possible.

The same rules about division of labor apply to bureaucracies, which can be extremely efficient in their own right. (It is much more efficient to have individuals with specialized skills focusing on their area of expertise than to have 500 people trying to accomplish 30 tasks, with no particular sense of organization.)

Traditionally, efficiency required stability. It required applying known processes to achieve predetermined results. Bureaucracies and traditional assembly line processes were efficient as long as they just continued to do more of what they were set up to do. What they were *not* was flexible. Coordinating the work of hundreds—or tens of thousands—of employees into a centrally controlled, unified effort required a great deal of structure and discipline. In order to be efficient, every role had to be played out accurately. Because of the interrelated nature of the parts and roles, a glitch in one area caused problems throughout the rest of the organization or process.

Having one key role missing for even a brief period of time delayed everything from that point on. Due to the "imperfect" nature of humans (i.e., they got sick or became otherwise unable to work at times), bureaucratic systems then required some level of redundancy. In the best of times, this excess capacity was wasteful and inefficient. Without it there was no room for error in operations.

The notion of bureaucratic organizations, of course, has long since fallen out of popularity and been replaced by many alternative metaphors and models. The term itself is outmoded, if not simply historical. Organizations now pride themselves on being flexible, if not actually "virtual." Old assembly lines have been replaced by flexible manufacturing processes which can run numerous small, customized jobs easily and efficiently, for instance. But whatever the new labels and packaging, much has not changed—and the emphasis remains on efficiencies.

As noted by long-term management guru Peter Drucker, it was the fifty-fold increase in the productivity of manufacturing labor that was responsible for both the economic and the social gains of the twentieth century.[3] And output per employee is still used as a primary indicator in most economic models.[4]

HUMAN KNOWLEDGE AND VALUE

According to Drucker, the challenge for the twenty-first century is going to be learning to manage the productivity of knowledge workers to the same degree that manual labor was managed in the twentieth century. The problem is that the kind of management needed for knowledge workers is almost the exact *opposite* of that needed for basic manual labor. For instance, in manual labor, the job or the task of the employee is already established at the time of hire. The employee is simply trained in this task, placed in the job, and monitored for accuracy and efficiency in getting it done. Knowledge work, however, begins with determining *what the task needs to be.* Given a problem to solve or a goal to be met, what will be required and how can it be accomplished?

This kind of approach to productivity creates a whole new set of roles and relationships. According to Drucker, knowledge workers need to be self-managing and autonomous, innovative, continuously involved in learning, and focused on quality rather than quantity.

The relevance to mergers and acquisitions is simply this—while most organizations (and management consulting firms, for that matter) have learned to say the right things about people and innovation and "new rules of business," very few show any evidence of it in the actions they take. In the great majority of ventures, people are still clearly dealt with as costs of doing business—as potential cost savings if they can be eliminated—rather than as assets. In general, we as yet have no way of even asking the question about each employee, "What could this person bring to the future of this organization?" What gets asked is, "What is the present economic value of this organizational role?"

To be very clear, this is not necessarily wrong. The great majority of organizations still function from an efficiency-driven model of production and economics. The point here is not to try to pretend that things are otherwise. It is another way of addressing the question of "what is being bought?" in a merger or acquisition.

HR professionals (and OD consultants and many others) have for too long attempted to paint a warm and human face on the exterior of very mechanistic organizational systems. Much of this can be traced back to the human relations school of management that began in the early 1900s. It tied productivity to the meeting of human needs such as recognition and participation. And while this and similar efforts and movements have attempted to influence the nature of business over the decades, they have ended up acting as the conscience of organizations, but not as the heart or brain.

In one specific instance, Levi Strauss & Co. began a very strong focus on human and social values in the early to mid-1990s. But its sales, revenues, and overall market share dropped. As a result, the CEO who initiated the effort was lambasted for his "touchy-feely management techniques" and lack of focus on the core business, "to sell as many Levi's jeans as possible by keeping its brand fresh."[5] Being politically correct and doing the "right things" from a human or social standpoint is applauded, but only as long as the company makes money. That's what the "bottom line" is all about.

While all of this may sound incredibly callous, especially in a book written for HR professionals, the point is simply to address the conflicts and apparent double-messages within which HR professionals often find themselves caught. Yes, the organization wants the talents and skills and ideas of the best and brightest people it can find, but it doesn't really want their personal and family issues. The people in the organization, including senior decision makers, may be genuinely concerned about the personal welfare of employees (in fact, in our experience, most really are), but this is always outside the basic nature of the employment agreement. And the nature of the agreement is essentially an exchange: *I'll trade you some portion of my time and expertise in return for some agreed-to compensation (usually monetary, or some equivalent thereof).*

For better or worse in business relationships, it's only when things get ugly that they get clear. However good and meaningful work and relationships may be when things are going well, when employees are terminated or their jobs eliminated, they are only "owed" whatever is specified in a contract or agreement, or is gratuitously granted by the company. There isn't anything legally due (other than possibly overtime pay) for nights and weekends worked or family holidays or birthdays or school plays and events missed or relationships lost in the process. There is no compensation for loyalty or effort or initiative, unless someone specifically decides to recognize it, because this is the nature of the relationship.

Clearly, this section won't look very good on a recruiting brochure. It's not the kind of image that an organization wants to portray. But what does it have to do with mergers and acquisitions, or the structure, functions, or purposes of an organization anyway? Actually, quite a bit.

WHAT IS AN ORGANIZATION?

The critical issue is the question, "What shapes the organization?" As indicated at the beginning of this chapter, most businesses begin as an idea. One person or a small group sets out to produce and sell something. Assuming multiple people are involved, different roles and responsibilities evolve or are assigned.

The structure of the organization is the pattern of relationships between the people and the functions involved, however formal and rigid or open and loosely defined these may be. Traditionally, of course, this was captured in an organizational chart. Higher ranking in the structure of the organization indicated more decision-making power and authority, and more compensation. It also equated with more experience and assumed knowledge about organizational processes. Like other methods for depicting organizations, structural representations have gotten much more complex through the years, and some organizations resist using organizational charts, for example, altogether. However it's depicted and displayed, there is usually some ordered relationship between the roles and positions of an organization.

The functions of an organization are the activities that occur within it. (Many organizational functions are now outsourced to external groups, so these may need to be considered, as well.) They are usually represented by departments and divisions (e.g., law, maintenance, various operational units, etc.). Theoretically, all the functions work together in accomplishing the basic products or "outputs" of the organization. And historically, functions were closely aligned with structure (the senior counsel oversaw all legal functions, each supervisor in an operational area reported to a manager who reported to a division head who ultimately reported to a chief operating officer, etc.). In many newer organizational structures, functions may be parts of multiple areas of a company at the same time. Many operational groups, of course, have their own HR function which may or may not report directly to a corporate HR manager.

The purpose of an organization would seem to be obvious—primarily equivalent to the functions. If a company runs paper mills, the purpose of the company is to make and sell paper, right? Unfortunately, of course, it's not always that simple. But the impact of these kinds of assumptions runs much deeper than it may first appear.

Most companies are made up of very complex networks of functions, according to the tasks that have to be accomplished (accounting, engineering, construction, maintenance, etc.), as described above. To the degree that each focuses on its own internal efficiency, there tends to be conflict between the functions. This is at the heart of the centralization vs. decentralization questions that organizations have faced for years.

Relatively small functions usually only need simple accounting systems, for instance, which would be entirely inadequate for the needs of much larger and more complex functions. But an accounting system with tens of thousands of codes and categories, designed to link to both inventory control and tax systems (for greater efficiency) of, say, an industrial chemicals operation makes little sense, and is still inadequate, to meet the needs of the internal medical department. There are no ready codes for bandages or medicines. So, does the medical department "force fit" its accounting into the larger system as best it can, or does it run a separate, customized system that may not link to the larger system?

Structurally driven organizations tend to run like bureaucracies. You end up with massively complex, one-size-fits-all systems with which no one is entirely satisfied. Complaints about how incompatible this may be for any one function, and how the requirement to use it hurts that function's efficiency and productivity, tend to go unheeded. Efficiency is determined by the degree of compliance with centralized controls. This answer to the medical department's question is, "Get with the program and use our system."

Functionally driven organizations tend to be highly decentralized, focusing on the uniqueness of each area and its individual needs for efficiency. Each function may be seen as its own small business, needing to operate profitably in its own right. But in the extreme, this raises questions about the degree to which the functions are actually parts of one, overall organization, and about the relationships between them.

If an internal service function, operating from a small business model, can get more profitable work from external sources, should it still have to give first priority to internal jobs? How should such a "small business" function be capitalized in terms of start-up costs and growth? Should the employees of each such operation be compensated according to profitability, or do they have to fit into the company structure for compensation?

Many variations of matrix-type structures have attempted to combine both types of efficiencies—to create unified functions that are individu-

Figure 2.3
Technological Business Model

ally responsive, for instance. (Organizations that have adopted a matrix type of structure seem often to be those that have abandoned organizational charts, since the reporting relationships don't seem to be that clear—or maybe that critical—anyway.) In some cases, they have created a compromise between the orientations. In others, it's a matter of which master gets served on which day, according to the law of the "squeakiest wheel."

Another way of viewing organizations is as defined by technology, products, and markets.[6] Similar to the model in Figure 2.1, technology is the know-how that is needed to produce the products that are delivered to customers in given markets, as shown in Figure 2.3.

In most traditional organizations, one of these is dominant and determines much about the other two. In a product-driven business, product managers and production functions are key. The search is for that "killer app" or the breakthrough treatment drug that will reap the hoped-for rewards. Technologies may be changed or replaced as needed to find newer and better ways to produce the product. Alternative markets are sought as needed for continuing the viability of the product.

A drawback to product focus can be a failure to recognize the larger or broader value behind a product. For instance, IBM spent an estimated $20 billion in its layoff of some 200,000 of the brightest programmers and designers around rather than use them to capitalize on extremely advanced technology that had been developed, applicable to the digital communications industries.[7]

Market-driven companies focus on delivery of as many different products and services as possible to a known group of customers. Manufacturers of household goods, such as Procter and Gamble, try to produce as many different types and brands of detergents, cleaners, sponges, and so forth, as they can keep flowing through grocery and department store chains. Similarly, producers of personal care products, or of pharmaceutical products, focus on specific target markets through certain retail chains.

Organizations defined by technology are those that tend to adhere very strictly to a sense of "core technology." They work from the basis of a certain know-how and exploit this in as many ways as is feasible and profitable. These would typically be companies heavily involved in and driven by research and development efforts, such as 3M.

"Systems" approaches to organizations attempt to balance and align all of these together within an organization, recognizing that all three represent critical challenges and opportunities.[8] Addressing a sense of organizational *purpose* is a way to attempt to deal with all three, and with their impacts on each other. In practical terms, most organizations' sense of purpose is identified with just one of the variables named: products, markets, or technology. In the best of circumstances, *purpose* is described by a company's vision statement and is closely aligned with its core competencies and values. It is the company's reason for being in existence.

The danger of defining organizational purpose too narrowly is that it tends to limit understanding and perspective. An organization that is driven by products or functional operations will most likely have persons with expertise in those areas in charge. They have risen through the ranks based on their success in product development, for instance, and see the success of the organization in these terms. Many construction and manufacturing industries are based in engineering principles, run by executives from engineering backgrounds, and tend to see the world in terms of fairly direct cause-and-effect relationships. Organizations driven by scientific achievements may tend to see success in terms of the next "breakthrough" and have difficulty balancing research investment with profitability.

Each perspective may well be valid within its own realm, but not necessarily apply to others. Products can be engineered to their highest levels of efficiency and effectiveness, but this does not work so well for management of people. And there are not necessarily best answers for business dilemmas in the same way as there are for problems of mass vs. strength.

In times of growth and stability, companies may be able to operate from a fairly narrow approach, and very nearly in accordance with their own ideals. At present, though, many companies are faced with situations of Darwinian survival—how can they move quickly enough to obtain needed resources (e.g., capital investment), maintain basic processes, avoid predators, and adapt to environmental changes? Changes in technology are driving fundamental changes in markets, and a hot, innovative product today can become just another commodity item, if not simply outmoded, tomorrow.

Computer companies are battling over whether software will continue to be a component of a PC or accessed through the Internet. At the same time, wireless communications devices are vying to displace PC's as the vehicle for accessing the Internet. Cable television companies, telephone companies, and utility companies are trying to circle the earth with fiber optic lines, while others are trying to get enough satellites in space to become the primary links.

Sometimes adapting to change is only a matter of altering existing processes, for example, producing updated versions of current products or streamlining production processes to make them more efficient. But other times, it is the entire approach to business that has to be reexamined. (The old analogy is something about making better buggy whips at a time when cars were displacing horses and carriages.)

The approach of many companies to survival tends to look like ongoing series of cosmetic surgeries and organ transplants performed by roving bands of consultants. Images are updated to keep the organization attractive and appealing. Systems are upgraded to provide power and agility. Excess weight is shed. Processes are stressed and fine-tuned to maximum efficiency so that every component is utilized to its fullest.

The practical result for employees has generally been longer hours, fewer coworkers, more demands with shorter timelines, and less job security. The outcome, organizationally, are companies with ever-increasing needs for change and innovation, but with decreasing capacity to do so. The faster that companies are forced to react to external pressures, the less able they are to internally contemplate what to change, or why. If everything is urgent, nothing is particularly important, and there is no realistic way to prioritize demands.

In many instances of organizational change, the real, unspoken goal is avoidance of change. If enough incremental change can be achieved, deeper fundamental changes can be avoided. And in organizational terms, "higher" is "deeper"—those at the top of the decision-making ladder will be the last to be affected by such changes, as a rule.

In a merger or an acquisition the strategic intent of the deal is usually related to a narrow sense of purpose. The decision makers of the deal see what they see of the target company from the dominant perspective of their own organization, and this defines what assets are considered to be of value. This way of perceiving also determines all the other attributes that exist, which may not only be missed in terms of value, but may not really be "seen" at all.

As applied to mergers and acquisitions, the "winning" company, whatever label is placed on the deal, is the one that is able to dictate the structure, function, policies, culture, and processes of the resulting organization. And typically, this involves just incorporating the desired aspects of the other organization into its own (or at least that's the goal). The dominant organization is able to perpetuate itself through growth in size and market share, increasing its efficiency through eliminating redundant administrative functions from the other organization.

The problems here are many-fold. First, despite all the apparent similarities of two organizations, in terms of products, markets, geographic proximity, and so forth, their senses of organizational purpose may be entirely different. In a merger of two convenience store chains with which we were involved, the dominant partner was focused on high volume and low costs. The less dominant partner had invested a great deal in building expensive and attractive store locations, attracting more stable, educated employees, and focusing on customer service as ways to create a high-end market niche. It was a marriage of convenience (pardon the pun) in terms of market geography, but a disaster in terms of organizational fit. In this kind of instance, the costs associated with integration may delay the return on investment in the partner much longer than expected.

Second, growth in market-share may be a red herring to divert real change. If a competitor is creating a marketplace threat through innovation, one answer is simply to buy out the competitor and kill the innovations. If the employees who come with the acquisition are needed due to the increased size of operations, they are not likely to be thrilled about being shoved back into "old technology" for their work.

Just as importantly, as long as the need for change is responded to with incremental steps from a single perspective, the adage that "change is constant" will be eternal. A technology-driven company is likely to respond to *any* pressure for change by looking for a technological "fix." In the case of mergers and acquisitions, this would be a company that would seem to offer more research capabilities and new ideas. Even if the target company was actually product-focused, what they had to offer in terms of R&D might be very good—and the R&D employees might initially be thrilled to get to move to more of a scientifically-oriented or technology-driven company. But the organizational results might be only temporary at best if the "fix" didn't actually fit the problem.

It's also possible to have a product-driven company understand, for instance, that it's dealing with market-driven issues and possibly acquire a division of a more market-oriented competitor—only to have major integration problems due to the differences in orientation. If all the "drivers" of the organization (e.g., compensation, incentive programs) as well as all the decision makers in the organization continue as they have always been, it's likely to end up as something of an "organ transplant rejection."

As long as organizations are focused on efficiency-driven processes, there will be limitations in their abilities to adapt and change. *Efficiency involves applying known processes to achieve predetermined outcomes.* In order for an organization to acquire and utilize a specific skill effectively, it has to know and understand the thing (e.g., the threat, the competitor, the changes) in the environment that it is facing. But to gain this understanding, if the "thing" is not already familiar, requires learning. And learning is not an efficient process from an input → output viewpoint.

Efficiency aims for zero defects and zero waste. A learning environment requires an expectation of mistakes. *Learning requires exploring things that aren't familiar and attempting things that aren't yet mastered.* To allow for this requires building in the excess capacity for trial and error and mistakes, and this is typically considered "waste" in efficiency-driven organizations. If mergers and acquisitions are used by organizations as ways to adapt and change, they need to be placed in this larger context of organizational change rather than being treated as mechanical additions or replacements.

Behind all of this drive for efficiency lie many deeper beliefs and assumptions that are so fundamental to organizational life that they seem out of place in this kind of book. Yet it is the nature of these kinds of assumptions that in fact create the conflicts for which there seem to be no real answers when things don't work. Such deep assumptions develop over generations, not just years, and tend to shape both "what we see" and "how we see it."

It goes without saying, for instance, that we are talking here about business organizations that operate in economic systems based on principles of free markets and capitalism. But not saying so means that we assume a great deal about your shared understanding with us of many issues. And when conflicts arise at a level outside the bounds of a current discussion, there is no ready way to address them—they are usually just dismissed as irrelevant.

One such fundamental notion is the idea that organizations are "rational," that is, that they can take basically irrational, selfish, and lazy people and direct their behavior in a desired way through systems of rules and order, through rewards and punishments. This idea dates back to the founding of the industrial age itself when conditions in factories were so oppressive that prisoners and paupers were the prime source of labor. And despite being challenged through social research and organizational studies since the early 1900s, the more "scientific" model of organizations has prevailed. But it is this same mental model that creates significant problems in organizational change.

Deep and fundamental assumptions form what is referred to as *tacit knowledge.* And it is this realm of tacit knowledge that will provide the thread that ties many of the organizational and personal issues of mergers and acquisitions together, as will be shown.

The chapters that follow provide increasing levels of detail about issues to anticipate and recommended actions and responses in relation to mergers and acquisitions. Initially they will explore a number of concepts that may sound simply like management buzzwords (and that may not seem to have any relation to the topic of this book)—such as *organizational culture, human capital*, and *organizational learning.* But as will be shown, these concepts are intimately intertwined with each other. And together, they help to explain the crucial nature of the human side of organizational change. Then will follow the more applied chapters, explaining how these concepts can be implemented in the process of a merger or acquisition.

You might use the ideas in this chapter to sketch something of a mental map of your own organization on which you can reflect to help organize the issues. As the key roles of the organization are determined, how do these affect the structure and what do they imply about the functions and the ways they will relate? As new functions are brought into or merged with existing functions in the organization, or as existing functions of the other organization are replaced by those of your organization, how is this likely to affect the ways in which things get done? Are they very different approaches that will take time for familiarization? Are there broader implications about reorganizing and realigning functions that can be expected to cause some communication difficulties at the outset? Do you anticipate functional difficulties due to conflicts between key role players?

Much of the emphasis of this book is on anticipation and planning. To the degree that you can maintain some image of the larger picture of the organization, and its role in the larger economic environment, it will help in your efforts.

NOTES

1. Katharine Mieszkowski, "How to Speed Up Your Startup," *Fast Company* (May 2000).

2. See Paul Roberts, "Getting It Done" and "The Art of Getting It Done," *Fast Company* (June 2000).

3. Peter F. Drucker, *Management Challenges for the 21st Century* (Harper-Business, 1999).

4. See, for instance, reports by Alan Greenspan, Chairman of the U.S. Federal Reserve, regarding the economy and interest rates, which utilize such indices.

5. Amy Kover, "Levi's Gets New Boss," *Fortune*, October 11, 1999, p. 55.

6. Jamshid Gharajedaghi, *Systems Thinking: Managing Chaos and Complexity* (Butterworth-Heinemann, 1999).

7. Ibid.

8. Ibid.

Chapter 3

Organizational Culture

What makes an organization unique are those qualities that are not found in any policy handbook or training manual, nor are they typically offered in any orientation session. Sometimes these qualities are referred to as the company's culture (defined at times simply as "the way things are done around here"). Often, they're captured in part in the stories that are told about the founding of the company or about some dramatic point in time in which the company's survival was threatened. Most often, though, these qualities are found in the unspoken rules and expectations over which newcomers or outsiders may trip, unknowingly causing offense or embarrassment, or simply a reaction like "You obviously don't know how things work here." They create the context for how a *faux pas* is defined in a given environment, as well as for how success may be measured.

Organizational culture begins with assumptions and beliefs. When a new company is begun, it has to have some sense of identity—some ways by which it can distinguish itself from competitors in the marketplace. The distinctions chosen are obviously those that the early founders and owners believe will be the most successful. And these beliefs are either reinforced, because they prove successful, or they are changed to something that works better.

There are two primary difficulties that tend to arise with culture though. One is that, once established, a sense of culture and identity becomes hard to change. After all, why would you want to quit doing what has created your success? The second difficulty is that the longer existing organizational culture and identity remain intact, the more ingrained they become. While at first the most important rules of operating may be reinforced directly and obviously, in the form of frequent statements (e.g., slogans or mottoes) voiced by owners or senior managers, later they simply become assumptions by which people operate, with little conscious awareness.

The role of cultural conflict in mergers and acquisitions is nothing new. Active investigation of its role in failed efforts dates back at least to the late 1970s and continued through the 1980s.[1] So why has such information not had a greater impact on M&A deals?

Despite the significant work done in the area of organizational culture in prior years, it seemed to remain removed from the core of business activity. Much of what we know about culture is grounded in social science, specifically in anthropology, and that was an academic discipline, not a business area.

It is Edgar Schein that has recently brought much more clarity and focus to the ways that cultural issues affect the real workings of organizations.[2] And for purposes of this book, the tie is through the concept of tacit knowledge.

The term "tacit knowing" seems to trace back to Michael Polyani, a Hungarian medical scientist turned philosopher. Polyani was apparently influenced a good deal by Gestalt psychology. One of his primary theories distinguished between *focal knowledge*, which is knowledge about an object being focused upon, and *tacit knowledge*, which is the background knowledge used to categorize and understand the object. According to this theory, knowledge is both a static collection of facts, ideas, and concepts and an active process of knowing through experience. People therefore switch between focal and tacit knowledge constantly, incorporating new information into what is already known or believed (understanding that "what is known" is largely a socially agreed or constructed concept).

From an anthropological standpoint, culture involves all those ways of thinking and seeing the world, as well as ways of behaving, that are "socially transmitted" from person to person. They are the ideas and beliefs with which children are raised that help them identify with a certain tribe or race or ethnic group. Cultural differences are seen most easily in "artifacts" such as special foods, music, ceremonies, holidays and events, and most importantly, language. You aren't get issued an instruction manual for learning these things as a child, and they usually only become obvious when compared with other cultures. Until then, they are "just the way things are."

The tie with tacit knowledge is that culture is embedded in the tacit realm. It can be made more conscious or "explicit," but it normally lies in the background of our awareness, forming the underlying assumptions through which we understand and act. And critically, culture is not usually a matter of what is *thought*, but of what is *felt*. While we may have some commitment to ideas that we propose, most people are open to debate about ideas, at least at some level. But more deeply held beliefs about religious practices, family values, national patriotism, and the like are not things that we're likely to change as a result of a casual conversation. New information may influence ideas, but challenges to basic beliefs only create defensiveness, as a rule. Our most deeply held beliefs are probably experienced through those things that bring a tear to our eye about "what's really important in life," or how the world should ideally be.

Just as social cultures are seen most obviously in contrast to each other, so are organizational cultures. And while there is no more obvious contrast than during a merger or acquisition, such deeply held differences are often overlooked or misinterpreted as personal issues of "resistance to change," rather than cultural conflicts.

While it's fairly impossible to trace the roots of our social cultures back to any specific origins, such as "When did this language begin?" or "When did people first cook this food?" the founding of an organization is something that we can watch in progress. As noted in Chapter 2, businesses usually begin based on an idea for a specific product or service. But ideas about how to develop and deliver a product or service, and ideas about ways of having other people involved in the process, don't develop in a vacuum. They come from professional training, from personal experiences, from ideas shared by mentors or friends, and from deeper beliefs from within segments of the social culture. (Business schools may teach some strategies about personnel management, but they don't typically shape basic assumptions about relationships with other people, about whether people are fundamentally trustworthy or greedy, about how to resolve conflicts, etc.) For our purposes, organizational culture is most importantly the *assumptions and expectations* that underlie organizational decision making.

Schein provides frameworks for understanding two aspects of organizational culture that are especially helpful.[3] One breaks cultural issues into three areas: artifacts, espoused values, and basic underlying assumptions. The other speaks to the differences in organizational culture according to the age and developmental phase of an organization.

DEVELOPMENTAL PHASES

Organizational culture is a product of the history of successes. If the ideas for delivering the product or services worked, they proved to be "true" at least in the minds of the company founders and therefore were repeated in order to continue the success. If the initial approach did not work, the company probably did not continue.

Organizational culture tends to reside inside the founders initially, but quickly becomes integrated into the organization through the many decisions that have to be made at the outset. Seemingly simple decisions set a precedent for how the organization is to operate—things like the style and location of offices (e.g., high-class or bare-bones), how aggressively to advertise and market, whether to focus on the quality of products and services or on salesmanship and relationships, whether management is tightly controlled and detail oriented or trusting and participative. In other words, the culture of a new organization is largely a reflection of the personality of the founder(s).

Once these first patterns are established, they don't have to be decided repeatedly—they become the routines by which the organization functions. Where very explicit instructions may be given initially about how to do certain things, work begins to flow more smoothly once everything becomes more habitual and familiar. As new employees are brought in, not only can current employees explain the basic routines, but also new persons can watch them in progress, speeding their learning. (Of course, there is always more to be learned than anyone thinks to explain because so much of it becomes second nature.)

In the natural evolution of a company, a major change occurs at the time that control moves from the entrepreneurs who started it to professional managers (typically MBAs) who are either promoted or brought in following the death or retirement of the top executive(s). By this point, most of the ways in which particular practices began have been forgotten by all but the most senior employees and only recounted occasionally in stories that may arise inadvertently. (Founders' stories are appearing more frequently now as books about companies become more popular, but the stories are typically "sanitized" for popular consumption if the book is authorized by the company itself.)

Professional managers tend to shift focus away from individuals and onto organizational and financial issues, which heralds in a new era for organizations. This more established "midlife" period is often focused on growth and expansion of both the business and the organization (e.g., more production and new markets as well as the hiring of internal staff to manage functional departments for law, human resources, security, finance, etc.). Challenges to the existing culture at the time of the transition are often seen in terms of challenges to the legacy of the founders, which may create problems for more senior employees, especially. Also by this time, those who have risen in the organization surely represent the culture in many ways, otherwise they would not have succeeded in it.

If the organization survives long enough, it eventually reaches a mature period in which the fundamental culture is so ingrained that it is extremely hard to pinpoint. But note also that culture is maintained through the activities of living persons, and therefore is an ongoing process. As organizations grow and mature, and as new and younger employees enter and move through them, many subcultures form, as well.

Subcultures (again, assumptions about the world and expectations about how one should or needs to act in it) frequently form internally around professions, organizational functions, departments, and even communities of practice. To be an effective part of any of these, one has to comply with certain norms that develop over time. And just as critically, many of these subcultures cross the traditional boundaries of the organization, both internally and externally.

Most people's original view of the world is shaped through the family or setting in which they are raised as well as any religious upbringing they may have. The educational system forms the next layer of this view, with Western societies relying heavily on principles of scientific "proof" as the basis for "truth" (or at least the best explanation). Then comes professional training, in which we learn to act "productively" as a part of our societies. Beyond that, personal experiences in the form of jobs, travel, ongoing religious or social affiliations (e.g., community groups or civic organizations to which we belong), and the writers and media personalities that we pay attention to continue to reinforce or shape the views we hold.

With respect to both cultural and job experiences, there are generational differences as well. People currently in their fifties and sixties (and older), who still hold power in many organizations, grew up with very different experiences in terms of technology, the economy, politics, and family life than people who are now in their twenties. These "older" people often had parents who lived through the Great Depression. They themselves lived through the Vietnam War and the 60's, grew up when color television and automatic washing machines were still new technology, and may well have been raised in a family where Dad worked and Mom stayed home. People in these generations simply have different orientations to job and financial security, relationships, and technology than people just now entering the workforce.

The whole spectrum of these issues can appear inside organizations in any number of different ways. Some of the most obvious come from professional affiliations because these form both the skill-set and orientation from which people work. Attorneys, engineers, research scientists, and accountants all play critical roles in many organizations. But each not only brings different skills and abilities, each often sees issues facing the organization in very different ways. In fact, what is a crucial issue for one may not even be of concern in the view of another. There are so many overlapping environmental and safety regulations, for instance, that if engineers tried to use them as the basis for their work, nothing would ever be built or produced. Building or producing anything involves some element of risk, which simply needs to be calculated and minimized. But in the more extreme cases, from the attorneys' view, engineers are simply either blind or ignorant of the "realities" of the potential consequences of problems.

Such issues of perspective arise commonly in organizations, but like many other cultural clashes, typically are dismissed as personality conflicts or power struggles. What is lacking in such cases is a deeper understanding about what is important, and why, from the other's perspective. And there is no natural method in organizations by which such understanding can develop. Usually, resolution to conflicts comes in the form of a decision by a higher power (for instance, the CEO), which often falls to the closer or more trusted in terms of relationships, or according to the stronger history and culture of the organization itself. (If this were a very risk-averse organization, the decision would probably fall in that direction, whatever the means by which it was made.)

In general, the existing culture(s) of an organization remains in place until one of several things occurs. First, the death or retirement of senior executives eventually makes way for successors. In the case of a family-owned business where a son or daughter or a long-time internal employee takes over, many of the more fundamental assumptions are likely to remain intact, though some efforts at change are likely as well. In a publicly held company, or one in which an outsider is brought in to manage, existing assumptions may be challenged, but even here they will be defended strongly, even if this has to be done covertly by loyal employees.

Second, the organization may face a crisis that threatens its survival. Usually such a threat comes from the larger environment, in the form of increased competition or changes in markets. It can also be in the form of a legal or financial scandal by key executives. But it can occur from a severe break in relationships between owners or controlling parties, as well, in which there is a shift in control of the organization. If the organization is successful in overcoming such a crisis, the way in which it was accomplished will usually create some change in the expectations about what success means and how the organization must now act in order to survive.

Third, of course, the organization may be involved in a merger or acquisition. In this case there are three apparent alternatives: (1) the acquired company may simply be absorbed into the culture of the acquirer, (2) the two cultures may be kept separate and intact, or (3) the development of a whole new culture may be attempted, utilizing the "best" of each culture.[4] Whatever the intent, the reality at present is that there is no simple, known way to purposefully create a new culture on the spot. As pointed out throughout this chapter, culture resides at a very deep level of human understanding and behavior. And culture is ever present. There is no way to design and implement a totally new culture without existing cultural elements being involved in the process.

So in the case of a merger or acquisition, or even of a joint venture, one culture always seems to end up dominating the other. While the larger stakeholder may feel that everything possible has been done to create a "merger of equals," the less dominant partner always seems to feel differently.

DEFINING THE CULTURE

The specific issues facing you as a HR professional trying to work through the cultural combinations and collisions of a merger or acquisition will be greatly dependent upon the age and stage of the organizations, on the size and the number of subcultures involved, and on how different the cultures turn out to be. They will also depend on the basic level of awareness that decision makers involved in the deal have about these human issues. If there is even a small understanding about organizational culture and the impact it can have on a transaction, then you have some leverage with which to work. If the structure of the deal is simply a financial transaction and the key players have no particular awareness that other issues could impact the success of the deal, you'll probably have to find different language and leverage points for action.

So where do you even begin to gather information about organizational culture—or in what ways can it actually be seen? As noted earlier, there are three levels of review that can help you to form a very useful framework: (1) artifacts, (2) espoused values, and (3) basic underlying assumptions.[5]

Beginning with the second category first, espoused values are essentially the public image of a company. As regards culture, they are the stated beliefs about what an organization says are important. Ford's slogan that "Quality is Job 1" is a prime example. So is the oft-recited mantra by companies in recent years that "People are our most important asset." Being "customer-driven" or "environmentally conscious" are further examples. The image of the company presented to financial analysts and investors is another type of espoused value. And as might be guessed from these examples, a company typically has not one image or espoused value, but many, each for different audiences.

Cultural artifacts are the more tangible or visible actions or behaviors of an organization. They are the actions and decisions of a company, on both large and small scales. These include very simple things, such as dress codes, hours of work, degree of formality in relationships (e.g., are senior executives addressed by their first names by *all* employees?), punctuality for work and for meetings, attendance at after-hours functions, extravagance vs. frugality in travel expenses, and so forth. They also include the ways that companies respond to competition, to threats such as lawsuits, and to the ways in which plans and directions for the future actually are decided and implemented. The primary problem with trying to understand organizational culture through simply observing or asking about it is that, while artifacts are the most obvious and visible characteristics, there is no easy way of knowing their underlying causes. You may know *what* is happening, but that doesn't necessarily tell you *why*.

Basic underlying assumptions are those beliefs so endemic to an organization that no one inside ever considers discussing them, even if they were aware of them, because such discussions would be considered pointless. They begin with the most basic concepts, such as "What does it mean to be in business?" Essentially, this implies a need to engage in economic exchange and, by doing so, to create enough profit both to cover one's costs and to build additional equity. Or at least this would seem to be so in capitalistic economies. There are different fundamental rules of success, for instance, in other types of economies and in other industries such as governmental agencies, educational institutions, and other not-for-profit entities (though all are frequently challenged now with questions about efficiency—but that is another story).

Basic cultural assumptions are embedded in and intertwined with national, religious, and ethnic concepts, as well. What, for instance, is the role of women in society and the workplace? What is basic human nature, and how are people motivated to work and to participate? As described earlier, it is this level of culture that is much more felt than thought. And it is this level that is most involved in driving the actual behavior of an organization.

Chris Argyris and his colleagues began looking at the differences between behavior and espoused values in organizations some time ago.[6] What they found was amazing consistency in *differences* between espoused values and actual behavior. While the values that people espoused varied widely, individual behavior, when observed, was almost entirely consistent and conformed to four "governing variables": (1) achieve one's own purposes, (2) win rather than lose, (3) don't acknowledge negative feelings, and (4) act rationally.[7] According to their research, the pervasive nature of culture in the larger society continued to drive such behavior in people despite their beliefs that things should really be otherwise.

Organizations also act in contradiction to their espoused values, and, according to Shein, it is at these points where an organization is particularly ineffective. Whatever the stated vision and goals of an organization may be, it actually operates according to more deeply held expectations and assumptions. This is, in fact, the downfall of most organizational change efforts that only work at the level of espoused values, in terms of developing vision statements, strategic plans, and the like. In order to create true, fundamental change, the organization must be able to incorporate changes back into the deeper levels of experiential knowledge, not just intellectual understanding. To do this requires first an ability to "let go" of older assumptions before attempting to incorporate new behaviors. It then requires that new models of success be developed and incorporated into the basic assumptions of the organization.

All of this becomes much more complicated, of course, since there is not just one overriding model of culture within an organization. As noted earlier, each profession and area of expertise brings with it its own set of assumptions and expectations. And though all may be focused on the ultimate success of the organization, each interprets what this means in a somewhat different way. The sales force, of course, understands that regardless of how well run the operations are, if products aren't sold at a profit, there will be no money for operations and very soon, no company. And that is true. And the security personnel understand that regardless of how much profit the company makes in sales, if all of it goes out the door through external or internal theft, it is as if no profit were ever made. And the accountants in many different functions understand that a business is ultimately an economic operation, and that if bills and taxes are not paid, and payroll not met, and so on, the organization will not continue—and that the final measure of a business is found in its accounting. But the government relations personnel know how intimately a modern organization is tied to the political realm, and how quickly a change in legislation can affect both markets and business operations, in the form of regulations, trade agreements, and so on. All of these are true, and none of them really any *more* true than the others. A business organization, especially a larger corporation, is a very complex combination of functions that must be aligned.

Just as complex, though, is the relationship between various aspects of culture, as described here. It is one thing to know how a company describes itself. It is another to see how it actually works in real time. But it is yet another thing entirely to understand the fundamental causes for why it is the way it is and acts and responds the way it does, because these are issues that can rarely be explained by those involved, at least in any coherent fashion.

A company may act very directly in concert with its stated beliefs. But given the complexities of societies and markets that would be rare. There are simply too many separate and varied audiences, each with their own agendas and ways of understanding, to allow many simple approaches. To provide *exactly* the same picture to financial analysts, environmental activists, legislators, and unions in a way that would be pleasing and understandable to all, for instance, would be difficult.

The greater the sense of coherence though between an organization's beliefs and values and its actions, the stronger the organization will be. And correspondingly, the greater the disparity, the more trouble the organization is likely to face. Generally, such disparities do not result so much from malicious intent as from competing pressures that require differing responses. Rather than intentionally violating their own rules or values, companies often find their stated positions and their actions "drifting" apart in order to remain viable. How does a coal or an oil company in the United States, for instance, act in an environmentally friendly way while competing against companies in other nations with no environmental regulations to speak of?

COMBINING CULTURES

Such obvious disparities can generally be dealt with, simply because they are so obvious. The more complicated issues, especially in the context of mergers and acquisitions, happen at a more subtle level. When an organization is chosen as the "target company" for a potential merger or acquisition, it will typically be based on some combination of beliefs and knowledge about its operations, markets, and finances. And at some point, there will be efforts to validate and quantify these beliefs through a due diligence process (as will be explored in a later chapter). But nothing about these efforts is likely to get at the most fundamental assumptions that drive the organization and that make it what it is.

In the case of the acquisition of a small, startup organization, such fundamental assumptions are likely to be much "closer to the surface," that is, much less ingrained in the organization, much easier to see, and much less difficult to change. But even this can be overestimated. If the owners and employees involved are only hoping to cash in on their efforts quickly, whether through a lucrative IPO, a merger with a well-financed partner that is likely to grant large stock options, or being acquired at a substantial premium, then they may be very agreeable with change, at least at the outset. If, though, you are dealing with a very creative and talented group of idealists who believe they have created something unique together, and value that at least equally with the financial aspects, then "capturing and assimilating" them will be a very different effort.

As the age and size of the organizations involved grow, so too will the extent of the issues to be addressed in a M&A deal. As noted earlier, the older the organization and the further removed from the original founders, the less aware employees are likely to be about how assumptions came to be the way they are. Also, the more complex the mixture of previous mergers and acquisitions, of nationalities and ethnic groups, and of changes the organization has already been through, the more complex the issues.

As a general rule, organizations with a greater degree of coherence between their beliefs and their actions are likely to exhibit a greater sense of loyalty by their employees. This might be found, for instance, in an organization that had recently struggled to survive some external threat and had done so successfully. Old assumptions would have been challenged more openly than usual, and successful behaviors chosen or confirmed more consciously. Acquiring the employees after such an experience might involve asking them to give up much more in the process than employees where there was already a good deal of discontent. But again, caution is in order, in that even in cases where the basic beliefs of an organization were being violated by those currently in charge, it might not affect the beliefs by employees about how things *should be*. In fact, if the violation of the basic beliefs is seen as the reason for the merger or acquisition, the beliefs themselves might actually be reinforced significantly. And there is no simple way to sort our such complex issues through questioning or observing employees, especially in an environment that is not your own.

Any effort to combine or merge organizational cultures must ultimately affect the tacit realm of underlying expectations and assumptions. Old habits do die hard, and even "young" habits can be very entrenched if they have created a specific formula for success of an organization. Argyris' primary technique for working with such organizational behaviors has been one of bringing them to conscious awareness so that they can be acknowledged and examined—essentially a process of learning and decision making. He did this by having participants write down details of real or imagined conversations about an organizational problem between themselves and a key decision maker, then also writing the things that were *thought* but not *said*. The differences between the verbal and mental conversations revealed many of the underlying tensions between the espoused values of the organization and the actual ways that it behaved.

Shein's approach deals with trying to "seed" new cultural elements into an existing organization. One method is to promote people who reflect the desired cultural characteristics into positions where they can begin to influence the broader organization. Another is to develop a "parallel system" inside the organization that is actually involved in real, ongoing work, but does it from a different perspective. The concept, apparently, is to spread "new successes" into an old culture.

Each of these approaches comes from thoughtful and well-researched work and may prove useful in your setting. The primary difficulty with these, as with any approach that can actually reach into the tacit realm of an organization, is that they require time for examination, reflection, and stumbling through learning new habits. The greatest enemy of this learning and embedding of new ideas is often the pressure of a merger or acquisition deal itself. Deals that are set up with such high expectations that everything has to go perfectly from the outset, as if everything can continue at full speed throughout the process and only get better, are often doomed. People can be pushed and forced into initially *acting* like there is no transition needed, but at some point reality will hit. The greater the underlying tensions, the more mess there will be to clean up when it finally happens.

The next few chapters will look at other aspects of organizations, closer to the "surface" of more familiar work and activities, but still tied to these same themes. They involve the processes by which work is accomplished, but also some of the assumptions that drive the processes. Those chapters will set the stage for some of the deeper-seated issues that must be understood and addressed to make a merger or acquisition successful.

NOTES

1. Bob Montgomery, unpublished doctoral paper, The Fielding Institute, December 9, 1998.

2. Edgar Schein, *The Corporate Culture Survival Guide* (Jossey-Bass, 1999).

3. Ibid.

4. Ibid.

5. Ibid.

6. See C. Argyris, "Tacit Knowledge and Management," in R. J. Sternberg and J. A. Horvath (eds.), *Tacit Knowledge in Professional Practice: Researcher and Practitioner Perspectives* (Lawrence Erlbaum Associates, 1999), pp. 123–140; C. Argyris and R. Putnam et al., *Action Science: Concepts, Methods, and Skills for Research and Intervention* (Jossey-Bass, 1985); C. Argyris and D. Schon, *Theory in Practice: Increasing Professional Effectiveness* (Jossey-Bass, 1974).

7. Argyris and Putnam et al., *Action Science*, p. 89.

Chapter 4

Human Capital

In every merger or acquisition there is intent to capitalize on the use of existing assets. There is a sense by one or both companies involved that overhead expenses could be reduced or production and distribution efficiencies increased or greater economies of scale in some other way achieved by combining the organizations. And the typical approach assumes that the physical and financial assets of the companies, as reflected in the balance sheets, represent the value of the assets.

But the notion that tangible property equates with organizational value has been eroding for some time, despite the fact that it continues to dominate the mindsets of deal makers. Peter Drucker used the term "knowledge worker" over three decades ago to describe a change in the nature of work. As he pointed out: "Modern society is a society of large organized institutions. In every one of them, including the armed services, the center of gravity has shifted to the knowledge worker, the man who puts to work what he has between his ears rather than the brawn of his muscles or the skill of his hands."[1]

Every organization that seeks to produce anything (e.g., information, services, or products) utilizes the intelligence(s) of its members in some way. The concept of an information-based economy is predicated on the idea of information itself as a commodity. Knowledge-work may be sold in the form of a computer software program or a book or a speech, or it may be a solution to a specific problem, be it a new organizational design or the right way to handle a difficult employee problem. The connection to mergers and acquisitions lies in the question of how such knowledge is valued, or what part it plays, in a transaction.

In general, there are three broad approaches that attempt to capture the intangible, human value of organizations. Scandinavian companies (primarily Swedish) have taken the lead in developing methods for measuring intellectual assets. U.S. companies have focused on intellectual property, primarily in the form of copyrights and patents. Japanese companies have purportedly taken a different approach, in fostering the ongoing creation of knowledge.

From a strictly financial perspective, the novelty of the idea of intellectual capital is the recognition and identification of knowledge as something of tangible value to an organization—something that can be captured on the balance sheets and used to leverage financial investments. Much of the attention focused on the topic of intellectual capital has been on attempts to "account" for the value of knowledge, most frequently attributed to efforts coming out of Sweden.

Apparently, the initial concern of the companies involved in Sweden was over the high rates of return being required by investors due to the lack of "tangible" assets owned by financial services companies. This led to their efforts to more clearly value "intangible" assets, so that they could compete more evenly for investment capital with the traditional, industrial companies.

The value of intangible assets has not been lost on the United States, though. In fact, while the overall trade deficit of the United States was $339 billion in 1999, it ran a $25 billion trade surplus in intellectual property revenues. Over $37 billion worth of "patented information" was exported in the form of licenses for software and even broadcasting rights.[2]

And while the assets themselves may be somewhat intangible, their monetary value, at least in some cases, is certainly not. In one of the more notable acquisitions of this type, IBM paid $3.5 billion for Lotus, which on paper was worth only $230 million. This was apparently due to IBM's belief that the technical and management talent of the Lotus employees would provide this high level of return on its investment in them.[3]

Skandia AFS, a Swedish company at the forefront of this movement, developed a "formula" for the idea:

Human Capital + Structural Capital = Intellectual Capital.[4]

Human capital referred to the intangible attributes that the company was clear it could not actually own. These included things such as the knowledge, skills, and abilities to innovate that resided in individual employees. It also included the values, culture, and philosophy of the company itself. Structural capital, on the other hand, encompassed those tangible things produced by employees that could be captured and retained.

Figure 4.1
A Basic Systems Model

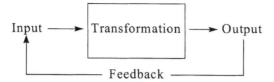

Figure 4.2
An Intellectual Capital Process

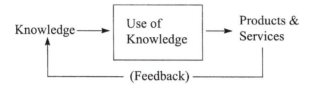

These included software programs, patents, trademarks, relationships with key customers, and so on.

A CONCEPTUAL MODEL

For purposes of discussion, intellectual capital might be viewed, as in Figure 4.1, from a very basic systems model.

In this case, *Input* would be the knowledge gained or acquired by the organization. *Transformation* is the way in which the organization utilizes that knowledge. *Outputs* are those products or services delivered by the organization, and *Feedback* is what is put back into the organization as a result of the process. This could be described by labeling the model as shown in Figure 4.2.

INPUT: HOW THE ORGANIZATION ACQUIRES KNOWLEDGE

Knowledge inputs come from a variety of sources. As described by Skandia, these can be broadly broken down into *human capital* and *structural capital*.

Human capital obviously comes from people. But just who represents the source of this capital for an organization is not so self-evident. The majority of writers on the topic of intellectual capital seem to take a "key employee" viewpoint, exactly in line with the typical view of most Western companies.

As shown in Figure 4.3, for instance, employees may be seen in terms

Figure 4.3
Employee Value Matrix

of the value their contributions seem to make to overall organizational success, as compared to the ease with which a given individual can be replaced.[5] The level of individual importance has to do with how much difference it makes to the organization who it is that fills a given role. Only key employees are seen as exceptionally valuable, both individually and professionally. Highly skilled technicians are increasingly necessary and valuable (especially those with information technology skills), but most organizations have little concern about the individual personalities that fill the roles.

In most organizations, key employees would most readily be identified as those at an "officer" level who had access to material information about company operations and dealings and would be subject to insider trading rules for purposes of stock transactions. But these may or may not be the persons who actually make the most difference to the organization, in reality. True key employees, from this framework, are those who create the reasons that customers continue to be attracted to this company rather than to a competitor.

Such thinking is contradicted by other writers, though. According to Pinchot & Pinchot, "Organizations become more intelligent when they find ways to bring the intelligence of every member into supporting the purpose and goals of the organization."[6] This is much closer to the ideas espoused within the "quality" movements (e.g., Total Quality Management and Continuous Quality Improvement), which are often equated with a Japanese style of management and which recognize that laborers closest to actual processes are the ones who know them best and have the greatest potential for improving them. It also fits with the Japanese approach to knowledge creation as described by Nonaka and Takeuchi.[7]

Most U.S. companies seem drawn to this "key employee" view of creativity and talent. While Nathan Myhrvold was chief technology officer at Microsoft, he recruited some 245 senior researchers from other corporations and universities under the assumption that bringing together a large collection of brilliant minds would have to produce exceptional results.[8] (Individual brilliance and collective creativity are not, of course, synonymous, but this doesn't seem to stop attempts to make it so.)

A critical issue within the arena of human capital is the question of intellectual property rights. As noted in Skandia's definition, individual intellect or creativity is not something that can be owned by a company. Yet it has long been the legal standard that any work produced by an employee within the scope of his or her workplace responsibilities or on paid company time was the property of the company, unless it chose to share it otherwise. This was true whether the product was a routine part of the employee's responsibilities or resulted in a major scientific or economic breakthrough (e.g., a patent for a new vaccine).

Ownership and protection of information has been a serious issue for some time. It is likely to continue to be one of the crucial issues for both businesses and governments in the near future for a number of reasons. One is the ease with which information can now be accessed and shared through such media as the Internet, which was developed specifically as a vehicle for communication between government and academic institutions. Questions about who should have access to and how to protect information range from issues such as the sale or exchange of books or music on the Internet to the formula for creating a nuclear weapon. On an individual basis the question of who owns a person's ideas, or the products resulting from them, is likely to become just as hotly debated.

This problem is manifested in the changing structure of organizations, and the nature of employment. When lifetime employment was at least a conceivable goal, there was the potential for a long-term, collaborative relationship between employee and company in that the employee was given time and resources, including training, to develop ideas and products which could then be marketed and sold by others. If the product did well, all in the organization stood to benefit (even if some more than others).

But under the "new employment contracts" that began to define different relations between employees and companies in the 1980s, there is little incentive for loyalty or long-term payoff. In the world of mergers and acquisitions, the loyalty of "acquired" employees to their former company has little or no meaning to an acquiring company in many cases, except that it may present resistance or conflicts during the transition. Unless an employee personally owns a patent or copyright or has some other legal claim to a product or idea, whatever was produced is the property of the company. Ownership of the product (software, patented formula, etc.) can be acquired and the employee that produced it simply dismissed.

Many computer software firms, probably the archetype of organizations dependent upon intellectual capital, have long since recognized the need to distribute ownership throughout the workforce. Typically, they have done so through the granting of stock options as a way of sharing future successes in return for an investment of expertise by current employees. This has been most typical in start-up organizations that lacked the funds to pay large salaries at the outset.

Where there was once an assumption that employees were either hired with the necessary expertise or would develop professionally from experience on the job, there now appears to be a growing demand for finding and acquiring the right knowledge and skills for new requirements by corporations. As the need for key employees grows, especially in high technology companies, it is becoming more common for teams of employees, or even whole companies, to be bought to acquire the necessary talent, as in the case of many of Cisco's acquisitions.

In fact, the need for upgrading employee skills is happening so quickly that many companies are now laying off "outdated" employees and hiring new ones at the same time, in a practice referred to as "churning." According to an American Management Association study, this was occurring at 36% of 2000 companies surveyed in 1999.[9] Just as the pace of change seems too rapid for companies to keep up with through internal growth or evolution (which drives more mergers and acquisitions), change also seems too rapid for traditional employee training and development. Rather than change and modify, we're now "disposing and replacing." But to borrow a term from consumer electronics, this assumes a "plug-and-play" ease of fit—that the new "parts" will be compatible with the existing structure, with no need for adaptation. And this is a very broad—and in our judgment, faulty—assumption.

TRANSFORMATION: HOW THE ORGANIZATION USES KNOWLEDGE

The key difference in intellectual capital as opposed to other forms of capital or raw materials is that intellectual capital is not depleted but in fact grows with use. To return to the basic systems model (see Figure 4.4 for reference), the transformation process involves not only producing goods or services, but also transforming human capital into structural capital—that part of intellectual capital which is most directly owned and controlled by the organization.

While the term *human capital* is used above in reference to the input

Figure 4.4
Focus on the Transformation Process

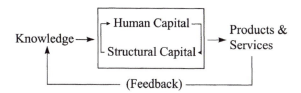

section of the model, it is the way in which the organization puts these resources to work that creates value. As shown in this evolution of the model, turning human capital into structural capital, which then creates an environment for developing more human capital, is a primary function of the transformation process. Referring again to Skandia's two-part definition of intellectual capital, structural capital becomes the more tangible evidence of the human capital of the organization. But what different organizations value, and the ways in which they harness and organize these assets, varies immensely.

The most obvious and tangible evidence of structural capital within U.S.-based companies is patents. This was the starting point for Dow Chemical's efforts to begin managing its intellectual capital. Reportedly, Dow had some 29,000 active patents in 1993 when the effort began, but less than half of these were being used.[10] The initial effort apparently amounted to creating a centralized method of actively managing the patents, applying those that had remained neglected, and weeding out those that were no longer useful.

Knowledge-based companies, such as management consulting firms, have attempted to capture and share internal expertise. In some, the approach seems to rely primarily on the voluntary input by employees into computer databases of knowledge gained during the process of projects for customers. At others, employees are evaluated and compensated based on their contributions to the company's store of information. This stored information can then be accessed by all employees, providing a means to distribute knowledge to the organization as a whole.

One of the limitations of such an approach to capturing intellectual capital is the future potential, as employees become more aware of the value of their knowledge and creativity, that they may become less willing to share it freely with their employer. If they can gain knowledge and experience, then turn this into valuable ideas or innovations, why not leave the organization and take this into an open marketplace where they might receive much greater rewards for it?

Such potential losses may occur in mergers and acquisitions, as well. What if most of the Lotus employees had decided to leave for other opportunities following the purchase of the company by IBM? There certainly would have been some tangible assets in place with which other IBM employees could have worked. But a great deal of the total value of the organization would have been lost as well.

Much of the complexity of these issues stems from the fact that information, knowledge, and learning cannot be entirely separated from each other. They are not raw materials in the same sense as coal or crude oil, nor are they specific and controlled processes of an assembly line nature. They are embedded in human interactions and ways of understanding the world. As the global economy shifts further in the direction of knowledge-based value, these issues will become more and more apparent. For our purposes, the point is simply to reinforce the idea that purchasing and integrating all or part of a business is simply not the same as gaining and realizing the true value that it may represent.

One of the most common approaches to trying to gather input from employees at many different organizational levels has been the use of workplace teams. The commonsense value of a team is captured by an aphorism such as "all of us (collectively) is smarter than any of us (individually)." But as many organizations have learned, creating such value does not happen automatically. (And as demonstrated by the phenomenon of "groupthink," collective decision making can be detrimental.)

For a time, workplace teams were considered a superior model of practice as compared to the traditional model of independent work common in the United States and other Western economies. This movement seemed strongest in the auto industry at the time when they were losing significant market share to the Japanese. The success of the model in Japan is typically attributed to factors that did not exist in the United States, such as lifetime employment and a culture of collective, versus individual, responsibility. The more likely explanation is that U.S.-based companies are so deeply steeped in Western ideas about individualism that true teamwork is "countercultural" in a very literal sense.

There is a fundamental conflict between individual and team approaches, which has been described as a tension between the "Me, Inc.", an approach in which the employment relationship is a "fling, not a marriage," and the self-directed team, which is responsible for its entire operation.[11] Further, until we learn how to practice collective, rather than individual, accountability, and to create corresponding changes in reward and compensation systems, we will continue to live with this conflict.[12]

An alternative concept to that of formal teams is what has been called "communities of practice." Communities of practice are informal networks that develop around common interests. These happen in neighborhoods and civic groups as well as companies. They would seem to have as much a social as a professional composition, in that they might be found in groups having lunch on some regular basis, or exercising together, or formed only through sharing of e-mail. These social bonds tend to create a basis for trust and sharing of communication such that information received from a member of this network would likely be relied upon more readily than formal communication from an organization.

The critical difference between these and more formal groups, such as teams, is that they emerge on their own rather than being planned and created, and that they are self-sustaining, not being responsible to any authority or hierarchy. When effective, they appear to perform two essential functions: knowledge transfer and innovation.

Gathering knowledge from people in an organization then is not like mining minerals from the earth. There are no deposits of facts stored away in places, waiting for discovery. But even more important, and more difficult, than gathering knowledge is spreading it throughout a workplace and putting it to use. Interestingly, a recent survey found that despite all the effort and money being put into the development of formal "knowledge databases" by organizations, most of the executives questioned thought that the most efficient means of sharing ideas and putting them to use were through informal employee networks.[13]

The idea of capturing and using the collective knowledge of a group of people in a company, or in any type of organization, then, confronts a multitude of both practical and basic theoretical issues. First, how does an organization recognize those bits of knowledge that create value, and then how does it extract or harness that knowledge for use by the organization? While people have been selling both their labor and their ideas for eons, as ideas and information become more clearly the raw material of commerce, it is not so self-evident that successive generations, with changing values and priorities, will automatically engage in the same exchange.

Knowledge becomes valuable only in its application.[14] Therefore, there are likely to be few persons who can simply auction their thinking or ideas on a free market; most will need the support and resources of others, within some sort of organization, in order to turn what they know into a marketable commodity. But the traditional organization is simply not going to be able to "purchase" the ability to create and innovate through buying a small, young, progressive start-up company and plugging it in to an old structure. There is a more fundamental level of change required than is apparent in most merger and acquisition activity at present.

Purchasing someone's ideas is not necessarily the same as purchasing their energy or time. Relationships between people and organizations may become much more crucial in the future, as work necessitates a different level of input. This is much of the underlying argument in the push for more "democratic" or "empowered" organizations, in which people have a much more authentic level of participation, even down to the lowest ranks and positions.

The primary arguments against traditional bureaucratic structures have been their inability to adapt to changing environments and their lack of responsiveness to individual customers. The idea of flattening organizations, that is, removing layers of middle managers, has been most often focused on getting persons in an organization closer to the customers of their services or products. In this way, the organization was to become more responsive.

Teams do not automatically create these necessary relationships. But in some cases, they may provide the type of environment into which people will want to invest themselves. A study of high-performance teams found that "real teams are deeply committed to their purpose, goals, and approach. High-performance team members are also very committed to one another. Both understand that the wisdom of teams comes with a focus on collective work-products, personal growth, and performance results."[15]

As studies have found, true high-performance teams are rare. This often has to do with the environments in which they are formed though, and the degree to which the autonomy of the team itself is supported. It may be that the basic generation of sellable knowledge in the future happens even more obviously within teams or other "local" (primarily meaning stable and familiar) clusters of people, who then self-manage its use.

But following this train of thought still leaves dilemmas regarding the transfer of knowledge into an organization in such a way that it becomes structural knowledge—something tangible and usable by the organization itself. Informal communities of practice are much more prevalent than workplace teams, especially high-performing ones, and they tend to form the basis of natural learning groups more than formal teams. In addition, there seem to be strong communication barriers within organizations created by cultures that reach beyond the organization's boundaries.

These arguments would seem to lead to the conclusion that little in the way of knowledge work could be getting done at present, despite the apparent evidence to the contrary. What, more likely, is true is that the efficiency of knowledge use within organizations is extremely suboptimal. If so, it is likely due, at least in part, to the fact that learning is still separate from work. There is no natural feedback loop within most organizations which allows for collective reflection about why things are done as they are or even why a process worked in one situation and not another. Efforts to record a group's experience on a project, for instance, and make this widely available to other employees may address the issue of most people not even knowing what others in the same organization are doing, but it is still a far cry from collective learning, or the creation of structural capital.

The Japanese approach to organizational knowledge, as opposed to that of U.S. companies, still seems to value both self-directed work teams and the ranks of middle management. This approach sees the role of middle managers as taking the strategic direction of senior executives and marrying it to the experiential knowledge of front-line employees. Workplace teams are given broad latitude in devising ways to implement the vision of senior managers. In doing so, teams may be involved in a significant amount of trial-and-error experimentation and cross-fertilization of ideas with other functional areas of the organization.

According to Nonaka and Takeuchi, Japanese companies work from a different philosophical base when it comes to the creation and use of knowledge. This is grounded in their use of experiential (tacit) knowledge, as opposed to a Western concept of "objective" knowledge.

As explained earlier, most U.S.-based companies see the value of intellectual or human capital almost exclusively in terms of "products." Valuable knowledge is something that has been transformed into a tangible "object," through a patent or copyright, or at least through its being recorded as a specific idea in a database in a way that it can be retrieved and transmitted. What began as a notion, or concept, or image in someone's mind is made *explicit*, and only *then* becomes of value.

Putting explicit knowledge to work usually involves combining it with other explicit knowledge to form complete plans or products. These might be the ideas that go into the development of a new marketing plan or the knowledge of various software programmers that becomes the code for a new application.

As long as the ideas or knowledge being worked with are "factual" or objective, they can be used and "engineered" like other objects. This works fine as long as the goal is simply to use existing knowledge to create products. But this runs into real problems when the goal is to use knowledge to create *change*.

As anyone who has ever struggled with a creative process knows, new ideas do not usually just appear, fully conceived, out of nowhere. They typically begin as vague notions or images or intuitive senses about something. Often, they get cluttered with pieces of other, already familiar ideas that may or may not apply in this case. Over time they become clearer and at some point can be articulated in a way that makes sense. But even this may be just the beginning of what eventually turns into a whole new idea.

Similarly, incorporating an idea from someone else is not just a matter of "swallowing it whole." It has to be "digested," if you will. To make sense of it, it has to be connected with existing ideas or things already understood. It's in this context that we typically experience that sense of *"aha!"*—where we go from recognizing the words we are reading or hearing to truly identifying with the understanding we think is intended. We have an "experience" of understanding.

For better or worse, moving to this level of experience is not a clear, rote, efficient process. It generally takes a lot of floundering about, "trying things on"—and requires room for experiment and failure.

When you begin to see how all these ideas converge, it creates a clearer sense about some of the conflicts within organizations. In the United States, knowledge is assumed to be the product of brilliant or enlightened individuals. The knowledge they produce is transmitted to others through educational systems where it can be digested and incorporated into each student's understanding (more or less). Students become workers in order to put this knowledge to productive use.

For the most part, academic institutions have been the places of learning—where people reflected and studied what *has* happened, in hindsight. Companies have been in the business of *doing*, and time for thoughtful reflection was a luxury, if not considered simply wasteful. Training and development in the workforce at large were necessary evils that hopefully paid off down the line but were generally viewed as impediments to production. Even organizations that relied heavily on research and development functions were focused on *applied* research, to produce *useful* knowledge, not learning.

It's no wonder that organizational change has been so hard since it requires not just application of existing ideas, but new learning by employees in order to happen effectively. And there is no natural place for this in most organizations today—with a few rare exceptions.

To be sure, organizations are using information to produce goods and services on a daily basis. Arguably, they are doing so with better efficiency than in the past. But there are still many important questions to be answered about acquiring and integrating human capital in the process of a merger or acquisition.

OUTPUT: PRODUCTS AND SERVICES

The value of ideas or intelligence or information for organizations is ultimately in their usefulness to other people (as individuals, communities, varieties of systems, etc.). Sveiby distinguishes between two types of organizations, according to the different ways in which they market and sell intellectual capital. One type uses an information-focused strategy, and the other a knowledge-focused strategy.[16] An example of the former type, a company that uses an information-focused strategy, is a computer software company such as Microsoft or Netscape. In this case, knowledge is sold as a product, specifically as computer programs. These are created and developed by large groups of professionals, sharing information and expertise, which results in a single product. The investment is measured by the cost of the time and number of people required for development of the program itself. Reproduction of the product, once it is developed, is insignificant.

The key to the success of this strategy is the degree to which this product is found to be useful or popular by large numbers of customers. Under this scenario, each product is made once and sold many times. Therefore the focus of the process is on efficiency. Organizationally, this strategy sees people as a cost of production. The greater the speed to market of a product, the greater the value of that product to the customer; and the lower the cost of production, the greater the potential profit margin.

The alternative approach, that of using a knowledge-focused strategy, is represented by management consulting firms such as McKinsey & Co. These organizations tend to sell knowledge as a process. Rather than creating products to be mass-produced, they focus on creating customized solutions (information) for individual clients. Their focus, then, is on effectiveness. They tend to see employees as sources of revenue, rather than costs of business, and therefore tend to invest more in the human than the technological.

These examples, of course, represent only two ends of a spectrum. There are companies which mass produce generic products, then customize them to the needs of individual clients. Other companies sell, or even give away, basic products, only as a means to gain service contracts, the basis of their real business. In each case the product or service is the outcome of the knowledge or expertise of individuals or of the organization as a whole, in some way.

While not traditionally thought of as a product or service, another output of the intellectual capital process is the information used to inform or persuade shareholders and potential investors about the value of the organization. Theoretically, financial analysts are swayed only by business fundamentals or financial results, but, as was noted by a growing number of corporations, the less tangible their assets, the more problematic the traditional assumptions became.

The simplest formula for attempting to capture such values seems to be what is referred to as Tobin's Q, which calculates intellectual capital by subtracting the book value (assets shown on the financial statements) from the market value (the actual selling price) of an organization.[17] Such intangible assets are traditionally captured in accounting terms as "goodwill." But these intangible factors represent a growing percentage of the total value of corporations, and the anticipation of future earnings appears, at present, to be more important than all the cash flow and buildings and materials that a corporation might own.

Figure 4.5
Focus on the Closed-System Feedback Loop

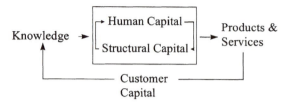

As noted earlier, work on finding ways to measure and demonstrate, quantitatively, the value of knowledge has primarily come out of Sweden. The original Skandia IC Annual Report, published in 1994, contained 91 different measurements grouped in five areas: Financial Focus, Customer Focus, Process Focus, Renewal and Development Focus, and Human Focus.

Edvinsson and Malone added an additional 73 indices to create what they believe should be a future, universal IC reporting structure.[18] They sorted and refined this list, noting whether each measurement represents a dollar value, a count, or a percentage and eventually pared this down to a list of nine indices:

1. Market share
2. Satisfied customer index
3. Leadership index
4. Motivation index
5. Index of R&D resources/total resources
6. Index of training hours
7. Performance/quality goal
8. Employee retention
9. Administration efficiency/revenues

FEEDBACK: MEASUREMENT AND REGULATION

The basic systems model introduced as the framework for this discussion is typically used as a representation for a closed system, one which only regulates its own given behavior, such as the mechanism of a thermostat. It serves to activate a heater or air conditioner but does not alter the mechanism itself, or change other parts of the environment in which it operates.

In one way, the feedback mechanism may be seen as the capturing of customer capital (see Figure 4.5). While the original Skandia model embeds this within the structural capital area, later models developed by other intellectual capital theorists and practitioners separate it, creating a third area of equivalent emphasis. This would imply a distinct relationship between a company and its customers, separate from but equal to that with its employees and strategic partners. The emphasis would seem to be on *relationship*—something of enduring value and duration, beyond a specific transaction.

Adding this third arena to the model creates an important shift of influence on organizations to factors outside the traditional boundaries. It is one that has been experienced by many companies, in very real ways, in their efforts to focus on being "customer-driven." In part, this has involved the recognition that it is more cost-efficient to keep existing customers and build additional business with them than it is to attract new customers. It is also apparent in the ways in which customer needs and satisfaction have become the measurement of quality, as opposed to internal or engineering-culture standards. Despite this growing emphasis, customer capital is probably the worst managed asset within the area of intellectual capital. Many organizations could not even identify who their customers actually are.

As used here, the term customer refers to persons outside the organization who pay money for goods or services. There is a growing emphasis, though, on recognizing and meeting the needs of internal customers (those inside the same organization for whom work is produced), and the same issues and principles tend to apply equally in both arenas.

Given the typical American understanding of intellectual or human capital as a patent, or copyright, or some other tangible product, dealing with the acquisition or merging of truly intangible characteristics like customer capital is going to continue as a major challenge. But it is one that will have to be faced sooner rather than later if companies are going to realize the value they have promised out of a transaction. Questions of what is valuable and who can produce value, are going to need to move to the forefront of deal making.

SUMMARY AND DISCUSSION

The concept of intellectual capital and the many related issues discussed in this chapter seem all to be tied to a vague but growing notion that, where we once lived in a world of things (tangible objects), we now live more in a world of thoughts. Value now comes not from physical objects, but from ideas. We have explored our physical world and know where and how to access its resources. We know the basic means of production and continue to refine the efficiency of these to the point that the physical materials themselves are only a minimal cost of end products. The raw material of successful organizations is quickly becoming its people and their abilities. But knowing how to access these resources and use them efficiently is an entirely new challenge.

This change in focus and emphasis, from physical resources and assets to human ones, shifts much of the burden of future economic success into what has been the traditional arena of human resources. But traditional HR skills are not going to be adequate to these future tasks.

The economic systems of the past, primarily represented by bureaucratic organizations, were established for efficiency. They could organize the repetition of activities between large numbers of people to reproduce vast quantities of limited types of products. But they required compliance, not innovation or independent thought. Advances in technology now allow mass customization such that large organizations can tailor products to individual customers, and this requires new skills.[19]

The more innovative of even the large, traditional corporations have recognized these changes. They are living with their realities every day. But understanding what to do about them is not simple. Early answers struggled with repetitive cycles of change and re-engineering. Lately, the "answer" has been seen in terms of faster change through mergers or acquisitions. But the challenges remain unmet.

Organizations are comprised of people (as they have always been), but the value of key people to the organization is changing dramatically under these new paradigms. Within bureaucracies, very few people think, but many people act. As organizations grapple with the issues of a knowledge-based economy and begin to move to new structures and relationships, it is not so clear whose knowledge is valued, or in what way.

An emphasis on "key employees" still prevails—it has simply shifted from an elitism of (physical) property ownership to an elitism of intellect. Those whose skills and knowledge are tied to the core functions of the organization will be more and more valued while others continue to be expendable (if not more so).

While these concepts are related to organizational structure, which will be dealt with more specifically in a later chapter, they directly affect the first model—the input. The model is not linear. It feeds upon itself, in a continuous cycle. The way in which the organization is structured will evidence the relationships that it has with each group of people. If core employees are valued in a significantly different way from the more peripheral employees in these models, then the intellectual resources available to the organization can be expected to be limited to them. Exchange of knowledge happens by way of some form of communication, and communication is embedded in relationships (if just the relationship of sharing a common language).

What is it, then, that can be provided by (or received from) individuals which is valuable to an organization? What do they provide in terms of input or human capital? They provide *professional knowledge*—in terms of their formal, academic training, as well as links to their own professional networks and communities of practice, *knowledge based on relationships with customers* (cycling back from the Feedback section of the systems model), *informal knowledge* of the cultures and understanding of the various systems with which the organization interacts, and much, much more, undoubtedly.

Attempting to capture these within a stable, existing organization would be a tremendous challenge in itself. Trying to capture the value of human capital from the process of a merger or acquisition, given all the other complexities involved, is going to require approaches that are probably only just being conceived.

This, then, leads to the question of how to access this knowledge: how to transform it into the structural capital that the organization can own and control? Directing employees to enter such information into a computer database for the good of the organization is likely to meet with limited success, at best. Continuing to tell employees (as has been the historical tradition in most companies) that any valuable ideas they have on work time belong to the organization, has about equal potential, especially as they begin to see the value of ideas become more obvious.

Organizing employees into truly functional teams seems to be a pervasive theme throughout much of the literature about human capital, and would seem to offer great potential. If levels of communication and trust can be established such that people learn with and from each other, there is the potential that much of the learning could be captured and made explicit, rather than being left to individuals' understandings and memories. But while some truly high-performance teams appear to have been developed, they are definitely the exception rather than the norm. (Highly functional teams tend to conflict with mechanistic, efficiency-driven structures.) And while few organizations today would describe themselves as bureaucracies, there are just as few that seem to support anything other than significant control, in some form, by those in the most senior positions (e.g., corporate directors and/or executive officers).

As ways of capturing knowledge evolve in the future, there will still be questions of how to transform it into something of value. The massive number of books, journals, newsletters, television channels and other popular media and press, as well as the Internet, have created an overload of information in which it all becomes equally insignificant. Therefore, not only capturing the right information and knowledge, but also transforming it into a useful product or service, will be a critical task. (Keeping up with the evolving concept of "useful" may become its own core competency, as choices continue to expand so dramatically.) The gap between concepts of "value" and "values" may begin to close, under this scenario as well as people reassess what is truly important to them in the face of so many choices.

Finally, it is within the "Feedback" section of the model used here for illustration where the most dramatic future changes may take place. As differences between organizations, members, and customers begin to blur, the very nature of relationships within economic systems may become unrecognizable, as compared to current standards. If customers are able, by way of interactive technology, to become a functional part of the design process (ordering exactly what they want and simply having the components assembled, for instance), and having their preferences learned by the organization, then, at some point, they become somewhat intertwined with the organization itself. (Possibly the high-tech equivalent of neighborhood food cooperatives of past generations.)

While outside of the scope of the typical literature on mergers and acquisitions, issues about people and human capital lie at the heart of value creation. Organizations that are able to recognize and capitalize on these less familiar issues, and that develop successful strategies for doing so consistently, will be the organizations of the future. The ways in which human capital connects with, and is actually embedded in, organizational culture and learning will be further explained in the chapters that follow.

NOTES

1. P. Drucker, *The Effective Executive* (HarperCollins, 1966/1993), p. 3.

2. Bernard Wysocki, Jr., "The Outlook," *Wall Street Journal*, April 10, 2000.

3. L. Edvinsson and M. Malone, *Intellectual Capital: Realizing Your Company's True Value by Finding Its Hidden Roots* (HarperCollins, 1997).

4. Ibid.

5. T. Stewart, *Intellectual Capital: The New Wealth of Nations* (Currency/Doubleday, 1997).

6. G. Pinchot and E. Pinchot, *The Intelligent Organization: Engaging the Talent and Initiative of Everyone in the Workplace.* (Berrett-Koehler, 1994), pp. 33–34.

7. Ikujiro Nonaka and Hirotaka Takeuchi, *The Knowledge-Creating Company: How Japanese Companies Create the Dynamics of Innovation* (Oxford University Press, 1995).

8. R. Stross, "Mr. Gates Builds His Brain Trust." *Fortune*, December 8, 1997.

9. Patrick Barta, "Firms Face Myriad Pressures to 'Churn' Employees as They Upgrade Job Skills," *Wall Street Journal*, March 13, 2000.

10. T. Stewart, "Your Company's Most Valuable Asset: Intellectual Capital," *Fortune*, October 3, 1994.

11. Stewart, *Intellectual Capital*.

12. Edgar Schein, *The Corporate Culture Survival Guide* (Jossey-Bass, 1999).

13. Pamela Sebastian Ridge, "Knowledge Sharing Isn't Always Best Handled by the Technology-Minded," *Wall Street Journal*, March 23, 2000.

14. Drucker, *The Effective Executive.*

15. J. Katzenbach and D. Smith, *The Wisdom of Teams* (Harvard Business School Press, 1993).

16. K. Sveiby, *The New Organizational Wealth* (Berrett-Kohler, 1997).

17. See J. Quinn, *Intelligent Enterprise: A Knowledge and Service-Based Paradigm for Industry* (The Free Press, 1992); Edvinsson and Malone, *Intellectual Capital.*

18. Edvinsson and Malone, *Intellectual Capital.*

19. T. Peters, *Liberation Management: Necessary Disorganization in the Nanosecond Nineties* (Alfred A. Knopf, 1992).

Chapter 5

The M&A Process

Most business combinations involve a number of fairly predictable stages or parts. While, as noted in Chapter 1, these stages may vary greatly in intensity and order, depending on the industry or the type of transaction involved, each represents some portion of effort that typically is covered in one way or another.

In chronological order, a merger or acquisition most typically includes the following stages or steps:

- Identifying target or candidate companies,
- Narrowing the field of choices,
- Selecting "first-choice" companies,
- Reviewing regulatory compliance,
- Conducting preliminary discussions,
- Signing a letter of intent,
- Conducting due diligence,
- Completing the financial negotiations,
- Signing the definitive agreement,
- Announcing the deal,
- Closing the transaction, and
- Integration of the companies.

Historically, HR professionals have not been included in the preliminary stages of merger or acquisition planning. Often, in fact, they have not been brought in until the substance of the deal was done, at the point of needing to implement what others had planned. Or if HR issues *were* addressed, it was only in terms of dealing with benefits-related issues such as medical plans and pensions. But each stage noted can be greatly affected by issues related to the people involved and/or have real implications for those who will be affected. Unless someone involved in the planning process has the requisite expertise about handling the human side of the transaction, this exclusion will probably be a major mistake.

IDENTIFYING TARGET OR CANDIDATE COMPANIES

Despite all the metaphors and buzzwords developed by management consultants over the decades, we still have a fairly mechanistic view of organizations. They are entities that exist to achieve given purposes. And beyond any rhetoric to the contrary, this view is increasing rather than decreasing. Therefore, when companies are looking for strategic partners, it is not the less tangible, human side of things that usually takes precedence.

As of 1998, nearly half of all American households held investments in the stock market through retirement plans and mutual funds as well as direct investments.[1] At latest report, stock investments accounted for nearly a third of total household wealth in the United States with total value of over \$13 trillion.[2] There is, then, a huge vested interest by the public at large in the performance of publicly traded companies. We may sympathize (or even identify) with the characters in Dilbert, but we also continue to support (at least subtly) the moves by companies to become more profitable. From an even larger perspective then, companies are primarily a means to an end—to create profit, and hopefully, shareholder wealth.

So the choice of potential merger or acquisition partners is primarily utilitarian. It is meant to add economic value. It is greatly a matter of finding another company in the right businesses and markets with current interest or availability in joining forces (often implying some vulnerability), at the right price.

But viewed through a different "lens," a potential M&A partner is also a huge complexity of history and personalities and relationships of people. And it is through this array of people and decisions that the business of each of the organizations has gotten done in the past.

Potential partners (whether by merger or acquisition) are, in most cases, in similar, or at least complimentary, lines of business. Often, in fact, they may have been fairly aggressive competitors, vying for the same customers in the same markets. The degree to which this is true will vary, of course, according to the age and stage of the companies involved. In mature industries, there may be years of such history. In the case of "dot-coms," there may have been very little history *or* rivalry.

Looking past the numbers, melding organizations means getting people to work together toward common ends and doing so in with the greatest efficiency possible. Typically, this implies cooperation rather than conflict; teamwork rather than self-interest. All the numbers may point toward success, but finding the right organizational partner also means finding the right people and dealing with each other in ways that achieve common goals. The best potential partners, in the end, may not be the most obvious strategic matches. But it is from this vantage that the process usually begins.

NARROWING THE FIELD OF CHOICES

Narrowing the field is partly a matter of getting realistic. Many companies might make interesting partners, but which are interested and/or available? And for those who are, what will it take to make the deal happen? Obviously, there will be a great deal of behind-the-scenes research and investigation that takes place, primarily from a strategic standpoint. But a great deal of human emotion can be built during this part of the process, including the potential for decision makers becoming somewhat fixated on one potential company that seems to be the "ideal" that will create what they are hoping to achieve. If this occurs, there is also the threat of having egos invested in a particular outcome, which can significantly influence judgment and objectivity about the deal.

SELECTING "FIRST-CHOICE" COMPANIES

The first-choice company (and as implied here, several may be under review at once) may be the ideal match—or it may be simply the best alternative available, given the circumstances. Obviously, external pressure can affect this choice a great deal. If there is significant M&A activity in a given industry, the pressure to grow increases, while the choice of available partners decreases. Once a first-choice company is (or several are) identified, both pressure to complete the deal and other accompanying activities increase.

REVIEWING REGULATORY COMPLIANCE

This stage of the process is primarily a search for "deal-killers." Are there any issues about the companies under review that are likely to turn into overriding liabilities? To some extent, this stage is preparation for second-guessing by regulatory agencies, such as the Federal Trade Commission. Will this combination of companies create an apparent monopoly or in other ways restrict free trade? (The FTC, of course, is having to review its own processes and guidelines in response to the current evolution of markets and industries.) In addition, there may be unforeseen environmental or legal pitfalls, just waiting to be found after closer scrutiny. And these may have to be reviewed not only in light of past events, but also of changing or pending regulations or legislation. Some of these may be large and obvious. Given current circumstances, for instance, does there need to be concern about cleanup of toxic production or storage sites? Or is there a history of poor employee or customer relations that might lead to class action lawsuits, in light of the current or pending environment? Others may be less obvious, but indicated by things such as a history of barely minimal compliance with environmental or safety regulations, antagonistic relations with state or federal regulatory personnel, or a long list of pending grievances by bargaining groups.

Some of the difficulty of this stage is the need to address issues in terms of probabilities rather than current realities. What may have been considered typical practice, or perfectly acceptable (even if less than ideal) within an industry in times past might be seen as a whole new issue in the present. (Witness the current situation affecting tobacco companies, for instance.)

Up to this point, the review of the companies will be typically based on their potential to *add* value. Due to the general timing of this stage, and the part that it plays in the scheme of M&A deals, information about regulatory compliance problems will often only be factored into decision making in light of the larger prospects for the deal. If the mood to this point has been that the deal is not only good, but possibly critical in order to save both companies, even fairly significant issues can become minimized, only to raise their ugly heads again later.

CONDUCTING PRELIMINARY DISCUSSIONS

Until this stage, most of the activity will have been done very quietly and behind the scenes. Now is the time when things become serious. In the case of a merger or some other cooperative alliance, both parties have probably been involved. In the case of a hostile takeover, the target company might well be totally clueless and caught off guard by the "opening shot" of the would-be acquirer.

Assuming there is some level of cooperation involved, even in an acquisition, this is the point at which the information that has been gathered is used to begin to frame the potential deal. An essential piece, of course, is the initial valuation of each company, to be reflected in the total value of the deal, whether in stock, cash, or both. This is also the point at which those closest to the deal typically begin to focus on their own interests—at least to the degree to which some decisions and issues can be predicted and controlled. Key roles and responsibilities may be initially agreed upon, and buy-outs and golden parachutes for executives not to be included are generally formulated and approved by both companies during this stage as well.

SIGNING A LETTER OF INTENT

If discussions are successful, plans for a deal are formalized between the parties. This moves the process from one of investigation to one of purposeful activity—the beginning of the creation of real changes in both organizations.

CONDUCTING DUE DILIGENCE

The due diligence process is the second step of looking for "deal-killers." Now is the time to determine how accurate all the preliminary data gathering turns out to be. Do the financial statements accurately reflect the condition of the company? Are there any irregularities about reporting or transactions? Essentially, is the company what it represents itself as, or appears to be, and are there any "skeletons in the closets" that will present later problems?

As insinuated here, the typical approach is aimed at very tangible fact-finding—primarily with a financial emphasis. What is often left out, of course, is any analysis about culture and people. In some cases, this is very conscious and intentional. If the only important assets of the target company are physical and financial, and it is irrelevant who actually runs the operations, then there is little else to be considered. If there is anything about the way the current business is operating, though, that makes any difference in its value, it is very short-sighted to ignore the human side.

COMPLETING THE FINANCIAL NEGOTIATIONS

In the current financial climate, with stock prices sometimes reflecting valuations of a hundred times earnings for companies that have never shown a profit, there can be fairly wide fluctuations in estimations of the worth of a company. As noted in Chapter 1, for deals that are done strictly through an exchange of stock, the attitude about valuation may even get somewhat cavalier. But at some point, numbers become expectations that need to be met. (A recent article estimated that in order for the AOL–Time Warner merger to meet expectations of 15% growth for the next 15 years, the company would have to grow to a market value of $2.4 *trillion* dollars, from the current estimate of $290 million.)[3]

SIGNING THE DEFINITIVE AGREEMENT

For those involved in "doing the deal," this step is the consummation of what often involves many evenings and weekends of work, and sometimes sleepless nights. It's no wonder that there would be a desire to celebrate this as an end-point. But, like saying "yes" to a marriage proposal, it is only the end of a decision-making process, and the beginning of putting plans and hopes to work.

ANNOUNCING THE DEAL

As noted above, there is a tendency to present this decision of intent as if it were a "done deal" already. In a great many ways, this point only begins what can be a very long process (depending on the nature of the deal and the companies involved) of questions, scrutiny, and second-guessing by everyone from employees to shareholders to media to financial analysts to government and regulatory agencies. The nature of the deal may be business, but the consequences of the deal may be much, much broader, involving such things as the closing of business sites, layoffs of employees, relocation of headquarters, and shifts in marketplace competition.

CLOSING THE TRANSACTION

As noted in Chapter 1, the time delay between the public announcement of a deal and its finalization can vary from days to months. Much of this depends on the level of scrutiny required by the FTC, SEC, or other regulatory agencies, but negotiations between the companies can sometimes drag on as well. Disagreements can arise about everything from asset valuation to key positions to executive perks to headquarters location choices. And what initially appeared to be settled may become a new issue, based on discoveries during due diligence or on the need to rebalance other agreements (e.g., "We'll give in on this one, but if so, we want to rethink that one.")

Sometimes, pressure to get a deal done can result in decisions being put off until after the signing of the agreement under the assumption that the details can be left to later. And in some cases this works (based on the relationship between the parties, not on the deal itself). But in a number of cases, what appeared to be a final agreement may also be "rethought" after the fact. Despite how deals are characterized, there are very rarely "mergers of equals," in reality. If there is enough difference in ownership (e.g., 50.1% to 49.9%) that one party can cast a deciding vote on issues, they are, in fact, the controlling party—barring extenuating circumstances. And it's wise not to consider decisions final until you actually see them being implemented by those in charge.

INTEGRATION OF THE COMPANIES

By the time that the investment bankers have congratulated each other, cashed their checks, and moved on to the next deal, the real and important organizational work has just begun. But it is through the mundane details that the "rubber hits the road." A deal that sounded great on paper is only as good as the newly combined organization that develops from it.

If it's a high-tech industry in which almost everyone stands to benefit from stock options, then at least a part of "what's in it for me?" is already covered. Also, the frequency with which employees tend to move to new jobs (and their marketability in doing so) may make changes significantly easier than in older or more traditional industries. But at some point, everyone needs to know, "So, what is this place now, and how does it work?" The more that employees feel wedded to their jobs and their locations, the more anxiety they will feel while waiting for these answers (and the less productive and focused they will be while waiting).

Integration planning often only begins after the transaction is final and the ink on the documents is dry. Accordingly, many companies and HR teams wait to develop their integration plans until after the deal is officially closed. But the greater the emphasis on, or recognition of, the human capital involved, the earlier the integration planning needs to begin. And in fact, in any deal in which there is a need to incorporate employees into new processes and expectations, the integration planning process should start at least as early as the beginning of the due diligence process (particularly if the view is that the deal is highly likely to be consummated). This early integration planning will help to expedite the eventual melding of the two organizations and will ensure that on "Day One" of the new venture, it will be clear to all employees that management has a well-conceived plan for the newly combined organization.

If team members are alert and sensitive to integration issues during the early stages of any due diligence processes, better decisions can be made about the problems or concerns that should be tackled early—*or even whether to proceed with the deal at all!* For example, significant differences in management styles and core values can often be identified in the course of the initial due diligence discussions. Conversations about these differences may help management take a harder look at the culture of the target company. In some situations, the management may decide that the integration of two companies with such vastly different approaches would likely be very difficult and contentious. On that basis alone, despite favorable financials, a company might elect to walk away from the transaction, or at least revise its approach to the deal, rather than risk the low probability of integration success. Ultimately, the success of the company is achieved only if the new organization actually comes together and can perform effectively.

What follows are some key issues about mergers and acquisitions, as well as some specific suggestions for integrating human resources into the process. Rather than making too many assumptions about the nature of the transaction in which you may be involved (e.g., merger, acquisition, joint venture or other partnership), or the specific process that it might follow, we've chosen to address these somewhat broadly. These are dealt with by topic rather than in order of typical stages so that you might interject them in the ways and places that seem to fit best—or simply at the time during when an opportunity presents itself.

- Review the strategies of both companies to ensure that the deal makes sense.
- Develop a vision and transition targets designed to focus on the key goals of the merger.
- Develop integration goals and a timeline for expected results, and use the goals and dates as a way to communicate successes to employees.
- Develop operating principles and critical success factors so that the new organization's core values and philosophy are clear to all employees.

STRATEGY

The strategic intent of a deal is the rationale for why the whole thing makes sense. What does merging these two companies, or adding one to the other, create that doesn't exist now? In the recent tidal wave of mergers and acquisitions, most seem to strive for some level of "synergy"—the idea that the combined companies will produce results beyond the sum of their current operations. Most deals are focused, then, on consolidation within a given industry, or expansion into related industries that appear to be converging (as opposed to deals of past decades, in which the trend was for companies to become conglomerates, putting excess cash into whatever markets or investments seemed most promising).

The Exxon–Mobil merger was a matter of consolidation due to competition. The primary rationale for this deal was the ability for the new company to capitalize its own exploration and investments (increasingly costly ventures) without the need for money from foreign governments.[4] (Many oil-producing countries have become direct competitors to major oil companies through running state-owned oil production operations.) Key goals, then, were essentially corporate size and the availability of capital. This is much the same rationale behind the recent wave of pharmaceutical mergers, where the need is for massive amounts of capital to finance research and development efforts, in the hope of finding a few blockbuster new drugs.[5]

Other recent deals, such as those involving financial institutions, are both changing markets and searching for synergies (in this case something like "one-stop shopping" for financial needs), blurring the lines between banking and securities, for instance, in the process. What were once separate companies in different markets then become direct competitors for the same customers, often starting further waves of consolidation as these new entities become more efficient.

But the merger of America Online with Time Warner is even another level of this process. It is an example of what can be anticipated of a much larger trend of emerging organizations—the combining of traditional, established companies with Internet powerhouses. The Internet and those who have developed it into a medium accessible to the masses have created an entirely new way of communication and access to information. Others are now ready to fill it with substantially more content. Future mergers and acquisitions of this type are likely to change old, and create new, entry industries, rather than just companies.

Price meets strategy very quickly in M&A deals. As explained by Rappaport and Sirower,[6] only about 20% to 40% of the price of a company's stock is based on its current operating performance. The rest is based on expectations about future performance. In a typical acquisition, a 30% to 40% premium is paid above the base stock price of the target company. This simply adds to expectations and demands for future performance.

Growth through acquisitions also incurs the full cost of the estimated value up-front. Rather than growing or expanding an area more gradually from within, according to results and profitability, the cost of the transaction sets a minimum level of performance and profitability that must be achieved for that business, regardless of market conditions.

The higher the premium paid, the faster and more perfect the integration process must be in order to meet debt payments and investor expectations. And this must happen during a time when there is typically a great deal of internal distraction, if not open conflicts or struggles for power. These struggles are prevalent and occur even in situations where management teams are full of highly intelligent men and women, purportedly with the best interest of their respective organizations at heart. A merger or acquisition also tends to heighten the awareness of external competitors who feel threatened by the change, and who may do what they can to undermine its success, both through increased business pressure as well as possibly using this time to lure away key employees.

The most critical part of the strategy process for HR professionals is clarifying where employees fit in the process. Based on the financial structure of the deal, what is going to have to be achieved in order to make this deal successful? Does this success hinge on key roles or skills, or is it more a matter of overall efficiency, cost reduction, and production (meaning that *all* employees will need to get on board with the changes)? Has the deal assumed certain levels of *inefficiency* by employees, which are to be corrected through employees doing "more with less"? If so, are there plans for achieving this new state, or only assumptions about prospective employee behavior?

Hidden behind the numbers of an M&A deal are typically many unstated assumptions about future organizational achievements. But these achievements will have to be accomplished by someone. A critical human factor in making future M&A transactions more successful is going to be making these human assumptions much more explicit, and incorporating plans to achieve them into the overall strategy.

ESTABLISHMENT OF THE COMPANY'S VISION

Part of any effective strategy includes an effort to create a sense of purpose about work for employees. In most change processes, it is also helpful to convey a sense of urgency about achieving goals or reaching the desired new status. To achieve this climate of understanding, it is important for senior management to establish and communicate a clear vision to help clarify the direction that the organization needs to move.

The vision should be a "picture of the future" that is relatively easy to communicate and that appeals not only to customers and shareholders, but most importantly to employees. Essentially, the vision needs to translate the rationale for the business transaction into "people" terms by answering the following questions for employees: *"Where is all of this headed?"* and *"Why should I want to be a part of it?"*

Communication of a vision for the company will begin to signal to employees what will be changing (as well as what will stay the same) in terms of the new organization's core values and principles. One effort at this, though, is not enough. Both the vision and the pervasive themes of the transaction should be repeated over and over again in order for employees to begin to actually hear and understand them. It takes time to incorporate new value and strategies into an existing culture, so it should come as no surprise if there is a delay in employees' response to the message. More importantly, any changes in basic values and principles which employees need to accommodate should be interwoven into the most basic of daily activities.

EARLY ANNOUNCEMENT OF "VALUE DRIVERS" AND TRANSACTION SYNERGIES

In addition to the development of a clear and compelling vision that will help explain to employees the *"why"* of the transaction and *"how"* they can help to make it successful, it is critical for an organization to determine the synergistic issues that will help it to achieve early value. These "value drivers" need to be identified, quantified or at least specified as much as possible, and communicated widely to employees.[7] This will help employees clearly understand on what areas they need to focus and where to expend the most significant energies. Tracking and monitoring of these transition targets will also send some positive signals to the organization that action items are indeed being accomplished, and that progress is actually happening, despite the apparent chaos they are likely to see around them. This should also help to keep the momentum of the transaction rolling.

INTEGRATION GOALS AND TIMETABLES FOR RESULTS

With each integration plan that is developed for each functional discipline (e.g., finance, human resources, information systems, etc.), it is important to develop timetables for the achievement of results and to install a process for communicating those results—sharing them frequently not only with management, but also with employees. This will help to assure employees that action plans are in place and that the effort is proceeding on schedule. The schedule and follow-up will give your workforce more confidence that the new management team has a well-thought-out plan and is moving quickly toward its execution.

Do not, however, make the mistake of assuming that a lack of vocal opposition to the plans means that everyone is working together in support of their achievement. Often, employees (even fairly senior ones) will passively watch and appear to be supportive (at least by their silence) as others move forward to carry out the organization's objectives. Yet, behind the scenes, these same employees may be subtly undermining efforts that they feel might be threatening to their positions or careers. Given that the deal is *just business*, don't assume that sound strategic objectives or some assumed history of trust will overcome individual fears which strike at the most basic core of a person's vulnerability.

OPERATING PRINCIPLES AND CRITICAL SUCCESS FACTORS

Much of the focus of a merger or acquisition, as outlined in the process of events, amounts to changing or creating an entity—an issue of "what." And based on what is being created, there are many assumptions about the expected outcomes, such as: the new organization will achieve tremendous efficiencies and synergies, significant increases in market share, and produce maximum shareholder value. Unfortunately, most of the thought about how this is to be achieved, at least among the deal makers, seems to rest in assumptions about what is being created. By virtue of combining two organizations, with their accompanying assets and customers, and eliminating the redundant personnel and processes, the general assumption is that increased profits will naturally result. Such assumptions can be very dangerous, indeed.

The key factors on which the success of this new entity will hinge need not only to be thought out, but also spelled out as well—in clear detail, to everyone who will be involved. If this is a relatively small acquisition, in which employees are being added to a much larger, existing organization with stable leadership and efficient processes that will remain in place, then clarifying operating principles is only a matter of orientation and time to get familiar. If the deal is much different from this very narrow scenario, then there definitely needs to be thought put into both clarifying and communicating these factors.

The emphasis, by the way, is on clarity, not necessarily detail, at this point. Operating principles can be fairly high level and general, but they need to give everyone an idea of what is important and what is forbidden or taboo in this new environment. If done well, they will be interpreted in more detail through things such as policies and procedures, which are discussed below.

- Determine the organizational structure.
- Decide on a headquarters location and physical layout.
- Establish the company's new name and legal structure.
- Develop processes, policies, and procedures.
- Understand differences in corporate cultures and develop a strategy for integration.

Many of these factors may have been taken care of at some point during the finalization of the transaction itself—but that's not always the case. Sometimes, even when the transaction itself doesn't seem all that big (e.g., acquisition of one division of another company), the changes that come with it can be greater than expected. Companies sometimes use these transitions as times to make other changes that were wanted anyway. Or the issues involved in assimilation of employees from a very strong company culture may prove to be a challenge. Again, remember that these tasks are not in chronological order, and may be addressed in different deals at widely varying times.

ORGANIZATIONAL STRUCTURE

To whatever degree the merger or acquisition changes the structure of an organization, employees need to know as quickly as possible what the new relationships will be. Depending on the size of the organizations, and the magnitude of the changes, there may be some lag time in finalizing all new functions and positions. But for many reasons, the basic structure needs to be outlined as quickly as possible. Delaying this process tends to create both frustration and anxiety among employees and may well feed into a decision by employees to leave the new company for other opportunities. In the worst case, you end up with a "manager for a month club," with the best people rotating through positions and leaving, until you're left with only those employees with the lowest skills and the fewest alternatives.

HEADQUARTERS LOCATION AND PHYSICAL LAYOUT

Location of a company headquarters is theoretically only a strategic decision. What location makes the most sense for the business, in relation to major customers, availability of labor, and access to transportation? Of course, given the global nature of many businesses, if there is one major headquarters, it cannot be near all the company locations. And in many cases, headquarters locations are purposefully isolated from other work sites. If so, then it would seem to make little difference where the corporate offices are located. But there are subtle messages that go along with these decisions, whether they are recognized at first or not.

Many executives choose to office in major cities for a variety of personal and business reasons. New York City was, of course, a favorite location for some time because of the access it gave senior managers to financial resources. Rising taxes drove out corporations such as Mobil and Exxon, and many corporate headquarters are now located in more remote areas, often at the perimeter of major cities and even some decidedly more rural settings.

There are, of course, other implications to the choice of headquarters locations, beyond just the strategic. These are both social and political. Cities and companies become associated with each other in many ways, much like major sports teams do. For small- to medium-sized cities, attracting a recognized company often "puts it on the map." The more well known the brand name, the more clout it brings. And having such a company, of course, brings other assets to the city—the tax base and rationale to improve infrastructure, including airports and new airlines, corporate donations to support local arts, and higher income individuals to patronize shops and restaurants.

But there is a sociocultural effect that boomerangs back to companies as well. Corporations headquartered in San Francisco tend have a more open view about diversity and personnel policies in general than those located in more conservative cities. The human side of things is that the issues policy makers are faced with day to day do influence them. And it's much easier to ignore issues that only come in as "data."

For the purposes of this book, the more important point is the way that decisions such as corporate location are interpreted by employees. What's the message about not only the location, but also how that decision was made? Was it really a strategic decision for the company, or was it primarily a personal preference for the lifestyle of specific key executives? Does the location really position the company competitively, or does it primarily insulate executives from the average employee? All the media hype and rhetoric the company wants to throw at this issue has little impact if the underlying message is more clear. This can be a seemingly small decision with a great deal of long-term impact.

Without belaboring this one point, the physical layout of company buildings, as well as the proximity between them, tends to send very strong, if subtle, messages. There are certainly practical aspects to all of this, simply in regards to costs and to getting work done—but there are also many discretionary choices. Architects and interior designers may go to great lengths (and expense) on exterior facades and impressive entrances, with art to fill them, but leave an internal working environment that makes little or no sense.

In one instance, a company made the popular transition from offices with walls for all managers, to cubicles for all but executive employees. While the idea of establishing a more open working environment was clear, employees soon found themselves having to learn to whisper on phone calls or when meeting with another person to keep from distracting coworkers or to maintain confidentiality. But things really hit the fan when it was learned that the cubicles also cost more and took more space per employee than the previous private office arrangement. And to add insult to injury, the copiers and file cabinets now occupied the window offices!

NEW NAME AND LEGAL STRUCTURE

The answer to "what's in a name" can, of course, be "a great deal." Marketing and advertising industries spend billions of dollars on creating names and attaching images and meaning to them. Like most other marketing issues, these tend to follow trends and fads over time, as well. At present, there's great value attached to being a "dot-com," and the most recognizable and popular Internet domain names are being auctioned for millions of dollars—even when there is, as yet, no actual business behind the name.

We'll leave the issues about choice of names to the creativity of marketing experts. In relation to the focus of this book, the problems we've seen have been in areas such as a failure to use the name to help shape the identity of the organization. Whatever the name chosen, it needs to become prominent throughout the organization as quickly as possible. Old signs need to be removed (respectfully—not dumped into waste containers behind the buildings), and new stationery, business cards, and the like distributed to all employees quickly.

The legal structure simply refers to whether the deal is a merger, acquisition, joint venture, alliance, or some other variety of partnership. This sets out the official nature of ownership of the entity, as well as establishing guidelines for decision making and control. From an HR standpoint, problems typically arise only in relation to contradictions between the official structure and the ways that things actually occur.

As noted earlier, there is rarely a true "merger of equal partners" in M&A transactions. To have a 50–50 split of ownership and control could result in stalemates in decision making. Therefore, one partner is almost always ultimately in control. Though people may not like being on the subordinate side of the deal, if this is the way that decisions actually are made, it's much easier simply to know this early.

There are surely circumstances in which the intent is honestly to share power—to preserve the best of each company and what it can add to the venture. But if this is the desire, a great deal of thought needs to put into how this is actually going to be accomplished. There are very real limits to how much most organizations can change without "losing themselves" (truly, losing their corporate identity) in the process. There are also real limits that each executive, as a person, has about what is acceptable and can even be considered. (This begins to touch in a very real way on the "tacit" realm of organizations.) But because these limits are not always explicit, or even within conscious awareness, they tend to arise emotionally. They may surface during the negotiation process, or not until integration is under way. But when they do, they frequently surface as major breakdowns in communication between the parties. They may appear as such divergent philosophies or points of view that there seems to be no point in discussing them. (And those involved don't have any ready way *to* discuss them.) So the party with the upper hand simply makes the decision and imposes the greater will on the lesser owner.

One of the great dilemmas in these cases is that it's often very hard to tell the real beliefs and intent of those involved. Was this a breakdown in communication, or did the majority owner simply wait until the deal was done, and then take over? The end results may be essentially the same, but the issue of trust by employees may be quite different.

Clearly, there are deal makers who take a very Machiavellian approach—you simply "kill off" (in this case, terminate the employment of) all those in any real positions of power in the other organization, and integrate new decision makers into the old ranks. There are thoughtful and intelligent persons who might still recommend this approach. But in an age of more educated and knowledgeable employees, with ever-increasing access to information, such an approach may have much different implications than in past times. Specifically, with low unemployment and tight labor markets, especially for the most skilled employees, summarily dismissing talented employees today would be something like burning down a production facility (in times past) because it didn't look like the rest of the facilities.

PROCESSES, POLICIES, AND PROCEDURES

Processes, policies, and procedures are the means for translating general concepts of vision and purpose into specific plans for action. How does this organization work and what are the means by which employees are expected to accomplish the organization plans? Is the organization looking for initiative and creativity, or loyalty and efficient compliance? Does this organization use incentives such as flexible working conditions to attract employees, or focus simply on financial compensation? In essence, what kind of an environment is this, how does it work, and what's the incentive for being here?

CORPORATE CULTURES AND INTEGRATION STRATEGIES

Despite what has become fairly common use of the term "corporate culture" in recent years, it is not always clearly understood. One definition is simply "the way that things are done around here." Another is that culture is something like the "DNA" of the company without which the organization would not exist as it is.

Corporate culture is closely connected to, or possibly one aspect of, what we've described as the tacit realm of organizations. It has to do with the overall environment of an organization and contributes to the uniqueness of it. And because of this, it's often easier to identify the characteristics of a corporate culture from the outside than from within it.

IBM was famous (or notorious, depending on your view) for years for their dress code. Men wore white shirts with blue or gray suits and a conservative selection in the colors of their ties. In the eyes of less formal or conservative companies, this was extremely rigid and "stuffy." EDS, under the direction of Ross Perot, was at least as conservative. But like Wall Street bankers (probably destined to be the last great bastions of conservative dress), the intent was to create an aura of unquestioned professionalism, and therefore to elicit trust by clients. Much like military dress, these "uniforms" created pride through association with others of exacting standards.

Silicon Valley, of course, is just as notorious for its *aversion* to suits and ties. The intent is to create a very different type of environment in order to accomplish a different type of work and to attract a different kind of employee with a more creative and freer style.

Many work places are shifting, of course, to more casual dress—including IBM, some years ago now. So within a given industry, where there are dramatic differences, they show up even more starkly. According to one former manager in Mobil, when the executives from Exxon showed up, it wasn't hard at all to spot them—they looked exactly like executives from IBM a decade ago. And one of the first changes made was to abolish casual dress on Fridays, which had been instituted within Mobil only five years earlier.

While it's easy to poke fun at more conservative ways, given the current swing of the pendulum, there really isn't an ultimate right or wrong here. And though they're one of the easier indicators to spot, dress codes are certainly not the most critical of corporate cultural issues; however, they are a visible signal about the kind of work environment that the company management wants to create.

The point is that lots of small things go into building an organizational environment. And much like broader sociocultural issues, people can be expected to feel fairly sensitive about them—even if they don't necessarily like them themselves. The same employee who may have complained for years about certain practices (like dress codes) within an organization may still get extremely offended by remarks from others in a new company about how "stupid" or "archaic" that same practice was.

Addressing issues of cultural differences between companies, then, requires a great deal of sensitivity. In most cases of a merger or acquisition, one of the existing corporate cultures is likely to end up being dominant (generally that of the new or the majority owner). But one of the easiest ways to stifle the integration process is to offend the employees of the acquired company.

As one specific suggestion, be very thoughtful when using humor, especially at first. People like laughing together, but no one likes being laughed at. If there are jokes to be made, make sure that they're always about "us"—*all* of "us," not just those of us who recently came here.

As noted earlier, planning for integration needs to begin at the first possible opportunity. If there are clear signals that the deal is likely to go through, discussions between HR professionals should ideally begin to take place as soon as there is legal clearance to do so. Issues like corporate culture can be discussed in a much more open and collaborative way than, say, details about severance packages or golden parachutes.

Given what's been said already, collaborating is not as easy as saying to your counterpart, "So tell me about your corporate culture." This could elicit some interesting responses, but generally will only get at the "artifacts" (as described in Chapter 3). This is also one of the reasons that visiting the other company's workplace locations can be helpful— some of the best information about the differences might be in your own reactions to the contrasts. Just remember that you're evaluating differences, not rights or wrongs. The goal is to transition people *into* whatever their new reality is going to be, and this is most easily done if they feel welcomed, not defensive.

To a large degree, you may only learn about the deeper levels of corporate culture when people *react* strongly to certain things. At this point, there might be an opportunity to learn more, but only through some careful listening that might help to uncover the thoughts beneath the feelings.

- Develop key HR policies (including severance, outplacement, and relocation).
- Handle consolidation and reduction of headquarters staff early.
- "Re-recruit" top talent and employees the company wants to keep.
- Provide technical skills and change management training.
- Clarify roles, responsibilities, and expectations.

KEY HR POLICIES

After the initial question, "Do I have a job?", policies regarding severance, outplacement, coverage of relocation costs, and the like are the real nuts and bolts of a merger or acquisition for the average employee. They are also often the most tangible evidence of what the companies really really instead, despite what they may be saying verbally.

It's actually very enlightening to hear how clearly and articulately even the lowest level employees can verbalize the pressures driving organizations to change. In most cases, they do understand. But this does not mean that employees are easily prepared for being terminated from their jobs or for watching friends and colleagues "get the ax." That's about relationships, not intellect.

From a functional standpoint, employees are a means to an end for organizations—they are a part of a production process, whether of goods or services. But they (we) are still incredibly intricate "mechanisms" full of emotions, perceptions, hopes, fears, and possibilities—for good and for ill. And despite the emerging new realities forecast about work in the future (virtual workplaces and corporations, etc.), the current realities of society are still tied to some very traditional ideas.

When financing a house or a car, loan officers still generally ask for proof of stable employment (almost regardless of what recent income you have had or for how long). If you want to participate in a tax-deferred savings plan, or want to purchase health insurance at better-than-average rates, it's still almost a necessity to work for a large organization.

The bottom line is that, at present, despite all the rhetoric about people being a company's "most important asset," the average employee still only shows up on the balance sheet as an expense. When a deal is contemplated, shedding "excess" or redundant employees is almost always a part of the plan. But for an employee, a job is a tie to the economic realm of society—virtually a survival necessity in modern times. Cutting costs by eliminating jobs may be not only prudent but also necessary, from a financial point of view, but the message that people are an expense, not an asset, is not lost on employees. It is a clear case of actions speaking louder than words.

CONSOLIDATION AND REDUCTION OF HEADQUARTERS STAFF

Changes in headquarters staff are, of course, some of the most visible and sensitive personnel issues that have to be addressed. While these are often the most redundant positions, and some of the most highly compensated, they are also frequently the most politically loaded. If there's anyone known throughout an entire organization, he or she probably works at the headquarters location. Employees here, as a rule, tend to be long-term (relative to the age of the company) and typically both loyal and intimately tied into the workings of the organization. These are the employees for whom special deals are likely to be struck, if such is going to occur.

If there is a place to consider Machiavelli's advice, this is it. And this is not to suggest a ruthless approach—only a very careful study of the decisions to be made. In an outlying location of a large organization, a simple change of name and logo, with little accompanying change in daily operations, may be just taken in stride. (This is especially so in cases where the workgroup has remained stable through numerous changes of company control.) At a headquarters location, the changes cannot help but be more dramatic.

Headquarters employees may well see future opportunities in a new organization and want to take advantage of them. But as a whole, they will also have the most "emotional baggage" to deal with and are therefore usually more vulnerable. If they want to make the transition, they need to be clear about their choice, about what they will be moving to (especially if they perceive it as a demotion), and about their commitment to do so. (Discussions about these positions can give a great deal of insight into the cultural issues mentioned earlier.)

The *process* for making decisions about positions needs to be determined early. If employees from both organizations will be allowed to apply for available position on an open basis of some sort, then they need to know this, and they need to understand something of the criteria by which selections will be made. If the organization in control plans to simply retain its own employees, then it's much easier to make that clear to everyone involved at the outset in order to outline the plans and avoid setting misleading expectations.

Transition periods are always delicate, at best. The controlling organization may very well plan to simply absorb most of the existing functions and retain few of the other company's employees—but still need to have those other employees keep things moving for a period of months. If discussions have gotten nasty between the companies in the midst of negotiations, employees will have lingering feelings about that. You obviously don't want to fuel that fire in the way that the transition period is handled. (It's just not a good idea to hack off the whole information services group when you need them to transfer and translate years of important data, for instance.) At the same time, headquarters employees are not, as a rule, the best on which to try "golden handcuffs" of monetary-only incentives. While retention agreements, retention bonuses, and the like may be necessary (and effective, in some cases), other methods ought to be considered as well. The cleaner and more honest the approach, the less likely that a major emotional blow-up or incident of sabotage will happen.

If you walk in with a clear plan about the structure, goals, and culture of the new organization, many employees may simply "opt out" voluntarily. It may just not feel like a good fit for them, and if that's the case, then they can begin to move on emotionally and prepare for a different future. But in such a case, it is *their* decision, not something being done *to* them. And that sense of control is an absolutely critical difference in terms of the ways employees (both those leaving and those who remain on the team) respond to these changes.

As for employees who will lose their jobs, it is critical that they be shown at least a modicum of respect through the process of a merger or acquisition. There are certainly restrictions on what information can be shared with whom, and at what point—according to legal and financial standards. But using "smoke and mirrors" strategies or putting "spin" on bad news will eventually only undermine the credibility of senior managers. *In the end, a hard truth is easier for employees to deal with than a sugarcoated half-truth.*

"RE-RECRUIT" TOP TALENT AND EMPLOYEES

To the degree that the organization is seriously committed to using the best talent available, it needs to devise and follow a strategy for doing so. From a functional standpoint this seems simple and straightforward but is, of course, much more complicated in real life application.

Star performers also have to be team players if the organization is to be successful. There must be a good fit between skills and the context in which they are used. This only reinforces the need to be clear about the kind of organization that is being developed, up front, so that skills and talent of key individuals can be assessed within that context. A really outstanding salesperson, for instance, has an individual style and approach, as well as the backup of other people who may provide a good deal of support (or a lot of cleanup, as the case may be). A salesperson also works within the context of a larger marketing scheme and relies heavily on production and distribution systems to deliver things as promised, for instance. If these relationships are conflict-oriented rather than cooperative, target goals are very likely to be missed, regardless of the talent involved.

Key personnel issues, then, include both "goodness of fit," as well as track records of performance. But during transition times, this can also become far more complicated with the overlay of politics and egos.

Senior executives tend to live in worlds at the convergence of politics and business. While some manage to avoid a great deal of public visibility, their decisions are generally subject to scrutiny and second-guessing in many arenas. Maintaining positions of power usually involves alliances and compromises. Relationships are crucial, whether based on trust and loyalty or based on debts and favors.

The selection of key individuals may run up against such issues, whether openly or not. In some cases appointments may seem to make little sense on the surface but are simply sent down "from on high" with little discussion. Only afterward does the fallout happen if the person's skills or personality are inadequate to the tasks.

If these kinds of decisions are to be influenced, it will probably have to happen early and quietly. As a rule, human resources is not consulted about such political decisions in the heat of battle, as senior executives are fighting for professional survival. This assumes, of course, some entry into these discussions, before the pressure of a deal is in the works. Early discussions about succession planning, participative decision making, or delegation of authority can at least set the stage, or provide a backdrop against which the issues can be raised later. In the heat of the discussions, it's probably only major organizational issues that can be raised (e.g., "You can put this person there, but it's likely that you'll have to replace most of that staff in the next six months if you do").

Ideally, of course, you want to remove the conflict and pressure from these discussions. If there's an abundance of exceptionally good people in a specific area, there might be consideration given to rethinking the positions. Current jobs might be redesigned to allow for a better fit in order to retain all of the individuals in question. (The downsizing mentality of the last couple of decades has so pervaded management thinking that it always seems to be a question of "How far can we cut back?" rather than "How can we take these great resources and do more than we had imagined?")

On the other side of the issue, you obviously don't want to create positions with no real work just to avoid tough decisions. Having people hanging around, "rusting out," is not a good alternative.

In the end, there will probably be many compromises. Some very good people will use this occasion as an opportunity for a fresh start elsewhere. Some new talent may emerge and have a chance to blossom. For those who are in senior positions and who expected to remain there, expect to have to acknowledge their importance to the organization—to do some "ego stroking." Change brings insecurity to even high-ranking individuals, on a personal level. And somehow, a new "team" will have to emerge from all this.

For those employees who will remain or those being brought into an existing organization, the first messages are often the most lasting. They will set a tone for "how things are" now. How can they participate in making this new venture a success?

TECHNICAL SKILLS AND CHANGE MANAGEMENT TRAINING

Just keeping existing employees in any given organization current on changes in technology, such as communications and data systems and upgrades in software programs, is difficult enough. Getting large numbers of employees familiar with the technology and processes of a new organization is yet another magnitude of scale. It begins with very basic things, like how supplies are ordered and bills paid. Achieving the efficiency of a "well-oiled machine," for the organization as a whole, usually requires a great deal of effort, and will happen somewhat in relation to the level of planning devoted to it.

This is one of the very tangible places where the promised synergies of the deal, as reflected in the value imputed by the financial analysts, can fail to materialize. Becoming familiar with new people and new routines is going to distract attention from other work, in the best of circumstances. It's simply part of a learning curve. If this is compounded by lingering feelings of bitterness or conflict, due to something about the way the deal was transacted, the learning curve can be extended dramatically.

It has been common in our experience to see retained employees who were extremely hard-working, loyal, and ambitious before a transaction, become only compliant, being at work when they had to and doing what needed to be done, but no more. Their hearts were just no longer in the work. There was no sense that loyalty or ambition made any difference for the employees who were terminated, so why should they now bother? Their response was simply to "check out" while remaining on the job.

Even at the level of technical training, there needs to be some thought given to the more subtle messages of being welcomed to and included in the new organization. Employees need to learn "how to do things" so that they can also be a part of the "new order" of things.

Both for the employees who are to be part of the new organization and for those who are preparing to move on to other things, it's a good idea to offer programs regarding change itself. Ideally, this should be coordinated with transition phases of the organization. In companies that might still not have experienced a great deal of fundamental change— where the basic corporate culture might still be largely intact—a first phase is simply to help employees deal with anxiety about what is to come following initial announcements about the deal. A second phase should be offered at the time that change actually starts to occur—when employees are notified about impending job losses, elimination of functions or departments, and so on. To the degree that plans are clear, separate groups can be held for those employees who will be terminated and those who will move on with the organization. A third phase of change workshops or programs should be offered once the new organization is intact, to have a place for specifically dealing with things like corporate culture and lingering feelings of conflict or bitterness.

One aspect of change programs is normally teaching about change itself—simply giving employees information about the phases and feelings that people typically experience when facing change. But a critical and usually overlooked need is for very real dialogue (not discussion, not debate, not argument—*dialogue*), in which people can listen openly and without defensiveness or criticism to the views and perspectives from "the other side." Ideally, these should be offered in as comfortable and informal a setting as possible and at least initially should be facilitated (not directed) by someone with expertise in listening skills. (See Chapter 3 for a better understanding of some of these issues.)

There are a great many organizational development and organizational psychology firms offering change management work now, as well as many management consulting firms. The key here is not just buying a canned program, but identifying and addressing the real issues and needs affecting the organization—those that are likely to become the stumbling blocks to its future.

ROLES, RESPONSIBILITIES, AND EXPECTATIONS

Once organizational structures and key personnel are in place, there is still work to clarify just how this organization is to function. Typically, this happens through something of a "trickle-down" method—each level setting its goals, objectives, and activities in line with that of the level above it. The more decentralized the organization, the more independently this activity may occur.

Our suggestion is that you not formalize this any more than necessary, but primarily that you have some sort of feedback system in place for seeing that it occurs. Once the work of striking the deal is finally done, senior managers and executives may feel a great deal of pressure to catch up on things that were put off. There may be a sense that, now that the deal is done, it's time to get on with things without delay and not worry too much about details. What may happen, instead, is that rank-and-file employees are left sitting and waiting for some real direction, or that, in the absence of clear decisions, they jump in and begin making some.

If the company is one that encourages initiative and self-direction—that's great. But even creativity needs boundaries, not a vacuum. There are undoubtedly *some* limits to what employees can initiate, and these need to be made clear.

If this is an organization that requires a great deal of close coordination of efforts and attention to specific detail—not free-thinking—then time has to be devoted to beginning these processes.

- Communication Issues
  - —Determine relevant stakeholders to be communicated with.
  - —Develop individual strategies for communicating with each group.
  - —Use multiple forms of media.
  - —Repeat messages and common themes.

It's an oft-used adage that people hear what they want to hear. Actually, people hear and interpret the way that they do for a variety of reasons. As much as we take it for granted, communication can be a very complex issue.

If you're delivering what people interpret as being bad news (for them personally), they're generally listening through a filter that screens out anything that doesn't seem relevant to them, personally, at the moment. The company may be delivering a message about long-term growth and success and value for shareholders. Employees are thinking about how to stave off foreclosure on the loan they just took out or how they are going to present the news to their families.

Part of the complication, of course, is that the same press release or message to employees carries with it many different implications for different groups. Some groups will be minimally affected and so may be more open to just getting information. If unions are involved (especially if labor relations have historically been strained or contentious), they need to filter the message through the language of their contracts with the company. Those who expect to be most directly impacted may barely hear any of it—except for the few words that they think are most relevant, and these may be distorted in any number of ways, depending on their current frame of reference.

It is in the communication process that senior managers may become the most frustrated and about which they may need the most coaching and encouragement. If you have a good relationship with your company's communications staff, begin talking as early as possible. If there's not a close working relationship, you may need to directly approach the senior managers themselves. (If you're dealing with major change in your organization, this is not a time to be bashful or reticent. There won't be second chances for some of these opportunities.)

If the magnitude of the changes expected is significant, this is an emotionally laden time for everyone, and that directly affects communication. Senior executives and managers who have worked nights and weekends putting the deal together, behind the scenes, are likely to be both physically and emotionally drained. They may easily lose patience with employees who "just don't get it"—primarily those who have only heard a fraction of what was said and may have distorted that information (in the deliverer's view).

For all these reasons, it's almost impossible during these times *to overcommunicate*. Messages need to be simple, clear, and consistent. But they also need to be delivered repeatedly, and in multiple forms. Different people learn and understand much better through some mediums than others. Some are more visual, some more auditory, and so on. But different backgrounds, language skills, ideologies, emotional states, and other factors can also greatly affect perspective and interpretation.

The greatest difficulty in communication may result from a deal that drags on and changes in the process. (Sometimes this is unavoidable, as in an intended deal that is made public, but then must undergo scrutiny for antitrust issues.) All that can be communicated at that point is what is really known to that point. The difficulty for senior managers may be that the changes make them appear indecisive or not really in control. The truth is they may not be in control of some aspects, and they are living in a "glass box" at that point. It's important to be sensitive to the pressures facing senior managers—both personal and professional. But also be mindful of the needs of the employees who will have to participate in the making of the new organization.

Once the deal is really done and in place, ongoing communication is critical to reinforce the key messages. If things have changed along the way, it's that much more important to clarify what the new organization is, where it's going, and how it's going to get there. People will only support what they believe they understand, and blind faith is not a part of the "new employment contract" that has evolved over the last few decades. Additional information dealing with the following subject areas is discussed in more detail on the pages that follow.

• Conduct employee/customer attitude surveys.
• Train employees on
  —Team building
  —Survivor skills
  —Merger sensitization
• Identify the issues and develop project plans.
• Monitor and track the critical 100-day path and results achieved.
• Communicate constantly.

EMPLOYEE/CUSTOMER ATTITUDE SURVEYS

As the transition progresses, it's critical to establish mechanisms of feedback about ways that organizational changes are affecting both employee and customer relations. As noted earlier, mergers and acquisitions are prime times for competitors to attempt to lure away both employees and customers. Regardless of how well the transition plans are made and executed, they're pointless if they don't end up addressing the needs and concerns of both employees and customers.

Some of this feedback process should probably be broad and formal, such as through confidential surveys that can be tabulated for examination by decision makers. Others should be one-on-one sessions to probe and listen for problems and concerns that are developing. Just as importantly, beginning such processes can begin to set a tone for listening and attending to issues by the organization as whole, much of which can be done more informally, in the long run.

TEAM BUILDING, SURVIVOR SKILLS, AND MERGER SENSITIZATION

Whether formal workplace teams are a part of your organization or not, a sense of teamwork in the organization is an important aspect of productivity. All three of these factors (team building, survivor skills, and merger sensitization) are closely interrelated and essential to the integration process. Parts of these issues may be covered in your change management programs—but not necessarily to the extent needed for full integration.

Both teams and organizations distinguish themselves not only according to what they *are*, but just as importantly through comparison with what they are *not*. In the best of circumstances, this results in friendly competition and rivalries that push everyone a little harder than they might push themselves otherwise. When competition gets out of control, in teams or organizations, it can cause too much energy to be focused on a competitor, and deter focus from the real goals of the group itself (e.g., satisfying customers through the best possible products or services).

The establishment of a group identity also draws boundaries—who is "in" and a part of the group, and who is "out." During the merging of organizations, these boundaries have to become very fluid, which is much more easily said than done. The closer-knit the group, the more it tends to protect its own turf and boundaries. (In the case of workplace teams, this happens through things such as taking pride and ownership in the work processes and products of the team and feeling protective about the decisions made about them.)

In the case of a merger or acquisition, it's very likely that some members of work groups have been lost, due to early retirement incentives, termination decisions, or the like. Losses to a group tend to increase a sense of protectiveness about the group. If "outsiders" are being added to the group at the same time, it's no wonder that tensions may rise. And reactions to such issues are generally emotional, not intellectual. In many ways, this only exacerbates the reactions, since those involved, both the existing group members and the new "outsiders," may fully understand the changes and even support them as necessary for both organizations, *intellectually*—but have very dissonant feelings about the changes emotionally.

Insensitivity to such issues by managers who may be feeling pressured to get things "back to normal" quickly is also counterproductive. If the message to team members is "just figure it out and get on with it," the more subtle message tends to be "teamwork here is really not important, regardless of company rhetoric," and employees will usually respond accordingly.

ISSUES AND PROJECT PLANS

Just as with the clarification of roles and responsibilities, it's important to have fairly specific plans and targets for individual workgroups (e.g., departments and teams) as quickly as possible. It helps for people to have specific projects or goals to work on in order to get momentum going and that these are clear and achievable enough that there can be some early, tangible successes.

In most cases, there is no lack of necessary work to be done—usually, in fact, about two to three times as much as seems possible. Early projects need not only to be achievable, they also need to be tied to the larger goals of organizational success, as much as possible, to help build a sense of participation in the whole.

A word of caution, though—people will rise to the occasion for what they believe to be extraordinary circumstances, but not everything is an emergency. You can't maintain adrenaline levels for extended periods of time. They get used up and then need to be replenished. Make early projects focused, tangible, and inclusive (requiring new and old team members to work together), and pick the ones that seem to have the most leverage in accomplishing organizational goals. Then prioritize the other "absolute necessities" in ways that feel at least remotely manageable, not overwhelming.

THE 100-DAY PATH AND RESULTS

Appendix 3 offers a sample 100-day strategic plan for getting basic executive decisions made and structures set in place. If such a plan is put into motion, it needs to be tracked and aligned with other organizational activities.

CONSTANT COMMUNICATION

As noted, there is virtually no way during an organizational transition to over-communicate. This is not to imply that there is any merit to "information dumps." In-baskets and e-mail systems don't need to be jammed with multiple copies of the same announcements, over and over again. What is more critical is listening and responding. Employees need all the input they can get that will help them anticipate their futures and provide "feedback mechanisms" to tell them whether the new behaviors they are trying are the right ones or not.

THE INTEGRATION PROCESS

Building a new organization is not entirely different from building a new family (allowing that the definitions of both have changed a good deal since the 1950s). Regardless of how much agreement you think there is at the outset, or how easily things *should* work, based on apparent similarities, each participant brings an individual set of understandings and expectations.

Actually, the trends in both families and organizations through the decades share a good deal. Organizations in the first half of the twentieth century, like families, tended to be structured and paternalistic. They started with a small nucleus and grew internally. Everyone had roles, and lines of authority were clear (at least in our nostalgic memories).

Organizations today may be as varied as family types. Where families were once fairly clearly defined as a male and female couple with children, this traditional establishment now accounts for only about a quarter of the households in the United States.[8] More and more, single-parent households, unmarried couples, same-sex relationships, single persons living alone or with fraternal roommates, and multiple other varieties of relationships are becoming accepted as commonplace.

Organizations, like these different family types, are no longer locked into specific forms or expectations. Rather than having to fit a specific structure, organizations may choose to focus more on "what works." If you communicate with your colleagues primarily through e-mail and phone messages, regardless of whether they're in the cubicle next to you or on a different continent, what difference does it make where your office is? If the company is running 24-hour operations in five different time zones, "face time" isn't going to happen on regular schedule, anyway.

But with the freedom from old routines comes the potential for stress and confusion. The less obvious and familiar that things are, the more openly they need to be discussed and communicated. Be careful about assumptions, even when dealing with employees who seem to "speak the same language" (literally or figuratively). Even if your merger or acquisition partner is a long-time competitor in the same industry with key employees from the same professional background, this does not mean that the new organization you are forming will happen automatically or that everyone will agree on what it should look like.

With that in mind, there are key roles that have proven helpful in putting things together in some successful ventures. They may not fit every scenario, partly because they necessitate buy-in from senior decision makers that can't safely be assumed without a real commitment. (Suggestion: Don't put people in these roles just for the sake of doing so. If they can't get real support for their efforts, don't use them to shield autocrats.)

In general, here's what we've found to be helpful in expediting a post-deal integration effort:

APPOINTMENT OF INTEGRATION LEADER

It is important that one (and only one) senior-level person be named as the leader of the integration effort. That way there is one voice of authority to answer questions about the process along the way, rather than numerous perspectives confusing each other. This person obviously doesn't *make* every decision but is the conduit or liaison through which questions get funneled and answered.

The role of integration leader is a full-time job that can be expected to last from 12 to 18 months. (In some companies, this is becoming a regular and ongoing position.) This person should be held accountable for the creation, delivery, and monitoring of a disciplined strategic plan for integration success and for getting the promised results on time.

If structured properly, management of the transition will be recognized as a distinct and critical business function, with sufficient time and resources devoted to the process. The role of the integration leader will help to build bridges between the acquirer and the acquired company that will allow information and resources to pass freely, with the integration leader actually serving in a consulting capacity to both sides.

Functions/responsibilities of the integration leader would likely include the following:

• Developing of new policies/practices and communication strategies,
• Identifying new functions and/or positions that need to be added,
• Advising employees about how to obtain resources,
• Educating employees about the strategic planning and/or budget process and the performance assessment cycle and process,
• Translating company acronyms,
• Helping explain the culture,
• Acting as a key point of contact for information requests, and
• Generally explaining to employees of the acquired company why and how things work the way they do.

The integration leader serves a role very reminiscent of "corporate cheerleader" and chief problem solver. He or she should be an individual with an easygoing and approachable personality style, but also one who is driven to achieve results. Individuals from both organizations are likely to approach this person with business *and personal* problems that will need to be addressed quickly, so he or she should be capable of juggling multiple and competing priorities and also have quick access to the executive suite.

If selected carefully, this assignment can allow the new organization to provide some intense leadership training to the integration leader. He or she will also have the opportunity to meet and assess members of both organizations and can help to place talent in key spots throughout the organization after the integration is complete as a result of this intense working relationship.

TRANSITION TEAMS

A critical issue when integrating any acquisition is how to speed the process of getting hundreds or thousands of people to work together toward common goals when the values and mindsets of the combining organizations almost always differ, and sometimes quite radically. How do you get people from different cultures with different management philosophies (who may have been rather fierce competitors in the not-too-distant past) to work together?

To coordinate postmerger decisions and activities, many companies have found success in forming transition teams. These teams are structured best when composed of managers from both companies who have a clear mandate to plan for and monitor the integration process. The charter of these teams is to advise management on all aspects of the new corporate entity—from developing recommendations for combining functions to the development of new policies and processes, the selection of information systems, and the design of new (or the consolidation of existing) compensation and benefit programs, as well as communication strategies.

The primary purpose of a transition team is to focus key players on decisions that stabilize the organization and help to build momentum. It is generally best to set up small teams of results-oriented functional experts whose task is to focus on the postmerger "value drivers." These are the most likely projects to advance business opportunities, better utilize resources, produce early "wins," and drive profitability.

It is recommended that these teams consist of no more than three to five participants. If there are too many people on a team, it is difficult to coordinate meeting schedules and to arrive at decisions efficiently. It may also dilute the accountability of the team as well as lengthen the time required for the team to complete its tasks. As a simple matter of efficiency, not everyone needs to be involved in every decision.

In some cases, it will make the most sense to have one team leader with ultimate authority to make decisions and report in to the integration leader. This person is the on-site central contact for the transition process. (See the section above about the role and responsibilities of the integration leader.) This critical person is the primary liaison between the two companies with central oversight, coordination, and control of the functional transition teams.

The most effective teams will ultimately be those who incorporate *change leaders* who are already aware of issues and taking action, even if quietly, or that allow new change leaders to emerge as a result of their involvement. While the teams themselves can be formally established, their true value can only be allowed to emerge. They need to be given the freedom to innovate and cross-fertilize ideas—*if* they believe that the project is serious. If decision makers have predetermined a "structural fix" to the entire integration process, it's better just to say so and not waste people's time and frustrate them in the process.

Some sample principles that may be helpful in guiding the work of the transition teams follow:

Transition Team Guiding Principles

• Communicate what we know, when we know it.
• Acknowledge when "we don't know" and describe the process/timing for making the decision.
• Treat people fairly and with respect.
• Move quickly to integrate the businesses (i.e., get it 80% right and move on).
• Stay focused on supporting the company's vision and transition goals.

There is a delicate balance to achieve between the need for speed and resolution and the need for thoughtful, deliberate action. Speed is of the essence in a merger or acquisition, especially because there is a high degree of uncertainty in the work environment that leads to high anxiety and dysfunctional behaviors. The human brain absorbs information best when it is produced at rapid fire—you don't absorb a movie frame one day at a time for a year.

Once a strategy has been established, moving expeditiously toward implementation is critical to success. It is important to announce an ambitious schedule and keep to it. Why? Because when people are essentially kept in an indefinite state of suspended animation, a company loses the element of enthusiasm and actually punishes the people involved by unduly extending the state of uncertainty. *It has repeatedly been said that it is better to be 80% correct and make the necessary changes happen than be 100% correct after the real opportunity has passed. We agree.*

These transition teams generally report to the integration leader to ensure cross-group communication and to also ensure that the teams do not overlap in terms of decision making or recommendations. By monitoring and managing team progress, the integration leader can identify personal and political issues (sooner rather than later) that might interfere with the successful realization of the merger or acquisition strategy.

By establishing transition teams, the acquiring company also gains an opportunity to preview talent from both organizations. Representation on these teams must include team members from both companies in order to get a balanced perspective. It is also critical that the organization dedicates enough full-time participation so those employees can perform the required tasks of these teams. This is doubly important when one considers that these teams provide multiple opportunities for informal communication that is truly critical to the process of merging the cultures and getting people "on board."

SUMMARY

While the amount of work outlined in this chapter is immense, we do not believe we are being naïve or unrealistic. In our opinion, based on experience, these are all critical issues. If going through a large scale merger or acquisition happens to occur only once in the lifetime of the organization, then accomplishing this work may just be a short-term survival test. But given the pace of change taking place in both organizations and industries at present, that's not likely to be the case. Instead, this is in part, at least, an argument for the necessity of continuing to decentralize decision making and authority in most organizations. In this case, it's simply a practical rather than a philosophical stance.

The decisions required to keep business going while solidifying all these kinds of change cannot be micromanaged from the top of organizations of any significant size. Many hands and minds will be required. And while tremendously challenging in some circumstances, success necessitates a level of trust in people who may not be "proven and familiar" yet. The result may, in fact, be a higher level of camaraderie in the organization. But strangling the process through micromanagement is often a guarantee of failure. To be sure, there are risks involved, either way. But the best approach is to build the kind of organization of which people are proud to be a part and in which they are willing to invest a part of themselves.

NOTES

1. Jacob M. Schlesinger, "Why the Long Boom? It Owes a Big Debt to Capital Markets," *Wall Street Journal*, February 1, 2000.

2. Yochi J. Dreazen, "Stocks Make Up Almost a Third of Household Wealth in the U.S," *Wall Street Journal*, March 14, 2000.

3. Carol J. Loomis, "AOL + TWX = ???" *Fortune*, February 7, 2000.

4. Personal communication

5. Robert Langreth, "Behind Pfizer's Takeover Battle: Rockier Business Than It Revealed," *Wall Street Journal*, February 8, 2000.

6. Alfred Rappaport and Mark L. Sirower, "Stock or Cash: The Trade-offs for Buyers and Sellers in Mergers and Acquisitions," *Harvard Business Review* (November–December 1999).

7. The term "value drivers" was coined by Mark Feldman of Coopers and Lybrand.

8. National Public Radio, Morning Edition report, November 24, 1999, citing University of Chicago research.

Chapter 6

People

Despite the critical role that people play in the ultimate success or failure of a business venture, it is the human issues of M&A deals that typically receive the least focus by deal makers and are the most poorly handled. Yet, as noted in numerous ways in Chapter 1, there is a growing awareness that the strategic assets of an organization are tied ever closer to the knowledge and ideas, and to the skills and abilities, of the people involved. Sometimes such assets have been formalized into patents, or copyrights, or software code, or other more "tangible" forms that can be bought or sold and put into use. But real value lies in the potential to continue both creativity and productivity. And as trends continue to move towards customization of products and services and customer satisfaction, there are fewer and fewer jobs that don't really count or for which just "any warm body" will do.

Organizations that learn to appreciate, and to manage, these "human assets" most effectively will find themselves at a significant strategic advantage in the future. And quite apart from misperceptions that human factors are "soft" and should ideally be separated from "real" business issues, it is through forming connections between people—employees, customers, collaborators, suppliers, affiliates, and so on—that future wealth is likely to be created.

At present, handling human issues remains more an art than a science. There aren't always clear and absolute ways to achieve a desired result. Despite the thousands of management "how to" books and courses or the myriad of personality profiles and psychological consultants available, putting together the right mix of people and talents at the right time for the right markets, and then getting them to work, doesn't really have a formula.

In the period leading up to and immediately following a merger or acquisition, it's natural for employees of the company "under siege" to begin considering their own personal situations. Questions that are usually contemplated include "Where am I going?"; "What do I want out of both my personal and business life?"; "Will I "like" the new company and its management group?"; and "Will I fit in?"

The longer the post-deal organization remains undefined, the more attractive alternative employment becomes. For some employees, new employment is a way to regain a sense of control over their future— making some decision on their own rather than feeling victim to the decisions of others. ("If I've got to make this big of a change, then at least I'll do it on my own terms.")

To make things more difficult, the best and brightest managers are the ones who are immediately targeted by recruiters attempting to lure them to other organizations. One of the chief marketing tools of recruiters during these times of tumult and transition is that the company seeking their expertise is stable and secure—or at least the recruiter can tell the employee whom they'll be reporting to and what they'll be doing for the immediate future.

Based on recent statistics, 47% of all senior managers in an acquired firm leave in the first year of acquisition. But the exodus doesn't stop there. Within the first three years, 72% of those in senior positions are typically gone.[1] (In some cases, of course this is actually—at least in part—by design, as a way to eliminate "excess overhead," or to rid the organization of potential rabble-rousers or mavericks. But the loss of human or intellectual capital may far exceed what was understood or desired by the organization.)

The loss of key employees can seriously erode the potential value of a transaction for the acquiring firm. Perhaps equally damaging and just as costly are those people who stay on the payroll but who emotionally "check out" and don't perform at their previous levels of productivity. In a transaction not done well, the acquiring company may end up with the least desirable of the company's employees—those who simply had the fewest employment alternatives.

Much of the "Day One" emphasis in contemplating a merger or acquisition, therefore, should be focused on human resource issues. Early placement of management is a critical factor in beginning to stabilize the organization. Any delays in placing key managers only lengthen and complicate the transition by increasing uncertainty, diverting attention, and fostering internal competition. The challenge for the acquirer is in deciding who to retain, who to redeploy, and who to terminate in both the acquired company and its own.

EMPLOYEE SELECTION PROCESS

Some of the most critical decisions in a merger or acquisition are not just about the most visible or highly placed individuals. Corporate officer positions obviously play a key role, both with respect to who ends up in them and in how the placement decisions are made. But especially in cases where greater organizational efficiency is the main goal, not every corporate officer position will remain highly valued. And more importantly, lesser-ranked positions and skills may form many of the "value drivers" of the future organization that is in the process of being formed.

In the language of intellectual capital, the key people are those who add the most value to the organization and are also hard to replace.[2] And again, these people may be found throughout the organization.

Many companies in manufacturing and distribution businesses, for instance, are exploring ways to move into e-commerce or at least to the use of the Internet as a way of expanding their scope. This obviously calls for people with data communications skills, but the individuals who typically ran the information systems (IS) departments in these particular industries were, for a long time, primarily mainframe computer engineers whose skills are not easily transferable to the Internet environment.

Preparing the organization for its move into the future includes both identifying and positioning the right skills. In the case of IS functions, this might mean reorganizing a function entirely, including moving more forward thinking people with the right skill-sets into more senior positions—or even bringing in new talent from the outside while changes are taking place. (This "upgrading" of a company's employee base is likely to be an increasing trend for some time to come as the skill-sets needed by organizations become increasingly technological. Just as organizations can no longer evolve quickly enough to keep pace with changes in their environments and are faced with more fundamental transformations, so too are employees faced with not just upgrading skills but learning whole new skill-sets—or becoming "outmoded" in their capacities.)

But, again, the *ways* in which these decisions are made will, in the long run, be as important as the decisions themselves. They will communicate a great deal about what is valued by the organization. Do loyalty and dedication count, or is everything only about short-term results? Is the organization most interested in the best people, or does this count for less than social and personal connections with senior executives? Is there a sense that teamwork throughout the organization is essential, or is anyone below a certain level easily expendable?

There are many cases where reductions in the workforce are a critical part of the strategy being implemented. And in most organizations, some persons create more value and have harder-to-find skills than others. The point of this section is the importance of focusing on the alignment of people with the strategy in a way that achieves the desired results.

The first step, of course, is identifying the most valued employees (who theoretically also produce the most value for the organization). Typical methods for conducting these assessments include interviewing and testing techniques, use of outside consultants or psychologists, or other strategies. One of the difficulties of these approaches, though, is in getting clear about the underlying assumptions and the broader context of each.

It was a very enlightening experience as part of one corporate HR department, to learn about a process in which a highly paid consultant was regularly brought in to conduct screening tests of new salespersons. In asking more about these, it was discovered that the screenings were really just personality profiles. Using the most successful salespersons in the organization, a composite picture of their personalities had been developed. The screening amounted to simply looking for similar personality profiles in new candidates. The testing was highly quantified, but the characteristics being measured had no necessary relation to results at all. The organization just kept "cloning" the same personalities and hoping this would produce results.

Identifying the "right" skills, of course, necessitates knowing not just the current culture and structure of the organization, but much more importantly, what the future of the organization needs to be. Managers and supervisors naturally gravitate to hiring those candidates who are most like themselves, and therefore with whom they feel most comfortable and at ease. And under the assumption that these people will have to work pretty closely together, there is a lot to be said for basic ease of relationships. But a totally homogenous organization is very unlikely to be creative or to be able to address the massive challenges of a global marketplace. And one of the strategies for effecting change in an organization's culture is to *purposefully* put people with different perspectives and approaches into key positions to begin to "seed" new ideas.

Selection of key talent and key employees begins with an understanding of the vision and the purpose of the organization. Moving toward these may require choosing a certain level of *discomfort*, at least initially. If the goal of the merger or acquisition has anything to do with creating necessary change, the persons who are going to help create this are going to challenge existing assumptions and ways of doing business. One of the key challenges of the HR role is to make some assessment of the readiness for change and tolerance for conflict of the organization.

Despite the need for change and the support voiced for it, current employees (including many senior level people) may not be prepared for the level of conflict that can result. This does not mean that bright, alternative thinkers should be excluded (as noted, they may be critical to the creation of change), but it does mean that they should be prepared, as much as possible, for what they might face if they choose to engage. (It's also helpful to have an exit strategy ready for these key change agents, in case it just doesn't work.)

Once all of this has been thought through and planned, immediate steps should be taken to "rerecruit" and place these employees into key positions of the newly merged entity. If the goal is to retain these "star" employees, management should communicate its intentions to these individuals as early in the merger or acquisition process as is legally possible. This means requesting access to conduct confidential interviews with key employees well prior to the actual closing date. Most importantly, management should be very careful not to *under*commit to these people or they can be expected to consider other options. And rest assured that these star performers know who they are and understand their personal and professional marketability.

Selection of "noncritical" employees tends to be a much more general process in most mergers or acquisitions. Decisions are made according to perceived staffing needs of various operations, departments, and functions, and then according to some individual selection process. Yet the criteria by which these decisions are made can have a profound impact on employee morale.

An important concern in many M&A deals is just retaining talented employees while other organizational decisions are being made. What follows is a list of some of the most common retention tools that may be used during the transitional period following a merger or acquisition. These are not all necessarily *recommended* approaches, though you may find some useful or even necessary—at least as a stopgap if things are not going well. They are outlined to provide an overview of frequent practices, so that you can assess whether any of these tools would be helpful to your circumstances.

RETENTION TOOLS

- *"Cease and desist letters"*—Drafted by your attorney from senior management to his or her counterpart at another company requesting that company to immediately discontinue its attempt to "woo" your employees away;
- *Noncompete Agreements/Intellectual Property Agreements*—Can "lock up" your key talent from leaving to work with a competitor or from taking key knowledge with them upon termination;
- *Focus Groups*—Discussions with 8 to 10 employees with a facilitator in order

to understand employee complaints and concerns so that you can take quick action;

- *Exit Interviews*—Individual discussions with departing employees so that you understand very clearly the reason for their departure;

- *Accelerated Salary Increases*—These are useful for vulnerable groups (e.g. IS, legal, marketing, etc.);

- *Adjustments to Your Salary Structure*—Adjust the amounts of your minimum, midpoint and maximum salaries for each job;

- *Lump Sum Payout*—Consider providing a one-time lump sum payout to those employees who are at or near the end of their salary grade. This allows time for the salary structure to advance based on changes in the marketplace and the company saves money since the increase is not added to the employee's base amount;

- *Retention Bonuses/Contracts*—Contracts and retention bonuses can be an attractive tool to retain key employees and management level people;

- *Sign-On Bonuses*—For hard-to-find employees, a sign-on bonus can be the differentiator for your company;

- *Relocation Payback Agreement*—Prior to receiving relocation benefits, you might require the employee to sign a "payback" agreement which requires the full repayment of relocation expenses if he or she does not remain in the new location for 12 months or more;

- *"Spot" Cash Awards*—Great tool for allowing managers to "surprise" employees with on-the-spot awards ranging from $50 to $1,000 for outstanding effort, above and beyond the reasonable expectations of the job;

- *Alter Waiting Periods for Benefits*—Shorten or eliminate the waiting period on your employee benefit coverages;

- *Tuition Reimbursement*—Increase the percentage of reimbursement or the range of courses covered;

- *Introduce New Programs*—Consider adding stock-based programs to your range of benefits or increase the company's share of plan funding;

- *Subsidized Child Care*—Consider adding referrals, on-site day care or discounts for off-site centers;

- *Employee Services*—Many companies are offering "concierge" services such as dry cleaning, banking, grocery shopping, take-out catering, and the like to ease the burden of work/family pressures;

- *Sabbaticals*—Offer paid or unpaid time off after a certain number of years of employment;

- *Flexible Scheduling*—Offer core hours when everyone must be at work but floating hours at either end;

- *Job Sharing*—Split the workday, shift, or workweek with another employee;

- *Rotational Assignments*—Can be used to enrich an existing assignment;

- *Virtual Office/Telecommuting*—Save on office space requirements and provide increased flexibility for employees;

- *Relaxed Dress Code*—Fairly standard in most workplaces now, but if not already in place, the main point is to treat employees as if they know how to make decisions about what is appropriate (though this can require a little coaching at times);
- *New Hire Orientation*—Infuse the culture of your new organization by communicating the core values through a common orientation program in which various executives are invited to speak to groups of new hires on a regular basis;
- *Timely Performance Appraisals*—This is a basic "given" that is often overlooked. People want and need to know where they stand with the organization, and feedback about performance is a great way to ensure that employees receive an annual "report card" about their contributions and standing with the organization; and
- *Effective Dispute Resolution Procedures*—Instill a feeling of fairness and employee advocacy by providing effective procedures for resolving conflicts.

In addition to the retention tools discussed, some companies have also been successful in retaining key management-level employees by offering "stay" or "retention" bonuses or employment agreements to entice critical employees to remain. Other companies have also offered stock options and other short- and long-term incentives (e.g., performance shares or units, restricted stock, and the like).

The reason that these types of programs and incentives are not necessarily recommended is that, while retention of talent may be the motivation, the real objective is to drive sustained value creation by energizing and focusing the behavior of people. These types of incentives are only a stopgap for the retention of key and critical talent who, if departed, would seriously erode the ability of the company to compete in the future.

Not only do you want good people, but you want to keep the good people good. There is a danger that "golden handcuffs" can actually increase inertia and obstruct progress. These types of financial incentives, in reality, capture only the body—but they do not capture the heart and the mind. They reward a willingness to stay instead of results, and they are not linked to the creation of economic value.

While these types of retention practices may be necessary, ultimately, it is really the employee's perception of the new management team's fairness, integrity, and objectivity that will keep people engaged in the work of carrying out a merger or acquisition.

But, career-oriented achievers seek two other things as well:

1. They want assurances that they will have opportunities to influence the direction, character, and shape of the company; and

2. They want clear indications that their opportunities for valuable learning and possibly advancement, are significant.

Some of the desire for influence can be met through participation—by allowing high-potential employees to participate in key transition teams and by seeking their input on functional matters within their specific areas of expertise. Such an exercise is not to be taken lightly, though. Once begun, it will create or reinforce expectations about management or operational styles. And there is no quicker way to kill initiative among employees than to ask for participation and then ignore or override it.

The move by many organizations to the use of formal workplace teams, for instance, has met with mixed success. While teams are usually formed around very egalitarian values, most organizations are not. The points at which these different value-sets converge tend to be points of conflict, whether readily acknowledged or not. Creating possibilities for participation is important, but only if participation is actually valued by the organization. Otherwise, employees are likely to feel resentful that their ideas were asked for in the first place. The key is usually establishing parameters for the decisions up front (i.e., deciding what range of authority will be granted for participation), and then sticking with it.

Sometimes the growth caused by a merger or acquisition can accommodate the desire for career opportunities through creating new and meaningful positions. Given the trend towards eliminating excess layers of management though, upward mobility in organizations is simply not going to be available to all of even the best performers. Rather than losing such persons, many organizations have begun using lateral strategies, offering employees new opportunities for growth and challenge at essentially the same "levels" in the organization.

Alternatively, younger employees, especially in high-tech areas, seem much more prone to move through both positions and organizations, gathering as much experience as they can along the way, but not counting on any sort of career path with any one organization. For these employees, it probably makes much more sense to accept a different type of relationship, with the employee and the organization each working towards a mutually beneficial but time-limited outcome. The key here is setting appropriate expectations, and being able to be flexible about structural issues, such as benefits programs that still only reward longevity.

EMOTIONAL REACTIONS

Employees from an acquired company—from the senior management group to the mail clerk—are often anxious, insecure, uncertain, and many times even angry following the closing of a transaction. They are acutely aware of the fact that when companies are purchased, the acquiring company often puts its own people in charge, changes policies and procedures, restructures, consolidates, and generally takes over. If new positions are to be created or existing positions vacated as a result of retirements, it's important to clarify the selection process for filling them, as one indication of creating a "level playing field" for all who are to be involved.

Employees' initial reactions to the announcement of a merger or acquisition, especially in more stable or traditional organizations, is often to become preoccupied with their own personal security and identity and with what the deal means for their jobs, location, and future career. They are questioning everything, from "Who are these guys and can we trust them?" to "Will we still have a job and will it be the same as before?" to "What's in it for the people who can really make it happen?"

Conversely, the acquiring managers close the deal with a certain amount of euphoria, ready to get on with the exciting challenge of running the new business. If left unrecognized, this vast difference in emotional states can be debilitating to the work of integration and can send the process quickly down the wrong path.

Among the concerns that need to be given highest priority are the "me" issues. These are issues typically raised by employees that most directly affect each individual, including title, salary, bonus opportunity, job location, position, reporting relationships, authority, scope of decision making, office space, key procedures, and other "perks" of their job. Beneath all of this, of course, lurk the more fundamental questions of "Am I really a part of this?" and "Where do I fit?" Unless these "me" issues are quickly addressed, progress on the company's key strategic objectives will be slow at best.

It is fair to say that most acquisitions involve some restructuring. Moving quickly to restructure is not easy, even when obvious changes need to be made. But the strategy to delay the pace of consolidation is a faulty one. There is no such thing as an acquisition that does not include some degree of change—in structure, philosophy, systems, strategy, or location (or, in many situations, all of these).

Given that change is inevitable, it is far better to make, announce, and implement decisions about management structure, key roles, office location, reporting relationships, layoffs, overall organizational structure, and other career-affecting aspects of the integration as soon as possible after the deal is signed. This should ideally happen within a couple of days. If these types of changes are going to occur, it's much better to get on with them, rather than allow anxiety and speculation to diffuse employee energy and focus.

Critical to a successful integration effort is the manner in which the restructuring is carried out. The highest priority is that the acquiring company needs to be straightforward about what is happening and what is planned. Even when the news is bad, the one thing that the employees of newly-acquired companies appreciate most is *the truth*. That includes being able to say "we don't know" about certain areas or "we have not yet decided" about others. It also includes sharing information about when and by what process a decision is expected to be reached.

The truth also means acknowledging some of the stress and other emotions that are undeniably present. Never tell employees that everything will be "business as usual." The reality is, change is occurring. Resist the urge to tell employees that they have "a wonderful future" to look forward to when they are still confused and grieving over the past. But most importantly, please don't call the deal a "merger of equals" when it is clear that one company is the majority stakeholder and has the ability to cast the deciding vote in a split decision—and there is *always* one side that ends up as the "big dog."

Once decisions are made about functions and people, it is critical to treat those employees who will be negatively impacted by the transaction with dignity, respect, and support. Not only is it the right thing to do, it is also a powerful way of showing those who remain what kind of company they are now working for and to help them begin to develop some positive feelings toward the new organization.

In organizations with decades of history, delivering news of impending change (often meaning loss of jobs and relocations) can be extremely difficult. While most business issues can be handled with some sense of factual objectivity, this type of news hits at a very human level. The simple reality is that many people's most familiar contacts and even strongest friendships revolve around the workplace. In fact, a Gallup survey of 400 companies found that the ability to have best friends at work was the *highest* of 12 indicators of a highly productive workplace.[3] (We personally knew a group of secretaries who had gone to lunch together weekly for *25 years* prior to the break-up of a company.) Such losses cannot be taken or treated lightly.

And while welcoming new people into the organization would appear to be much easier and more positive, employees from an acquired company (or the "lesser" of the merged partners) aren't automatically going to be grateful for the change or the "opportunity." The ways in which such issues are handled will be closely watched and remembered long by those involved—for good or ill.

Chapter 10 covers the legal aspects of making people-related termination decisions and how best to notify the affected individuals in a humane and legally defensible manner. Appendices 7, 8, and 9 provide additional resources as you consider workforce reduction or how to handle the actual termination discussions and other issues related to downsizing.

THE NEUTRAL ZONE

Once management has made the new job assignments and sorted out the key transition policies, some managers start to "crack the whip" to get things moving as soon as possible. Unfortunately, there is usually a period of time immediately following the deal when it is common for people to drift and be somewhat confused. The better the integration phase is planned, the less dramatic this time should be—but a new organization won't emerge automatically or without some time and effort.

Employees who survive a merger often feel threatened by the new system of values and beliefs about the best way to get things done. New performance standards and methods often seem foreign and, all too often, seem to be "forced down their throats". People who are learning to adjust to new ways of doing things will naturally be more hesitant as they test how familiar skills work in unfamiliar settings or attempt to operate in a new culture.

This is the "neutral zone" (as it has been dubbed by William Bridges, author of *Managing Transitions*[4]), the time during a merger or acquisition when people are caught between the old ways and the new—and neither provides satisfactory answers. As Bridges puts it, this is "the nowhere between two somewheres." "This is a time," as Marilyn Ferguson notes, "when you've let go of one trapeze with the faith that the new trapeze is on its way. In the meantime, there's nothing much to hold on to."[5]

One of the most difficult aspects of the neutral zone for most people is that they don't understand it. Most of us expect to be able to move straight from the old to the new. But it doesn't work that way. It's a journey from one identity to the other, and that journey takes time.

So how do you give structure and strength during a time when people are likely to be feeling lost and confused? Some thoughts:

1. Try to reduce the number of unrelated and unexpected changes that are announced while people are trying to regain their balance.
2. Review policies and procedures to ensure that they address the ambiguities and uncertainties that are causing people to be confused.
3. Determine if new roles or reporting relationships need to be developed or better defined.
4. Set short-term goals toward which employees can aim, and establish checkpoints along the way.
5. Don't set people up for failure by promising high levels of productivity while the organization is in the neutral zone.
6. Determine what types of issues supervisors are having problems with and provide targeted training programs on those subjects.

Although the neutral zone can be a time of confusion and fear, it can also be a time of great innovation. It is during the gap between the old and the new that the organization is most likely to be receptive to truly creative solutions. It is generally when the old way of seeing things begins to disappear or weaken that the new way can begin to emerge.

Right after the closing of the transaction, the company needs to communicate to employees that this is a time to question the "usual" ways of doing things and a time to come up with new and creative solutions to both past and current problems. This is a good time to schedule professional retreats, policy reviews, employee surveys, and suggestion campaigns. It is important to schedule into these efforts a way to keep employees informed about what is being done with the ideas generated and the suggestions made. If there is no feedback loop, employees are likely to feel that their good ideas have been forgotten or are not being taken seriously.

But there is a natural impulse in times of ambiguity, uncertainty, and disorganization for management to push prematurely for certainty and closure. It is tempting for executives to rally the troops to "pull together" in the neutral zone and to follow the new management and strategy. Be careful not to move toward closure too early or employees will likely feel resentful and will consciously or subconsciously undermine the effort, feeling defeated and resentful in the process.

Significant changes can take place within people during the neutral zone. This change represents a kind of inner "sorting" process in which old (and no longer appropriate) habits are discarded and new patterns of thought and action are developed. This can be a time when people are able to let go of old assumptions and allow themselves to learn new approaches. It can be a time in which deep and intense dialogues occur between groups with differing perspectives from which new understanding and appreciation may emerge. It may offer an opportunity for new informal networks and "communities of practice" to begin to form. But these are not changes that can be "engineered" into a process. If any of this is to happen, people must be given the time that they need to get through it and the freedom and encouragement to tread into unfamiliar and uncomfortable territory.

TREAT THE PAST WITH RESPECT

Many managers, in their enthusiasm for a future that is going to be better than the past, ridicule or talk negatively of the old way of doing things. In doing so, they consolidate the resistance against the transition because people strongly identify with "the way things used to be." They feel that their self-worth is at stake when the past is attacked. But managers who are tempted to denounce the past are not all wrong either.

They are right in wanting to distinguish what they are proposing from what has been tried in the past or what is being done in the present. The challenge is to make the distinction respectfully.

Rather than attacking the old organization as inefficient and old-fashioned (with comments like "Nobody in his right mind would run a business like *that*!" or "That's archaic!"), a better approach is to credit employees and management for bringing the company to the successful point where it now stands, emphasizing the new challenges that call for new responses and approaches.

It is important that in urging people to turn away from the past, leaders don't drive them away from either an alliance with the new management or the new direction that the organization needs to take. Honor the past for what it has accomplished, and the people who were part of it. Be clear about what now needs to be created and how this is to come about. And allow people the creativity to figure out ways to make the necessary bridges to get from one to the other.

HUMAN ASSETS

As described in other chapters of this book, there is a strong tendency to treat people as expendable assets or only overhead costs in most M&A deals. And there is an equally strong bias about HR functions being primarily administrative data processing, or concerned with nontangible, nonprofitable issues.

As far as we know though, there are no organizations that have succeeded in going "people-less." Rather than being extraneous to operations, they are, in fact, central to them. The problem is most often the conflict between roles and resources.

In strictly efficiency-focused organizations, the ideal employee would be a mechanism that would need no rest, no rewards or incentives, and have no personal issues or complaints. The majority of tasks that need to be accomplished in most organizations don't miss a beat when they are transferred to nonhuman processes because the tasks themselves were set up as boring, repetitive processes. While we may personally rebel against innovations such as automated phone systems, it is our individual human needs for contact that are affected, not the needs of the organization. Such systems have essentially replaced live persons because, from an organizational standpoint, they are more efficient. People simply do not make very good machine parts.

Attempting to keep mechanistic processes interesting is also not an optimal answer, as this typically only runs counter to efficiency efforts. Rotating individuals through various roles may keep things from getting so boring, but also reduces the efficiency of the function while a new person masters the learning and the tasks required of the position.

The relevance to mergers and acquisitions is simply the assumption that maximum efficiency equals optimal results. As noted already, the perfect model for many organizational strategies would be a people-less company—just pure process and output. And this basic model, though rarely put in such caustic terms, is what drives many M&A deals. Buy a competitor, take what is useful, and discard the rest. And while there are important human characteristics to organizations, they always seems to be in conflict with this idea of perfect efficiency.

Round-the-clock operations provide an interesting example of this. Twenty-four hour rotating schedules have been standard in some large industries for generations. Many large operations, such as oil refineries and other processing plants, simply could not be stopped and started on a daily basis, and the equipment and machinery required human monitoring. Workers and their families simply adapted the best they could to odd cycles of sleeping and eating—and in their interactions with "normal" schedules of the rest of the world (e.g., schools, etc.). Similar schedules, of course, were taken for granted in hospitals, police departments, and other emergency operations. But 24-hour operations are now standard for many department stores and grocery stores, communications and media companies, sales-order functions for catalogues and other retail ventures, and on and on. People manage to adapt, but it is the operational needs, not the human needs, that drive the schedule.

Intercontinental travel is now becoming standard for many employees of global companies, demanding not just schedule adjustments but extended time away from home as well. Often these demands are coupled with increased workloads in companies that have to cut as many employees as possible in an effort to realize the value built into the inflated costs of a merger or acquisition. As long as people choose to comply, either out of economic necessity or from a sense of this being normal and expected, there will be people to fill jobs. But to the degree that organizational emphasis continues to be on process efficiency, there will be a real and significant human cost as well.

One of the problems in asking for these kinds of sacrifices from workers is the motivation for doing so. It's simply not very inspiring to sacrifice oneself for an increase in shareholder value. And being "expendable overhead" doesn't tend to increase devotion. Programs and incentives such as those described earlier in this chapter may help support the increased and dedicated efforts of people, but they don't provide more fundamental answers.

Culturally, we look to our occupational roles to provide a sense of identity and meaning. As long as there are no ready alternatives to this, people will continue to make the best of what they can find at work. But there are limits to the current trends.

To think about this differently, it might be helpful to look at some of the same issues from another perspective. Many of the pressures for organizational change are being brought about by rapid changes in the larger environments with which organizations interact (including customers, markets, competitors, etc.) These changes, in turn, are a result of larger changes (e.g., cultural and technological), but organizations tend to recognize demands in terms of things they are most familiar with.

Making structural adjustments to alter functional processes (reorganization efforts, etc.) have proven to be minimally effective at best, in terms of adapting to environmental demands. And worse, these kinds of changes have to continue, time and again. An adjustment made to a fixed process, aimed at delivering a specific, known outcome, is only effective for as long as the environment stays static (or remains stable enough for the "fix" to hold). When the change occurs slowly, such remedies remain adequate for long enough to suffice. During times of rapid change, the "fixes" can barely be completed before new changes are initiated—and often one is simply abandoned midstream while the next begins.

From a human side, what is engaging is what is novel and challenging, but within achievable limits (and these differ for each person).[6] When people are involved in activities that inspire them to be and to do their best, interestingly, time and energy seem to increase rather than be used up. Learning happens naturally when people regain a sense of the magic of discovery that was lost in formal education. When work is actually fun and relationships are good, people look forward to being there.

The better that organizations can anticipate changes in their environments, the more successful they are likely to be in responding to them. The more engaged employees are in the real purposes of organizations, the more they truly feel a part of them, and the more aware they are likely to be about customers' concerns and activities by competitors, and proactively addressing them. As noted by a veteran manager at Kodak, "As employees became more invested in their work, waste levels dropped significantly. So did overtime. Productivity increased . . . they started taking more initiative both inside and outside work."[7]

Human aspects of work and productivity have been recognized for decades and lie at the heart of many organizational movements (e.g., human relations, sociotechnical systems, etc.) The problems have been that such movements have acted only as overlays to still fundamentally mechanistic organizational systems. They lasted as long as business and profits were good and there were excess resources and capacity to support them. When competition or pressure for profits increased, they typically fell victim to cost-cutting efforts. The current challenge is that while employee support services and family-friendly programs continue to flourish, they can only attempt to counterbalance ever-increasing demands on employees for efficiency and production. (Interestingly, it is many of these same human issues that are driving demands for executive coaches, a more acceptable, "business-like" response for senior managers.[8])

Even more complicating is the fact that many of the conflicts that employees feel are not just within or about their jobs, but between the various roles they play in society—each of which seems to be increasing in expectations or demands. The really complicating part is that each of the demands, in its own right, seems to make sense. It's just a further evolution of its own process.

Competition seems to pressure people to excel at *everything*. Kids don't just participate in sports anymore. As sports mature and evolve, kids become involved at earlier ages and spots on teams become more competitive. So kids go to more and more camps, acquire more individual training, and teams have ever more training to keep up.

In academics, students competing for admission to the most elite colleges no longer just need near-perfect scores on admissions tests, such as the SAT or ACT, and top ranking in their classes. They must have additional ways by which they can set themselves apart.[9] Traditional extracurricular activities, of course, include arts and athletics. But in order to really stand out, exceptional students need more than just participation in *common* activities, such as band and soccer. Exceptional students must excel at uncommon activities. Elite schools tend to like top-ranked chess players, for instance, and to prefer athletics such as fencing and crew, and musical expertise with orchestral instruments.

While most students won't ever have the chance to seriously compete for spots in Ivy League schools, those expectations tend to set a broader standard. Kids feel pressure to be not just involved, but to excel in as many arenas as possible. Schools continue to raise standards to achieve "academic excellence," increasing workloads on students and simultaneously pushing for greater and greater parental involvement. Extracurricular activities almost invariably necessitate transportation arrangements (kids don't just ride their bikes to these events any more). In short, expectations to excel at everything—academics, arts, and athletics for kids; careers, parenting, community involvement, and so forth for adults—are creating increasingly unrealistic scenarios.

The point? Your organization has just completed negotiating an acquisition which is to be priced at a 43% premium over the current stock value of the company. In order to meet the profit expectations inherent in the deal, more costs will have to be cut than first anticipated, and this will include people. But if it works, this acquisition should better position your organization for a move into the e-commerce realm, both business-to-business and with customers. Key personnel and technology of the target company are being counted on to provide the answers. Profit margins in the industry have been down, competition increasing, and it appears that significant industry consolidation is beginning, so this may be only one of more mergers or acquisitions to come.

Anxiety in your own organization has been running high since rumors about the deal first leaked out, and calls are starting to come in about relocation issues for senior managers of the target company—availability of selective housing, quality of schools, special needs of specific family members, and so forth. Key managers are said to be wavering in their decisions about making the move and joining the company pending final decisions about roles and responsibilities and compensation packages. Several key managers also have spouses with similar level positions in other companies, and finding comparable employment for them in your own area is going to be a challenge.

Both of your organizations have been through the typical rounds of downsizing and reorganization in recent years, but each has also maintained a fairly solid sense of its own identity, and a number of long-term executives are still in place. Unfortunately, not all the executives in your organization agreed on the acquisition strategy, though they all support it publicly, of course. But you anticipate some ongoing turf battles behind the scenes as the deal progresses.

Each organization has a fairly strong culture of its own, but employees of the target company are much younger, on average. There was a strong sense of loyalty among your company's employees, but many became somewhat jaded after numerous rounds of layoffs and changes. Employees from the target company just seem to have a different attitude about work, from what you can tell. Your employees still work hard, but not with the enthusiasm they once had. The target company's employees just seem a lot more "self-invested" and interested in short-term, personal gains. And you're sure there's going to be some real resentment by your own company's employees when preference seems to be given to the employees of the target company because they have the more valued technical skills.

Your job as the HR guru is to somehow make the people side of this deal work. You must put together plans and incentive packages to retain key employees. You also must prepare to lay off employees from both organizations and see that the agreed-upon benefits and programs are provided. Several locations of the target company will have to be closed and appropriate records and files transferred. And in the midst of all these and many, many more details, you anticipate that some major integration issues, based on differences in corporate cultures, will undoubtedly find their way to your HR group.

Addressing the details of this kind of scenario is the reason that we've put so many suggestions about plans and approaches into this book. But this all lies within a much broader context of changing roles and expectations about work in general. As the value within work moves from repetition of known processes (i.e., efficiently accomplishing given tasks) to awareness and anticipation of changing environments, and innovation in ways for the organization to respond effectively to these, the basic nature of the organization begins to change. *Awareness and innovation are not mechanistic processes. At this point, they're still human characteristics.*

Acquiring additional assets or combining operations to gain economies of scale or new technologies or greater market share are temporary organizational solutions. Learning better ways to engage and unleash the collective skills, talents, and creativity of employee groups—across global markets and in the face of increasingly fragmented social networks and economic demands—is the challenge of the future.

NOTES

1. Mihaly Csikszentmihalyi, *Flow: The Psychology of Optimal Experience* (Harper & Row, 1990).

2. Thomas A. Stewart, *Intellectual Capital: The New Wealth of Organizations* (Currency/Doubleday, 1997).

3. Sue Shellenbarger, "Workplace Upheavals Cost Employees Some Friendships," *Wall Street Journal*, January 12, 2000.

4. William Bridges, *Managing Transitions: Making the Most of Change* (Addison-Wesley, 1991).

5. Betsy Morris, "So You're a Player. Do You Need a Coach?" *Fortune*, February 21, 2000, p. 152.

6. Csikszentmihalyi, *Flow*.

7. Morris, "So You're a Player," p. 152.

8. Ibid.

9. Lee Clifford, "What Does Harvard Want?" *Smart Money* (December 1999).

Chapter 7

The Role of Human Resources
in M&A Strategy and Execution

An HR practitioner wears many "hats" during the planning and execution stages of merger and acquisition activities. Traditionally, most of the HR role has centered around employment, compensation, and benefits issues. And most of the activity has been in the form of processing employment and termination forms, enrolling employees in benefits plans, and the like. But HR professionals often find themselves consulting with senior managers about specific personnel cases or issues, listening to worried or angry employees, and sometimes acting as the "temperature gauge" of the organization, as well.

In a formal way, there are six major stages that human resources can or will likely be involved in during M&A transactions. These include target screening, planning/pre-acquisition strategy discussions, due diligence, negotiations, integration planning, and the actual post-deal integration process itself.

It is important to explore each of these actual stages to determine the strategic areas in which you and your HR team should be involved, and how, as a group, you might maximize your collective contribution to the success of the transaction. These stages are outlined in more detail as follows:

TARGET SCREENING

Target screening is the process of gathering preliminary information about companies seen to be potentials for acquisition or merger. Given the delicate legal nature of such investigations and the potential effect that even rumors of such activity can have on company stock values and customer relations, this activity must be taken seriously and conducted carefully.

During the target screening phase of transactional activity, HR practitioners can perform "reconnaissance" by talking with other HR professionals who know the target companies. These discussions will focus on learning about the target company's HR policies and practices, their culture, leadership strengths, and operating and employee communication styles.

As noted in earlier chapters, much of the focus by financial and operational analysts will be on assets, markets, brand values, customer base, and so on. A good deal of what will be gathered here can be summarized in comparative numbers and maps. In an acquisition, is there potential financial value that can be realized through buying this company, merging what is most useful into existing operations (or using these for expansion), selling at a premium what does not fit, and disposing of assets that show no value? In a merger, it is typically a matter of combining efforts and assets to produce a larger company with more assets and market share that is able to attract more capital investment at lower costs. (In recent mergers, the stakes are actually much higher it seems. In some high-tech industries, leaders are seeking not just market share but market dominance and the ability to set the standards for emerging industries—for instance, what protocols will dominate the digital communications industries and whether these will be primarily through cable or wireless transmissions.)

From an HR standpoint, a first look at target companies needs to be a broad assessment about "fit." If there's a secret to this, it's probably that it needs to begin with some careful introspection before any analysis of other companies begins.

Primarily, you need to have some sense about what makes your organization unique and what makes it work. It might be really helpful to begin this work with some discussions with HR colleagues or executives from other organizations to get their views about your organization. It is, by nature, very difficult to be objective about oneself or one's own place.

Once you have some sense about your own organization's current strengths and weaknesses and its cultural peculiarities, you are better positioned to be able to anticipate some of the issues that might arise with other organizations. But do be aware that regardless of how consistent the feedback from your colleagues may be, this is a very subjective area, and others (including key decision makers) in your organization may have extremely different views.

In one instance in our experience, part of the rationale given for a deal at the time of its announcement was the wonderful cultural fit between the organizations. This was based on the sense of business approach and philosophy that emerged as the early discussions were carried on between key executives. As talks progressed from announcement to finalization of the deal though, things became much more contentious. As other employees travelled between company locations during the due diligence phase, the information coming back was extremely different. The other company's location was described as something out of a 1940s black-and-white movie, and their HR practices apparently a reflection of this. Though many employees did finally make the move to the new company, it was primarily because of the lack of alternatives at the time, and was done with a great deal of anguish.

In an ideal world, of course, we would all have ideal partners and ideal positions. But the world is simply not that way (as far as we can tell). As merger and acquisition activity continues to heat up, even as we sit and write this, the pressure to "eat or be eaten" seems to drive deals. But this does not negate the value of HR issues.

In the current climate, it may be difficult to know who is the pursuer and who the pursued until the deal is done. In the Vodofone–Mannesmann merger in Europe, there was a great deal of eleventh-hour negotiating before Vodafone emerged as the dominant partner.[1] But regardless of the nature of the deal or the process by which it is struck, at some point the integration process will become real. The better prepared you and your HR team are for the eventualities, the better the planning for them can be.

Obviously, given the confidentiality of these discussions, you must be very careful about the manner in which you and your team approach third parties to do your advance screening for key issues. In fact, it is prudent to talk with your internal or external legal counsel prior to actually engaging in these types of conversations so that you do not inadvertently violate any confidentiality provisions of a tentative agreement or stumble into securities law violations.

PLANNING/PREACQUISITION STRATEGY

During the planning/preacquisition strategy phase, the HR team will most generally be involved in the following types of activities:

Advising Senior Management on Retention and Benefit Packages

Much of the interest by senior managers in this information is generally only for purposes of financial accounting, though there may well be questions about the rationale for the recommended packages in order to justify costs. From a HR standpoint, these recommendations can't be made in isolation. While companies often have fairly clear philosophies about such plans (e.g., providing fairly rich packages in order to attract the best employees versus not wasting any more resources than necessary on these), these philosophies may or may not fit the requirements of the proposed transaction. It's not unusual for a company that is being acquired to require, for instance, as a point of negotiation, that equivalent healthcare and other benefits be maintained for its employees, at least for a specified period of time. If this happens, the acquiring company either has to maintain a patchwork of disparate benefits between different subgroups, which can be a reporting and record keeping nightmare, not to mention a source of contention between employee groups, or to update its own plans in the process of consolidation. The primary task at this point is simply to make senior decision makers aware that this process may entail more than just adding new employees to existing plans.

Talking to People to Gauge and Anticipate the Impact of Changes and Reaction of the Workforce

The greater the pressure to get a deal done, the more that decision makers are likely to work from their existing beliefs and assumptions about the organization. It's important though, to have current information about issues that are likely to trigger reactions by employees. If other senior managers are buried in facts and details at the moment, they are unlikely to be soliciting this information. Human resources is often in the best position to provide this kind of input—introduced strategically into discussions as a deal progresses.

Planning of Communication and Follow-Up Activities in Support of the Transaction Announcement

While there are often many rumors flying around workplaces during the initial stages of a deal, only at the official announcement does that particular deal become real. (And what it really turns out to be may not yet be fully determined.) So at the time that an official announcement is made, there needs to be a plan in place for all the questions and activities that the announcement will trigger. Much of the communications plan, of course, will be keeping employees informed about progress since their most basic questions about "How is this going to affect me, personally?" probably can't be answered at that point.

Planning Key Processes (e.g., Selection, Relocation, Outplacement, etc.)

Given the somewhat chaotic nature of the way in which deals actually are finalized, it's extremely helpful to have as many processes as possible planned in advance. To be sure, they will not always go according to plan, but at least the issues will have been reviewed, providing some basis from which to work as things change.

Policies for selection, relocation decisions and expenses, outplacement services, and the like are critical "me"-type questions for employees. They will frequently come up immediately following the announcement of the intended deal. While the final answers to the questions have usually not been determined, it's helpful to be able to give some response as to how they may take place. Otherwise, it tends to leave employees thinking that their careers and livelihoods are being left to the whims of some arbitrary decision maker who doesn't even know them—an incentive for the most talented employees to begin looking at alternatives.

In the case of a very simple acquisition of a small company by a large one, and in which little negotiation needs to take place, it may only be a matter of outlining the strategies in preparation for implementation. At the other end of the spectrum, negotiations may drag on at length, even as to which company will be the acquiring company or dominant partner. In these cases, it is not advisable to give specific details too soon—but think them through strategically.

In a case with which we were familiar, a very comprehensive plan for employee selection had been devised and proposed by one partner in a joint venture—in this case, the less dominant partner. As negotiations progressed, it became clear that the dominant partner had little interest in this plan. And since their employees were the less likely to be affected by the changes, they also showed little interest in informing employees about the processes. In the end, the process was relegated to a "horse-trading" system, with each company simply putting names into slots, according to the percentage of interest in the venture. Needless to say, this did not begin the new organization in the optimal manner.

Selecting the Integration Leader

Specific ideas about the selection and duties of an integration leader were covered in Chapter 2. In preparation for this, it's helpful to think through this role with senior executives in light of other plans for key employees. The integration leader will be a highly visible position. The person selected will be assumed by most employees to be a "rising star," if not someone already in a senior role. At the same time, this person will have to be able to work with senior executives and managers across both organizations for some period of time.

This is a highly visible and very important—but only temporary—assignment. Depending upon the size and magnitude of the transaction, it is likely that this person will not be able to carry these responsibilities and a new executive or senior management role simultaneously. But it may not be possible to simply hold a slot open for this person, pending completion of the transitions.

Such a role is sometimes filled by an executive nearing retirement (or one who only has a temporary assignment with the new organization). Otherwise, it is likely that his or her duties will have to be shared for a time in order to give adequate attention to these responsibilities.

It may take considerable thought and discussion to find the right person for this role. The person filling it needs to have a strong commitment to it, for they will be caught in the crossfire of organizational conflict at times. He or she also needs to have the support of senior executives in doing what's right for the organization, even if it's not the popular thing at the moment.

Advising Management on Structure, Makeup, and Processes for Separation/Integration/Transition Planning Teams

As with the integration leader, employees in these critical but temporary roles need to have the time and resources to allow them to be successful, but not end up professionally sidelined for having served. Much of the work in this preparation phase involves securing senior level commitment to the work of building a strong organization, not just achieving early numbers-results.

Assessing Strengths and Weaknesses of Businesses and Functional Leadership

This is a critical level of assessment that needs to be done, not in opposition to the political alliances that exist between senior managers, but alongside them. Despite the growing emphasis on human and intellectual capital in organizations, people still do not rise through the ranks of organizations based primarily on their leadership and people management skills. Some executives are exceptional leaders, but many are not. Getting the best combination of talents (human and operational) into key roles is optimal. But once in place, an organization tends to protect those in senior roles until problems are blatant and can no longer be ignored.

You may or may not be able to influence decisions made about key leadership roles in any significant way. You will, however, have to live with the outcomes of them. It is best to have as clear a picture as possible of the general style and approach of all the candidates in question. With regard to your own organization, it's probably good to begin discussions about strategic placement of personnel early on, in just an informal and speculative way. With regard to the other organization, some of this information about leadership ability can be garnered from discussions with colleagues, but probably not in any depth until discussions become somewhat open and formal. In some cases, there may be opportunities for exercising creativity in restructuring roles, so that individual strengths can be emphasized and the effects of weaknesses diminished— or at least identified as needs to be addressed through coaching or mentoring.

Identifying Potential Barriers to Integration Success

Whatever the characteristics of the partner company for the transaction it will not be a perfect match. Some problems will be irritations and some will be major hurdles. Some may even be deal-killers. Obviously, the earlier these potentially problematic issues are identified, the more thought may be put into addressing them. As emphasized throughout this book, the key to success is looking beyond the work of the transaction itself to the organization that is to emerge from it.

As in a pending marriage, the emphasis between the partners always tends to be on the positive—sometimes with the same naïve bliss that whatever the potential problems, they will be minor and will work themselves out. It's healthy in both cases to be aware that there will be major differences and even to work on strategies for resolving them as they arise.

Understanding the Culture and Key Policies/Processes of the Target Company

In addition to differences that might become stumbling blocks, as noted above, there may be strengths in the target company that should not be lost in the process of the deal. Identifying aspects of each company from which the other can learn can be *extremely* helpful to the integration process. These should not be created artificially, but they really don't need to be if one takes the time to try to "walk in the other's shoes"— to understand from their standpoint what has worked and been successful, or has created a sense of pride in that company. At the least, understanding the logic and rationale behind the company's business processes will make integrating them into the new organization much simpler.

According to one former manager, a major reason for a recent oil industry merger was the dominant partner's admiration of the other's approach to marketing and "downstream" operations, including its relations to it customers. Unfortunately, this was also a case in which the dominant partner appeared to plan to impose its own cultural norms on the other. It will be curious to see how the results progress.

DUE DILIGENCE

The best way to ensure that your merger or acquisition does not turn sour is through due diligence. A properly conducted due diligence study of a business goes far beyond examining its financial records. A checklist developed by human resources should be an essential component of the due diligence phase, which involves examining every aspect of a company's operations, especially its HR functions. See Appendix 1 for a recommended due diligence checklist that should be tailored to your specific company issues and style.

A due diligence checklist should begin with a wide overview and should examine each functional responsibility of human resources—such as benefits, training, and employment. The next step is to list the primary responsibilities within each function. While it may be tedious, it is critical to perform a careful and thorough examination of all HR-related issues at all levels.

There are a whole host of activities involved in the due diligence phase of any transaction. The most common areas of due diligence focus for HR practitioners include a review of the following: culture, employee competencies, key talent, compensation/incentive programs, employee benefits, policies and practices, and employee relations/labor issues. Most HR teams also review the financial costs associated with worker's compensation, unemployment, and employee benefit liabilities, sometimes in conjunction with the accounting or finance department.

Due diligence is a critical point of the transactional process. Key issues must be reviewed and considered in advance of actually deciding to move forward from that point. Some recommended due diligence practices for HR include the following:

Get Familiar with the Target Company, Its Businesses and Markets

During the due diligence phase of a merger or acquisition, information gathering gets more direct and more specific. In general, it will be based on discussions with representatives of the other company, and/or on review of documents or records. While there are certainly needs for care and scrutiny in verifying the information provided, due diligence does not have to take the form of an inquisition. Accuracy of data is crucial, but achieving a sense of understanding is no less important.

Even if the target company is a direct competitor operating in many of the same locations as your organization, they probably have some differences in approach and in the problems they encounter. It can be helpful to begin this phase, from a HR standpoint, by simply learning the other company's HR perspective about the proposed deal. Do they see this as a potential win, in any way, for their employees, or is it viewed as the death of their organization if it goes through? Do they really see potential synergies, either from combining similar operations or integrating operations into a larger whole?

If there are basic business aspects of the target company with which you aren't familiar, it's helpful to get some initial information, off-line (e.g., through public documents, advance market research, etc.), just to be able to formulate good questions. But being genuinely interested in learning about their operations also goes a long way toward establishing understanding.

Understand the Acquisition Strategy and What Senior Management Really Wants as a Result of This Transaction

In some cases, there are multiple target companies being considered in parallel fashion. This can continue into later phases before a final decision is reached. As discussions become more serious, it's critical to make sure that you are as clear as possible about the essence of each deal. There may be a great deal of public relations information being formulated for the press and financial analysts about both the tremendous synergies and cost savings that will be achieved. But in order to look for the right information during due diligence, you'll need to look past this public relations information to focus on the real value drivers of the transaction—and how likely it is that they can be achieved, given all the variables involved. Is the real essence of the deal the physical assets, and are the people ultimately extraneous? Or are there business operations and processes which, if they quit working successfully, will kill the value of the deal?

Know the Timeline

As described in other chapters, the process of a merger or acquisition is not necessarily precise and orderly. (As one senior executive explained to us, "it's like making a sausage. Most people really don't want to know what's in it—they just want it to be good.") Negotiations may take many twists and turns, with many changes made, revoked, and renewed along the way. And because of this, original timelines can slip a good deal. The HR problem that often results is an expectation that all that "people stuff" can be condensed, or even skipped if necessary, to try to catch back up with the schedule. If this is likely to happen, you really need to plan for it and to defend the need for still accomplishing the most essential components.

Minimize Disruptions by Planning Ahead

Much of the emphasis of this book is on planning and preparation. Preventing illnesses is better than trying to cure them. In the real world, of course, planning is sometimes considered a luxury for which there is no time. (It never makes sense in the end, but it continues to be the way that many people and organizations operate.) Simply put, the better prepared you are for both the tasks you need to accomplish and the inevitable alterations that will occur, the more likely you are to achieve them.

Develop the Acquisition Question Set in Advance of Going to the On-Site Visit

Going on-site to another company's location for a due diligence process is not likely to get you a red carpet reception. Hopefully, it will be polite, though it will probably also be a little tense. If you need to gather specific information (and at this phase, this is the point) it's best to have the questions outlined in writing, with space to make notes, to make sure that you cover all the issues and do so with some sense of order.

Understand the Areas of Discipline Overlap (e.g., Payroll, IS, etc.) and Work Out in Advance of the Actual Due Diligence Review Which Team Will Review Which Specific Issues

Different companies have various departments and functions split up and reporting in all kinds of creative ways. There is no rule or magic to it. What is critical is that the person from your organization with the right expertise be the one to gather the information. (In the case of reviewing multiple target companies at once, it could mean some shifting of due diligence team membership in order that this is accomplished.)

At the time of your visit to the target company, some advice is in order:

Stay Attuned to Confidentiality Issues

If possible, you might try to have a quick legal review for the due diligence teams just prior to the start of their work to make sure everyone is up to date about the process and structure of the deal at that point. This would also be a time to review specific areas of confidentiality for both organizations—the kinds of information that should *not* be shared as well as the kinds of questions that should be avoided.

Ask Questions in Interview Fashion

While you do want to use any on-site visits to establish a sense of trust and understanding on the assumption that the organizations might well be joining together, this is also a formal process and the information gathered will be shared with and used by the decision makers in your organization. So it's wise to keep the questions focused and on target, rather than just "conversational," so that all important issues can be covered and the data organized clearly.

Probe in a Respectful Way, Knowing That the Target Company's Employees Are Likely to Be Sensitive and More Than a Bit Wary of Your Visit

When you arrive at the target company location for a due diligence visit, you may be the first real "face" that those employees have to put with your organization. The assumptions that they make about you, even prior to your meeting, are likely to be based on media information and internal rumors about your company. They may see you as their potential new boss, or as an outsider who will make decisions about their careers. Needless to say, they are likely to be anxious or even defensive. The best way to deal with these issues is simply to be respectful of their position and to gather the information you need in a professional (but not "cold") manner.

Concentrate on the Critical Information

If you work from questions that are prepared in advance and use the interview format, you should be able to gather the information you need. In some cases, employees of the target company may react to the visit by providing loads of information (though much of it possibly extraneous) in an attempt to impress you with the quality of their operations and therefore the necessity of maintaining their positions. Again, it's important to be respectful, but to make sure you gather what you came for.

Don't Ask Multiple People the Same Question (Unless You Are Receiving Different Answers and It Is a Key Piece of Information)

This suggestion applies both within and across the due diligence teams. You need to try to connect the right people on your teams with the right people and areas of the target company, as much as possible, up front. If you use a "shotgun" approach to data gathering, you are likely to end up with a complicated array (or mess) of answers that will have to be sorted out. If you have difficulty getting straight or complete answers about critical pieces of data, you may have to probe further, but this can be done in a purposeful and targeted way, about those key issues specifically.

Follow Through on Commitments and Timelines

If you make commitments to get back to target company employees about decisions or answers to any questions they might pose, be sure to honor them. If you end up working together after the deal is finalized, these first interactions will set the tone for your relationship.

Use This Interaction to Start Building Relationships

As with the issues of timelines and commitments, basic issues of trust and integrity (or the lack thereof) begin from these first interactions. The golden rule is treating others as you would want to be treated.

Prepare Recommendations and Review the Issues Noted Against the Value Drivers of the Transaction

Analyzing and making sense of the data that your team has gathered must be done in light of the overall rationale for this deal—which is one of the reasons that truly understanding it is so important. You might find really impressive systems and procedures in place in the target company, say in its approach to enrollment in benefit plans, or communications with employees about key issues. Hopefully, these will be of value to your organization and be treated as such if the deal is consummated. But it's an ever-present tension of "staff groups" in organizations that what might be a model program from a professional standpoint is seen as excessive and wasteful from an organizational view. For better or worse, the functions of your teams have value only in light of the overall value drivers of the transaction.

Review the Analysis with Senior Management

In general, your analysis of the due diligence findings will be presented in a business model format, comparable to findings from the other teams. But this might also be the time to raise other issues, from a strategic HR standpoint, possibly in the form of a second, alternative analysis. This would allow you to introduce concerns about integration issues that might not be covered in the financial and operational categories but that could have substantial impact on them. Again, you'll need to couch such an analysis in terms of the rationale for the deal as framed by the deal makers, but it may introduce alternative ideas and ways of viewing the transaction.

For instance, "It seems obvious that the real value of Company X to our organization is. . . . From what we've been able to determine though, getting it to work that way took a great deal of effort and cooperation between a number of their groups. Our groups have struggled with the same tensions. Putting their processes in place might well solve one of our biggest headaches, but if we ignore how they got there, we may end up killing the value of what we're buying and be right back where we started. Could we look at this further?"

Prepare the Final Report and Deliver It on Time to the M&A Business Team Who Will Actually Negotiate the Purchase

The formal results of the due diligence process are used primarily to place a financial value on the deal and in negotiations about it. The initial interest in the HR analysis, then, will focus on costs and liabilities. But as shown elsewhere, the final valuation of the deal, if it succeeds, will have significant implications for the people in the organization who must fulfill the expectations and commitments set by it.

Your work at this juncture is delivery of input into the valuation decisions. But the input of all the teams needs to be kept in mind as the deal progresses, in light of the need for clarity of expectations among those who must fulfil the goals and commitments.

When a company initiates a due diligence process, you cannot assume that the acquisition is a "done deal"—it is actually just the opposite in most situations. Many due diligence studies conclude that a transaction is a bad business deal or a poor organizational fit. While HR issues typically are not the only dealbreakers, there is real potential for raising potentially dealbreaking issues through the due diligence process that might not be uncovered otherwise. Some of the most critical issues for due diligence review are covered next.

THE LEGAL MINEFIELD

The first step that HR might want to take in a merger or acquisition process is a thorough review of the target organization's legal position. The myriad of workplace laws and regulations mean that there is considerable room for error or even mischief. All policies and plans should be scrutinized during the due diligence phase to ensure compliance with applicable employment laws.

Companies can inadvertently assume significant liability if careful due diligence is not conducted. The target company can have pending charges or litigation from the EEOC or face unfair labor practice claims from the NLRB. Each of these potential legal problems needs to be addressed specifically in the acquisition agreement, and the purchasing company may also want to secure an indemnification in the agreement as well. Such an indemnification provision will keep a company from assuming unreasonable risks, especially if litigation is currently pending.

While one or two cases of discrimination or sexual harassment can normally be resolved fairly easily, what your HR team needs to be concerned with is examples of systemic problems (e.g., underlying problems in the company's policies or programs that are have creating the widespread problems). These systemic issues can be much harder to address and also harder to remedy. They also mean that the company could be exposed to class action litigation, which can be very costly—both economically and also from a public relations perspective.

Beyond pending claims and litigation, the Fair Labor Standards Act also has some real potential to create problems in a merger or acquisition. A failure to properly pay employees can expose the acquiring company to a wage-and-hour audit and back pay issues that can be expensive to resolve.

Companies should also include an audit of the target company's Form I-9's during the process. Statutes such as the Americans with Disabilities Act and the Family and Medical Leave Act do not seem to pose significant problems in the M&A context, but policies in these areas should also be closely scrutinized.

RETIREMENT LIABILITIES

In the HR arena it is retirement benefits that have the greatest potential for creating problems and for turning into "dealbreaking" issues during a transaction's due diligence. The questions surrounding defined benefit plans, defined contribution plans, vesting, valuation of liabilities, and overfunding or underfunding of plans are complex issues that can create real challenges for members of your HR team. These issues can create real sticking points during the negotiations of price.

The cost of retiree benefits must be incorporated in a company's purchase price. However, the extraordinary growth in the stock market over the past decade has created a situation in which many pension plans are overfunded, which can make companies prime targets for takeovers. In these cases the pension plan may be terminated and then replaced with the acquiring company's plan. This means that the excess assets can then be put directly into the acquiring company's general accounts.

HEALTHCARE ISSUES

In order to fully understand the cost of a merger or acquisition, you must conduct a full analysis of the target company's healthcare benefits and costs, as well as its worker's compensation costs. This means examining all ongoing claims, especially including large claims (e.g., those involving a debilitating or terminal illness). Because full disclosure of health-related benefits can run afoul of privacy issues, you must tread carefully when reviewing another company's benefit experience. This can typically be accomplished by requesting reports that include social security or employee numbers, rather than individual names.

NEGOTIATIONS

During the actual process of negotiating with a potential purchase or merger partner, HR practitioners are generally not much in demand. However, to the extent that key issues (e.g., benefit liabilities, worker's compensation exposure, etc.) need to be considered in negotiating the deal, members of the HR team must proactively bring these issues to the attention of those individuals who are actively negotiating the transaction—early in the process.

INTEGRATION PLANNING/EXECUTION

It is during the transition and integration effort that HR practitioners can have the most impact. By taking a lead during this process, HR can drive performance and help to create the organizational climate needed for real change and increased employee satisfaction.

This is the point at which plans that were drafted at earlier stages, based on what was known up to that point, are finalized and implemented. The key activities that HR must be proactively involved with during the integration phase of a transaction include the following:

Finalize an Integration Plan, Including the "100-Day" Plan (Outlined in Appendix 3) and Employee Communication Strategy

The integration plan that was outlined earlier can now be completed, based on details from the actual agreement. In addition to the 100-day plan which outlines the most critical activities for senior managers, plans for integrating specific functions and departments can be made.

Part of the rationale for all the advance planning recommended in this book is the tremendous activity level that typically takes place in an integration process of any size—and which will continue for some months, in most cases. Without a good deal of preparation, many issues won't be addressed or questions answered, or else they will be done "on the fly" by whoever happens to be available at the time. Job positions have to be filled, employees relocated if necessary, unneeded locations shut down, materials, files and equipment transferred, and on and on. And ideally, all this has to be accomplished while the company still conducts regular business activities and meets customer expectations.

Involve Senior Management and Ensure That They Are Seen by Employees Frequently

Providing a sense of leadership is crucial during the transition. All employees need to know who is in charge (most importantly, that *some-*

one is in charge) and generally what their own roles are. Remember, though, that many of these persons may have been involved in the negotiation process and, depending on their role and how the deal proceeded, be exhausted and ready to get on with business.

It's important not to subject these persons to endless meetings and the need to answer the same questions over and over. This is another reason that the communication strategy is so important—so that the crucial issues can be addressed through formal channels and senior managers don't feel bombarded by questions at every turn.

Introduce the Integration Leader to the Organization

As noted before, it's extremely important that the integration leader be introduced and remain visible and that his or her role in gathering questions and disseminating answers be made clear. This is an additional help in allowing senior executives and operations managers to move ahead with other business.

Orient New Executives and Key Managers to the New Company Values and to the "Non-negotiables"

This is probably the most critical of the "cultural reviews" that needs to take place. The most senior persons, especially those who had parts in the transaction of the deal itself, will undoubtedly have basic information about the company and its workings. They may, in fact, be very familiar with both its history and its business process, depending on how closely they have worked with (or against) your organization or peer professionals in the past. But be careful not to take this for granted.

The most important information is simply the practical business of knowing their way around, in terms of who to call about what issues or problems and how to get basic things accomplished. It can also be helpful to tell some of the company "war stories" that you think are most significant, especially those that point out foibles and faux pas that others have committed in the past. These should obviously be done in a way that is respectful to those involved (especially if they're still in the organization) but can be a valuable way of communicating a sense of company culture and expectations.

Provide as Much Information as Possible about the Expected Reorganization, Reductions, and Selection Process

As noted before, this is an extremely anxious and volatile time for employees, and they may react to it in a multitude of ways. One of the worst mistakes for senior managers to make is assuming that employees somehow know where they stand with the organization and therefore know the likelihood of their jobs being eliminated, or them being replaced in their positions. A good way for an organization to lose some of its most talented employees is by simply leaving them in limbo during a transition period.

If details about individual positions take some time and effort to work out, try to find some way of letting employees know at least how this is to occur. It's much easier to stay in the same organization than to move to a new one, both logistically and emotionally. For some employees, organizational change creates a good time to make a move, and they may have been ready for a change anyway. Most, though, are willing to wait and see how things work out and what the opportunities look like for them. If you have talent that you want to keep, don't waste it by simply failing to pay attention. You need to talk to key people early to be sure they know you understand their importance to the new organization's success.

Educate the Workforce about the Psychological Aspects of Change and Transition

The third segment of the suggested change programs, noted earlier, should be implemented during the integration phase. These should be targeted to the various transitions to be made by different groups—those who will be leaving the organization and those who are remaining or merging into new places.

Address Questions about How the Transaction Will Affect Employees

Despite all the effort you may put into the communication strategy, there will still be individual questions by employees who either did not hear or understand the information provided, or who are unclear about how to interpret it in their own cases. For some, you can try just pointing them back to the answers already provided. (It's usually very helpful to have an ongoing list of Frequently Asked Questions and answers specific to this transaction, readily available to employees for this purpose.) For others, it ends up being easier to simply do some "hand holding" and get them through the process.

Coach and Facilitate Teams through Separation, Integration, and Transition Planning Processes

Work groups will typically be losing and gaining members at the same time during the transition process. Generally, people handle these issues

in a professional manner, despite the emotional issues. But if not addressed, the emotional aspect of the changes can create quiet barriers to
initiative and cooperation for long periods of time.

A minimal strategy is simply to look for areas or groups where obvious problems arise. A better approach is to have a comprehensive plan
for work groups using the change workshops in a very tangible way, to
begin team building between the members at the outset. This does not
have to be inordinately time consuming or approached in a "touchy-
feely" manner. The business of getting business accomplished requires
at least a basic level of cooperation between people, and the sooner this
begins, the better.

Drive the Employee Selection and Retention Strategy

For a host of reasons, the selection and retention decisions about employees need to be as clear and fair as possible. Allowing this process to
create the appearance of a contest of political favors simply opens the
organization to accusations about discriminatory hiring practices. This is
an area in which HR needs to take a clear lead at the outset.

Finalize Culture Audits to Anticipate and Minimize
Clashes Between Employees

Culture audits should ideally be done in conjunction with the change
programs and used to begin teambuilding within the workgroups. In
addition, the process it might provide some background and understanding should deeper problems about the organizational difference
surface later.

Partner with Senior Management on Status to Design
Compensation, Incentive, Recognition, and Benefit
Programs; Training and Orientation; HR Policies; and
Other Transition Tools

A number of special programs may be needed or found helpful during
the transition process. These are discussed in more detail in Chapter 2.

Additional information about the actual work of integration can be
found in Chapter 4.

Given that there is so much real work to be done during these stages,
why is the HR group so frequently not a player during M&A activity?
The answer varies among companies but is often that human resources
is the company's "weak sister," accorded a correspondingly low level of
confidence by the management group.

The lack of confidence frequently stems from a belief that human resources does not have either the technical competence or the necessary acquisition experience to be effective in an active role. This low confidence, coupled with a general view of human resources as an administrative function, causes human resources to be left out of many deals. But that view is rapidly changing as HR teams are increasingly becoming key contributors during these transactions.

In some companies, this lack of confidence is on target. But in most companies, the HR team has the necessary competencies to help make any deal more successful. Just to review, the specific competencies that your HR team needs to exhibit during the process of a merger or acquisition deal include the following:

• Knowledge of the business and the value drivers of the deal,
• The ability to identify strategic and tactical opportunities, an understanding of the cultural attributes of the business, an ability to translate HR issues to value drivers, the ability to use other expert resources, as well as to collaborate both within and outside the HR function, and
• The technical skills in disciplines such as human/employee relations, compensation, employee benefits, communications, and change management.

  Specifically, human resources needs to be prepared to

• tailor the HR elements of the acquisition process,
• develop the due diligence checklist,
• conduct the due diligence process,
• prepare the HR section of the acquisition analysis report,
• support the integration planning process (e.g., process the leader role, identify and address strategy issues/philosophy, identify people implications and costs, and select the project head),
• monitor the integration process, and
• plan for and support of the employee communications effort.

  With these skills and competencies members of the HR team can play a pivotal and critical role in the success of their company's merger or acquisition. Some critical factors for future high impact and success:

• Get involved in the target screening and strategy development discussions.
• Factor key HR issues into the pre-deal discussions.
• Conduct thorough HR due diligence.
• Take the lead in integration planning and results tracking.
• Understand the vision/strategy before beginning people cutbacks.
• Design training to support the new strategy (e.g., orientation, dealing with

change, vision/values, new policies/practices, new systems, employee benefit changes, etc.).

- Use a disciplined assessment and selection process based on knowledge, skills and abilities, job performance, special skills, and length of service.

NOTE

1. Gautam Naik and Anita Raghavan, "Vodafone, Mannesmann Set Takeover At $180.95 Billion After Long Struggle," *Wall Street Journal*, February 4, 2000.

Chapter 8

Leadership

The need for leadership is never more apparent than during times of crisis or dramatic change. But despite the fact that companies reportedly spend some $15 billion per year on training and development of leaders, there is no firm agreement on what characteristics leaders evidence, nor even on what leadership really is.2[1] So during the upheaval of a merger or acquisition, when many employees are searching for some sense of guidance and direction, what can or should your HR team be providing?

First, it's helpful to distinguish between leadership and management. In a nutshell, management has to do with fulfilling a purpose or meeting objectives. Within a given context, certain things need to get done. Management is not a matter of *determining* the purposes of an organization, for instance. Managers are generally hired in order to see that results get accomplished.

Leadership, on the other hand, is about something larger. It has to do with focusing people's attention and energy in a way that makes them feel a part of something greater than just themselves. (And in this way, it taps into that tacit realm where things like culture reside.)

While the focus of this book is on HR roles and issues, this chapter will not attempt to distinguish leadership in a HR role from other organizational roles and responsibilities. In some organizations, human resources has a key position of authority and decision making. In these, the comments and suggestions can be applied directly by the HR professional to the organization as a whole. In others, HR plays only a supporting role. In those, the HR professional may need to provide leadership directly to his or her own areas of responsibility, but more indirectly to the larger organization by working through persons in key positions of authority.

HISTORICAL VIEWS OF LEADERSHIP

Interest in, and research about, leadership dates back to the late nineteenth century and seems to have begun with the "Great Man" theory.[2] This was the concept that "leaders were born" (not created through training or experience), and therefore that leadership characteristics were biologically based. Some people simply "had it." This concept fit well with hierarchical structure of organizations and with the centralization of power and control in the hands of a relatively small number of men at the time. Interestingly, this concept from the Industrial Era has continued to color perceptions of leadership since that time, though in various forms.[3] A range of leadership theories and references for them is included in Table 8.1.

As can be noted in the references column, much of the confusion about definitions of leadership has to do with not only the variations in definition, but also with the overlapping time frames in which they are used. There is no simple progression from one concept to the next, but various ones appear to fall in and out of favor over time.

Most importantly, all of these theories remain fundamentally grounded in an industrial organizational model. They simply amount to variations on a common theme and therefore are not models likely to lead to new and more progressive forms of organization.

James MacGregor Burns identified two leadership models: transactional and transforming.[4] Transactional leadership came from the Industrial Era. It emphasizes the communication of powerful ideas and values in order to motivate others. As part of this model, there is an exchange of either symbolic or tangible rewards for accomplishments. Transforming leadership, on the other hand, is based on collaboration and shared, interactive leadership by way of change, common purpose, and equitable distribution of power.

One of the necessary distinctions in this shift of thinking is that "leader" is not synonymous with "leadership." Transforming or transformative leadership requires that "leaders" (i.e., those in positions of power or authority) also learn to be effective followers. Rather than those in elevated positions defining both the nature of a situation and the correct response (the traditional "command and control" model), transforming leadership requires that all relevant information be gathered and considered to arrive at the best solution possible. Those with the highest positions may not be those with the most critical information or perspective at the moment. For purposes of this chapter, we will focus on leaders as those who exhibit leadership, regardless of rank or position.

Table 8.1
Leadership as Good Management

Leadership Theory	The Leader	Leadership = Good Management	References
"Great Man" Theory	Person who is able through natural abilities to exercise power and control.	Leaders influence followers to do what the leaders wish.	Crocker (1999), Haywood (1997), Jennings (1960), Moore (1927), Peters & Waterman (1982), Strock (1998)
Trait Theory	Person with distinguishing superior traits of a leader.	Leaders attract followers to the "right" direction of the leader.	Bennis (1984), Bogardus (1934), Stogdill (1974)
Behavioral Theory	The leader's behavior cues followers' task behaviors.	The leader directs the activities of subordinates toward a shared goal.	Coons (1957), Hemphill (1949), Luthan Kreitner (1975), Sheridan, Kerr & Alberson (1981), Vredenburgh (1978)
Situational Theory	Person emerges as leader due to time, place, or circumstances.	Leaders distinguish themselves from followers by demonstrating special skills to fit specific circumstances.	Nebeker & Mitchell (1974), Osborn, Hunt & Bussom (1977), Yukl (1981)
Contingency Theory	The task-oriented or relations-oriented leader.	Leaders demonstrate to followers how to adapt their approach to fit the context.	Fiedler (1967), Hersey & Blanchard (1988), House (1971), Vroom & Yetton (1973)
Development of Leader Traits	Through prescribed personal development, a leader with certain traits emerges.	"New" leaders attract followers to the "right" direction of the leader.	Cashman (1998), Conger & Kanungo (1998), Covey (1992), Jarworski (1990), Terry (1993)

Source: Larry Magliocca and Alexander Christakis, *Creating Transforming Leadership for Organizational Change: The CogniScope System Approach* (John Wiley & Sons, forthcoming).

By example, Ford has begun a massive leadership training program aimed at creating a more flexible and responsive organization.[5] The goal, according to its CEO, is to create leaders at all levels in the organization. And rather than focusing on traditional, authoritative approaches, the program works on personal growth and team development in order to generate and implement as many groundbreaking new ideas as possible.

CHANGE LEADERS

Katzenbach and his colleagues provide one of the best descriptions we've found for leadership, in the context of the subject of this book.[6] The real change leaders (RCLs) they describe are not the typical high profile, charismatic figures. In fact, they're typically found in the middle ranks of organizations and, as described, are more interested in getting things accomplished than being noticed or promoted. And the "real change" they help to create is the fundamental, transformation type that requires new learning and new skills throughout an organization.

Much like the middle managers described by Nonaka and Takeuchi, these change leaders manage to transform visions into workable methods and goals that can be accomplished. But somewhat different than those Japanese managers, they also seem compelled to *provide* a vision and some direction, even if on a more local or limited basis, when these are lacking.

These change leaders are both *pluralists* and *pragmatists*. They tend to believe in the value and contributions of employees at large, not just those in key positions or special roles. And they frequently accomplish change by working through teams, other work groups, or even informal networks. But they also seem to understand the realities of individual contributors and make the most of these, sometimes through using single-leader (more traditional) work groups, or even partnering with "mavericks."

Interestingly, the strategies used by change leaders are not entirely different from those employed by more radical facilitators of social change such as community organizers.[7] In both cases there appears to be an understanding of the need to work both with and through other individuals and of the reality that this cannot be accomplished, long-term, by wielding overt power. Power in these cases comes from the trust and credibility they can establish with their "constituents" and with the sense of hope they can provide to them.

Change of the magnitude initiated through these leaders is not a short-term venture. It requires time, and this necessitates commitment and the ability to maintain focus and momentum. It means recognizing successes along the way and building on them. The process of such change does not always occur according to a specific, predetermined plan. In some ways, it has to find its own path and grow in its own direction—but still according to an overall vision or primary goal. And while the goals may be large, or even lofty, they at some point must also connect with the personal needs of the individuals involved.

Working through others requires that the change leader not get ahead of participants. Humans seem to need novelty. They cannot maintain focus indefinitely and have to be encouraged and reassured. It also means recognizing the limitations of the individuals involved and understanding that such limitations will always be present, and always be a factor.

Both organizational change leaders and community organizers challenge the status quo, and both risk the ire of those in power. The key difference is that organizational change leaders generally seek to maintain the overall structure (the organization itself) within which they work, while community organizers sometimes seek to overthrow the power structure against which they struggle. In the current environment of mergers and acquisitions, an essential question is the degree to which current structures can be maintained while still achieving the necessary level of change—that is, just how radical does change need to be to be enough?

LEADERSHIP IN M&A TRANSACTIONS

In a merger or acquisition the obvious need for leadership is focused around achieving the stated goals of the deal. In the case of an acquisition, the overall purpose of the organization may never seem to be in question. It is only a matter of bringing new sources of talent and skill into an existing process. Even in the case of a full merger of organizations, the overall goals may seem to be apparent—or at least seem like they should be.

But in times of great change, what may have been obvious in the past can no longer be assumed. For the people directly affected, the most basic assumptions may need to be clarified or reinforced. Essentially, are people being asked to use their existing skills in new ways, or are they being asked to change the ways by which they get things done?

When an organization experiences change there is much more to it than typically meets the eye. And much of what isn't seen (or understood) is the "softer," human side that is the realm of human resources.

Because basic assumptions are largely unstated, they can be the source of great frustration. If you're simply acquiring a small production unit which is similar to other existing operations, it would seem that very little transition should be needed. And sometimes you get lucky and it goes that easily. But often initial targets are missed, not because of real production problems, but because people are working from different assumptions and interpretations. What seems "obvious" in one setting may not be at all so in another, simply due to history and experience. In the context of a full merger of whole organizations, these problems become magnified exponentially.

"Soft values" such as the ability to attract and retain talented employees, a company's reputation with both customers and peer companies, the integrity of a company's products and services, leadership, and community responsibility have been found to account for as much as 40% of market value.[8] Unfortunately, serious inattention to these factors is commonplace. Company executives often come primarily from financial or operational backgrounds and may or may not have any real expertise in such issues. When they do not, the "softer" issues tend to be dismissed, as if they will simply take care of themselves.

Leadership, in this context, requires both understanding and attention to these issues. They may be time consuming and frustrating, but ignoring them can be disastrous. If new expectations are to be set, this needs to happen at the outset of any changes. Otherwise, people will quickly gravitate into routines based on limited or incorrect information or simply based on their own assumptions. And once established, these routines and mindsets become much harder to change.

As noted above, leaders are not just those in formal positions of authority. Leaders work through other people, by helping to focus collective attention and energy and often by helping others find a sense of purpose. *Leadership is much like a catalyst in a chemical reaction—it sets things in motion by releasing the energy needed to get them going.*

These "soft" issues are crucial, but many executives are totally unprepared for dealing with them. As an HR professional, you will likely be required to take some risks during these transitions that you would not normally be comfortable with. For example, if you are not directly a part of the senior management team, you might find yourself working outside traditional lines of authority. But critical times are not times for timidity. Simple missteps in actions or communications by the organization at such junctures can cause years of employee relations headaches, and can take years to undo.

From the moment that rumors of a potential merger or acquisition first begin, and until the organization regains a sense of stability following the integration of the parties, there will be feelings of ambiguity and uncertainty. Emotionally, what people feel is a sense of potential threat, and they may respond to this in a number of different ways, depending on their own life experiences and their current circumstances. Those who feel secure about their positions, or feel certain they have other options, may take it all in stride—but may be prime targets for competitors to recruit. Those who have fewer options are more likely to look for assurances from someone inside that their positions are secure, or to try to demonstrate in some overt way their value to the organization. In more extreme cases, stress reactions may show up in the form of anger, fears about exclusion and lack of control, ego struggles, and often very real fears of termination or failure.

Rather than fulfilling the expectation of employees that either senior management or the HR team will provide answers, leaders need to reinforce employees' own sense of competency. Most importantly, they need to help keep employees active in a way that is productive. Many persons who have ended up in large organizations are not by nature risk takers. During stressful times, they may quickly abdicate decision making rather than take a chance on jeopardizing their position, casting your HR team or senior managers into something of a "parental" role.

In order to allay these anxieties, visible and accessible leaders are required—leaders who are physically and visibly present and from whom employees can get frequent information updates. Most importantly, this includes *you*, as well as members of your HR team who must "step up to the plate" and take on the uncomfortable role of leadership during this time of anxiety and transition.

Following a merger or acquisition, leadership can be scarce, especially when senior executives have similar feelings of insecurity and fear. Structurally, it's helpful for those making the decisions to get people into roles as quickly as possible so that everyone has a sense of what the organization is to "look like" going forward. Executive and senior management positions are, of course, the most visible roles.

Those in charge of determining who will fill the senior management roles must proactively recruit these individuals to "come on board" and be part of the new team. An enthusiastic welcome (including some ego stroking) is important, even for those in highly placed positions, in order to create a sense of confidence and trust. If there are no early overtures that a key individual is respected and wanted by the new team, he or she will likely be evaluating other employment options and may well "jump ship" before the new management decides to offer a position.

Following a merger or acquisition, employees are generally starved for direction and information. If changes in the organization have been, or are to be, significant, then it's probably clear that expectations are changing, but often not clear what they are changing *to*. People will look first to those they believe to be in charge but will listen most closely to those they trust.

To maximize this post-deal time frame, leaders should focus on the following types of behaviors:

- Providing direction and strategy,
- Being visible and accessible,
- Acting decisively,
- Expecting change—providing the why, how, and what necessary to effect real change,
- Communicating constantly and repetitively,

- Linking strategy to the "value drivers" of the transaction,
- Acting positively and communicating an enthusiastic message,
- Clarifying organizational strategy and the company's future vision (if these exist),
- Valuing participation and input,
- Setting high expectations and "stretch goals" to accelerate performance, and
- Inspiring confidence and trust among employees.

Remember that you are working on not only *what happens* in your organization, but on *what makes things happen* in general. In the end, many regular things may remain intact and familiar. But during the process, it may not be at all clear to the average employee just what will be the same—or whether they will be a part of it. At this juncture, leaders play a special role in maintaining or establishing the "basic fabric" of the organization, and their actions will be observed and scrutinized more closely than ever.

When decision makers do not act quickly and decisively during a merger or acquisition, the organization often flounders. Clearly, no decision will please everyone, but leaders *must* make the tough decisions. And they must make them early and quickly or the organization will suffer.

In order to maximize the potential for integration success, leaders should focus on several key actions:[9]

Leaders Need to Exhibit Ambition and Drive, Competence and Expertise, and Integrity and Moral Fiber

The character and integrity of leadership is of paramount importance in assuring employee buy-in. One set of guidelines is the six key "pillars of character"[10] (trustworthiness, respect, responsibility, fairness, caring, and citizenship), which can help to instill that sense of confidence that is the basis for real leaders' power.

Each of these character traits must be present and in balance or the leadership will not be effective. A leader who has only drive but not competence and integrity is a demagogue. A leader who has competence but lacks integrity and drive is a technocrat. And if a company is unfortunate enough to be seduced by someone who has ambition and competence, but lacks integrity, that leader is a destructive achiever.

Leaders Must Sequence and Pace the Work

Too often, every project or idea during an M&A transaction is portrayed as equally important. New initiatives are started without stopping other activities, or too many initiatives are commenced at the same time. It is important to prioritize projects to ensure that employees understand how to focus their early efforts. If employees somehow become overwhelmed with the message that "everything is critical," it will be difficult to achieve any significant results.

The real work of leadership is to generate a "creative tension" between the vision for the future and the current reality. This must create an *imperative for change*. This means that leaders must talk repeatedly and consistently about the future—how it will look and how employees can positively contribute to that vision. More traditional (transactional) leaders must "show" employees the future and why it is worth striving for in order to motivate employees to move in that direction. Transforming leaders should help to bring this same vision to view from within those who are to be involved in its creation.

By using narratives, such as stories, leaders can most effectively shape employee attitudes and behaviors. Individuals listen to stories and the meaning behind them far more than they read company "missives" or other documents that may be dismissed as "corporate junk." And through the use of stories, employees can begin to build shared concepts or "mental models" of an organization's culture.

At Nike, for example, telling stories of the company's founders and the spirit behind their efforts has become a way of life.[11] This is not just about shoes, but about athletes, and their coach, and their dreams. Nike was co-founded by its CEO, Phil Knight, and Bill Bowerman, Knight's running coach and the developer of the original waffle-soled shoe. The story is also about Steve Prefontaine, an Olympic hopeful for whom Bowerman designed the shoe, but who was killed in an auto accident before he had the chance to compete.

New hires at Nike reportedly spend nine days in Rookie Camp at the headquarters. One of these days is spent in Eugene, Oregon, at the track where Bowerman coached, and includes a visit to the spot where Prefontaine was killed. Needless to say, Nike takes its history and its culture very seriously.

In addition to creating positive tension, leaders must also help people in their organization learn to live with that tension. That means listening to their concerns, complaints, and frustrations in order to know when to take time to celebrate successes, when to back off and diffuse the conflict or stress, and when to play the role of "corporate cheerleader."

All organizations need a corporate cheerleader during times of transition and stress. This is a leader, frequently from the HR group (though not always), who is continuously positive about the deal and who works diligently to focus attention on the benefits that will come, in time, from the merger or acquisition. The corporate cheerleader is not a "patsy," nor is this person out of touch with reality. To the contrary, this leadership role can be difficult for an individual to take on. Very often, it requires that the leader constantly handle the "toxic" aspects of both people and organizational politics, sometimes even to the longer-term detriment of the individual's career. (This "toxic" aspect can result from taking on critical issues that senior managers do not want to address and which can therefore result in tension or conflict on a personal level with them.[12])

Transitions will not always go as planned, and changes may mean that those who were prepared to gain an increase in authority or position may lose out. The person who has been promoting the positive promises of the future can become an easy target for feelings of disappointment. He or she needs to be prepared for this possibility so that it does not come as a surprise.

It is far too easy to see the negatives during any time of transition. This time is typically fraught with problems, delays, and frustrations. It is far more difficult to view the positives when the negatives are so close at hand. Leadership requires individuals who can "see through the smoke" to the future. It requires people who can make believers of the employees in the organization who cannot, or don't want to, see that far ahead.

Leadership Is Not about Rank, Privileges, Title, or Money; It Is about Personal Responsibility

Authority figures sometimes become so involved in the perks of their personal success that they appear to care more about them than they do about the overall success of their organization. Also, power can be intoxicating, and people in positions of authority may get so caught up in the protecting theirs that they neglect working on making the tough decisions necessary to move the company forward. In times of change, there is a strong tendency for people to focus on themselves and their personal needs, sometimes meaning that larger organizational issues are only attended to secondarily.

Leaders need to consider the "mirror test." When they look themselves squarely in the eye, do they believe what they are telling others and are they confident about the decisions that they are making for the organization? If not, it isn't only a question of personal character or judgment. There may be issues about the deal itself that need to be questioned but that no one has been willing to voice.

If key decision makers are spending excessive amounts of time and energy negotiating their own perks and positions, this will not go unnoticed by the "rank-and-file" employees. The "grapevine" of information is never more active than in periods of change and uncertainty, and rumors about organizational decisions that primarily benefit executives, personally, only serve to undermine the organization itself.

As a leader, you need to be conscious of these issues. As a key "people expert" in your organization, you may need to raise these issues for other executives with an emphasis on the effect they are having on employees. This message may not be welcomed, but it may save larger problems from building if the message is heeded. Often, those involved are not aware of the change in their own behavior or of the fact that others are paying such close attention.

At times, leaders may have to forego their own popularity in order to do the right things and understand that not everyone will agree with their approach. But most importantly, they must carefully maintain their integrity in the process. (If it helps, you might think in terms of *structural* integrity, as in a building or a bridge. It has to do with how sound and well-integrated the parts are and therefore how sturdy the object is, and how much stress it can withstand.) Without integrity, neither the leader nor the organization will succeed in the long-term.

Leaders Are Responsible for Direction, Protection, Orientation, Managing Conflict, and Shaping the New Reality

A leader must provide direction to the organization by framing the key questions and issues and orienting people to the company's new mission, vision, and values. Leaders must help orient people to new roles and responsibilities by clarifying the new business strategy and outlining the company's expectations for decision making and accountability. Leaders must also work to bring conflict out in the open in order to generate organizational creativity and continuous learning.

Leaders must challenge those employees who don't seem to be "getting it" and who need to make further changes—initially through motivation and information, but after some time, through difficult transfer and termination decisions. If leaders do not take fair and immediate action to move poor performers or others who simply refuse to participate, employees will begin to doubt their ability and may lose confidence in the new team. Have no doubt that employees know exactly who is and who is not an "A" player. If it takes management too long to come to a similar conclusion, then employees will quickly develop a mistrust of the new leadership's judgment or leadership abilities.

The company's leadership must make the hard decisions about people. Those decisions, however painful they may be, must be made as soon as they are clear—for everyone's benefit.

Leaders Must Have Presence and Poise, Exhibiting Confidence Every Step of the Way

Leadership demands a deep understanding of the fears and sacrifices associated with the readjustment required by employees after a merger. But it also requires the ability to hold steady and maintain the tension while communicating collective confidence that the tasks ahead can be accomplished (without becoming too anxious personally).

Employees will be fearful of decisions being made and will likely be distrustful of a new management team. And while they do not want to hear bad news, they *do* want information. Leaders must provide a constant flow of information to employees. Employees want to believe that management knows what it is doing and has a clear plan. They may become highly anxious if they believe that management is "floundering" or is not "on top of things."

The signals from the management team must be of both high confidence and high expectations. But most importantly, there must be a constant stream of information about the rationale behind the transaction, what's in it for each employee, and why people should be supportive of the new direction.

Leaders Must Protect the Voices of Leadership from Below

Giving a voice to all people is the foundation of an organization that is willing to experiment and learn in order to grow. However, the reality is that whistle-blowers and other people who "march to the beat of a different drummer" are often unheard, unheeded, or even punished in various ways by those in positions of power.

These people generate tension and anxiety—and while these may be uncomfortable, they can also be catalysts for change if channeled positively. The easiest way for an organization to restore order is to neutralize these voices (e.g., through termination of their employment or through peer or political pressure)—sometimes in the name of "promoting teamwork" or "alignment." But to do so is likely to undermine any verbal message about the need for change.

The "voices from below" are often not as articulate or diplomatic as one might wish. People speaking beyond their positional authority usually feel self-conscious and sometimes have to generate excessive passion to get themselves geared up to speak out. But buried inside a poorly packaged thought sometimes lies an important issue that needs to be more fully considered.

No one that we've run across really likes criticism. But if there were no problems, there would be no need for change. It may take some significant patience and tongue biting to hear through the messages to the constructive points, but if you want people to become involved and take initiative, you cannot stop this flow of energy.

Leaders need to provide "cover" to employees who have enough courage to raise tough issues or point out internal inconsistencies occurring within the organization. Those individuals often have an alternative perspective that can provoke rethinking old and unspoken assumptions if management will stop and listen. And the unspoken message to other employees that "we're willing to hear you and want you involved" may be much louder and more effective in the long run than any official statement or speech could ever hope to be.

Great Management Requires Respect for the Employees Who Make Up the Organization, as Well as Other Executives in the New Organization

Great management requires respect for all people, understanding that it truly is the work of the employees that will either make or break the transaction. The leaders that people name with admiration are nearly always the ones who have been willing to delegate their authority and make subordinates feel powerful and capable.

Leadership has to take place *every day*. The demands of merger and acquisition work require leaders who take personal responsibility and who "stir our souls" a little.

Leaders Must Also Respect the Past

Leaders must show respect for past practices so that employees are not alienated early on during the merger process with a feeling that the ways they did things in the past were wrong or "dumb." (There was probably a good rationale for them at the time, and there is something about them that made the company worth buying or joining with now.) In order to incorporate new learning and skills, employees need first to be willing to let go of what is familiar, and this requires a sense of safety and trust. Criticism of their past, regardless of how innocently it is intended, will only serve to create defensive feelings and significantly impede change.

But that does not mean that critical—and often painful—changes should not be made early and decisively. Quite to the contrary, leaders must be decisive and announce changes as early as possible to help employees anticipate new expectations and start their process of recommitting to the new company. Employees must know what that new company stands for before they can begin to make a commitment again.

Leaders Must Remember That the Attitude, "We Bought You," Is a Corporate Cancer

Acquiring companies tend to dominate decisions and force their methods on the acquired company's management. Not unexpectedly, this approach dampens expected synergies and leaves the acquired staff feeling defeated and resentful.

Neither new equipment nor technology nor funding nor corporate policies will determine the success or failure of a merger or acquisition. When it is all said and done, successful integration will depend upon individual people and their collective actions. By showing trust in and respect for all employees (regardless of the "side" they came from), management ensures the greatest probability of success.

Leaders Should Not Declare "Victory" Too Soon

While it is important to celebrate organizational successes along the way, declaring that the deal is "done" too early can be catastrophic. Until changes sink deeply into a company's culture, new processes and approaches are fragile and highly subject to regression. It is all too typical for senior executives to signal that the deal is "over" once they have suffered through their own stress, secured their assignments, and set their minds on their next strategic issue. At the same time, middle managers and supervisors are still contending with the "details" of actually making the transaction work.

It takes time to work things out—especially when rules and relationships are in flux. Time, emotional space, and support from the top are needed to help employees get through the process of integration. And a recognition that the deal will take months (and sometimes years) to work out will be much more realistic to employees than an early announcement that it is "done"—when the real and painful work of integration has only just begun.

How will you be able to identify the good leaders developing within your organization? Within the sphere of a leader's influence, people will be reaching their potential and going beyond typical expectations; people will be learning and working together; and they will be achieving results.

Ultimately, structures, systems, and programs do not drive real and lasting change within an organization—leaders do. Without leadership an organization will flounder rather than reach its potential. With strong leadership, particularly on the critical HR front, great things are possible, and the probability of your organization's success increases exponentially.

NOTES

1. Joseph Boyette and Jimmie Boyette, *The Guru Guide* (John Wiley & Sons, 1998).

2. Larry Magliocca, "Leadership Concepts and Issues," unpublished manuscript.

3. Based on work by Rost found in Larry Magliocca and Alexander Christakis, *Creating Transforming Leadership for Organizational Change: The CogniScope System Approach* (John Wiley & Sons, forthcoming).

4. Ibid.

5. Keith H. Hammond, "Grassroots Leadership: Ford Motor Co.," *Fast Company*, March 2000.

6. Jon R. Katzenbach, and the RCL Team, *Real Change Leaders* (Times Business/Random House, 1995).

7. Saul Alinsky, *Rules for Radicals: A Practical Primer for Realistic Radicals* (RandomHouse, 1971).

8. John F. Budd, Jr., "How to Cope with Perceptions of Performance," *Directorship* (September 1999).

9. Ronald R. Heifetz and Donald A. Laurie, "The Work of Leadership," *Harvard Business Review* (January–February 1997).

10. Developed through the Josephson Institute for Ethics. See www.charactercounts.org.

11. Eric Ransdell, "The Nike Story? Just Tell It!" *Fortune* (January–February 2000).

12. See Peter Frost and Sandra Robinson, "The Toxic Handler," *Harvard Business Review* (July–August 1999).

Chapter 9

Employee Communications

Mergers and acquisitions are case studies in uncertainty. This problem cannot be completely avoided given that there will always be questions for which immediate answers simply cannot be provided to your employees. Many of the restrictions on communication come from federal regulatory agencies, such as the Securities and Exchange Commission and the Federal Trade Commission, limiting preliminary disclosure to corporate officers and other "insiders." But these legal limitations are not always understood by, or made clear to, the employees who will be affected by the changes.

Once a deal is announced, the first thing human resources should do is work with company management personnel to schedule employee meetings to discuss the upcoming changes and to announce any and all decisions that have been made to date. You must be prepared to answer tough questions. Following questions about job losses, the issues that generally receive the most attention include anything to do with employee benefits and policy issues. For example, health, retirement, and vacation benefits typically draw the most attention from long-term employees early after a deal is announced. These are also the issues that generate the most employee anxiety until answers are provided.

At the time of the announcement of the deal, you will probably not have solid answers to these questions. When a quick answer cannot be given, people need to be told honestly and frankly that a decision has not yet been made. In addition, employees also need to understand the likely timetable for such future decision making.

You must, though, say more than "we don't know yet" or "we'll get back to you on that" during these early meetings. Employees will quickly conclude that you are trying to avoid the issue if you fail to give any timetable for providing answers to these "me"-type questions.

In preparation for any merger or acquisition, it is critical to create a well-planned communication strategy. This strategy will generally have four primary considerations: audience, timing, mode, and message. The strategy should also

- include the identification of all relevant internal and external audiences (e.g., employees, shareholders, customers, media),
- anticipate the questions each group may have about business and organizational issues,
- script position statements and orientation meetings, and
- determine what channels (e.g., newsletters, personal letters, intranet, Internet, question-and-answer pieces, meetings, mailers, telephone hotlines, press releases, community speeches, etc.) are planned in order to communicate with each group.

The plan should be reassessed and updated frequently in light of feedback from each of the stakeholder groups. With frequent feedback, the delivery of messages can be tailored and modified for each group in terms of content, timing, and medium.

Because not everything can be changed at once, some organizations have used "demonstration projects" to enhance the change process while other decisions are being made. This is a single event or program that receives high visibility and communicates tangibly to employees that the new company is clearly different from the old. Some examples are as follows:

- To replace hierarchical, formal structures with flatter, more entrepreneurial structures and attitudes, a company might change its dress code to permit casual attire every day.
- To promote stock ownership and shareholder alignment, an organization might implement an all-employee stock option or stock purchase plan.
- To promote success sharing, a company might implement an all-employee cash profit sharing plan or arrange a gainsharing pool to be split if/when the benefits and synergies of the merger or acquisition are realized.

None of these ideas will single-handedly change the new organization. But they are visible, tangible signs to employees—ideally delivered early during the integration process—that the world has changed and that the new company is committed in a visible and demonstrable way to changing itself.

Below are some general tips for establishing a successful communication program:

1. Communicate rapidly, honestly, and frequently.
2. Consistency will generate credibility, so say what you are going to do and then do it!
3. Establish multiple routes of communication to reach employees (e.g., one-on-one meetings, group sessions, newsletters, letters to employee homes, bulletin board postings, Intranet updates, etc.).
4. Focus on the themes of change and progress by highlighting projects that are going right and action items that are being delivered on time.
5. Repeat the common themes of the merger or acquisition to increase employee understanding of the rationale behind the transaction.
6. Share information widely and frequently.
7. Choose your opening moves carefully, with the understanding that your selection of issues to address early on will send significant signals to employees about what the new management team deems to be of greatest importance.
8. Provide opportunities for employee involvement and feedback.
9. Promise that there will be problems, but provide a commitment that they will be identified and addressed as early as possible.

In order to communicate effectively with your employees, it is important to review the issues, understand the audiences and target groups, and identify the themes and messages that you want to communicate to employees. Ideally then, the strategy should be committed to a written document. Each action item, the person responsible for completing the item, and the timeline for completion should be included in the document.

Implementation will vary by company and based on each situation; however, the following communication strategies should be given careful consideration as you develop your own company's plan. While not all appear at first glance to be communication issues, in a formal sense, all are geared to conveying various types of messages to employees.

IMPLEMENTATION STRATEGIES AND SCHEDULE

These strategies have been grouped according to the suggested implementation schedule (e.g., within 30 days, within 60 days, within 90 days, within 6 months, within 12 months and other ideas for future consideration).

Implementation within 30 Days

Strategy #1: Conduct a Vision/Strategy Meeting with All Members of the Senior Management Team and Key Operations Personnel to Outline the Future Direction and Strategic Goals for the New Company

The most frequent concern raised by employees (at all levels) during most mergers or acquisitions is the need for a clear vision for the future and an understanding of the newly combined company's specific strategic goals and objectives. While the acquiring company may have already thought through this process, it is important to update the vision and strategy in order to reflect the direction/goals of the newly combined company. These are likely to be substantially different, given the potential for diversified product lines, an expanded customer base, an increased number of employees, and so forth.

There is real potential value in bringing together the new senior management team and key operating personnel for two to three days (at an off-site location) to talk about their views of the new company and to "hash out" the future direction and strategy together.

By working together on these critical issues as a group, each individual will have an opportunity to influence the debate and offer ideas for consideration by all parties present. At the conclusion of this "visioning conference," the participants should leave with a clearer understanding of the company's future direction (and the rationale for same) that they can then better explain and "sell" to employees.

The close contact over several days can also help begin the process of relationship development and should result in a better understanding of the perspectives and views of each member of the group. The meeting may also help to "bond" the participants into a more cohesive group that should improve future communication between and among various individuals and help to improve working relationships.

It is recommended that a professional facilitator be used to help lead the meeting, particularly given that two independent groups with different management styles will be meeting for the first time to discuss significant issues. A facilitator can help to ensure that a constructive exchange of ideas takes place and that all participants actually contribute, even those who may initially be reluctant. A facilitator will also help to ensure that no single individual will dominate the discussion and that all views are entertained and respected by the group.

Strategy #2: Assure That an Adequate Communications Function Exists, Including the Resources Necessary to Make It Successful, Such as a Professional Staff and an Adequate Budget

In order to maximize the potential success of your internal communications effort, it is necessary to staff the function with professionally skilled communicators. Effectively handling employee communications requires a high level of expertise; accordingly, any key staff must be added at a fairly senior level in order for the individual to be privy to newsworthy information and to be considered a true business partner.

An adequate budget must be allocated in order for the function to truly contribute company-wide. Clearly, the organization does not want to send inconsistent messages to employees by sending out glossy, expensive magazine-type publications at a time of cost cutting and constraint. However, there is an expense associated with any form of communication that must be recognized and provided for so that appropriate internal communications can be provided and other special communications can be distributed in a timely manner as well.

Strategy #3: Finalize and Announce the New Company Name to Employees and Aggressively Work on the Development of the New Corporate Identity

Companies sometimes become so caught up in operational details of the integration that they fail to take care of the simplest issues, such as deciding on and announcing a new name for the combined company. This delays what is typically a highly visible and symbolic signal that real change has occurred. It will also hinder the ability of employees to embrace the new entity.

The new company name needs to be announced to employees immediately, if possible—preferably on the day the deal is finalized. In addition, other visible signs of the old entities (e.g., business cards, stationery, signs, electronic references, internal forms, job postings, promotion/transfer announcements, internal communications forms) need to be changed over to the new name and logo quickly, rather than wait for old supplies and forms to be used up. Expense should not be the primary consideration in delaying the purging of these materials. It will likely be much more costly to delay the new organization's identity than it would be to toss out all old letterheads and such and start over from the outset.

In the case of a merger, you might also consider having an event to announce the new name and to symbolically help employees move into the future. Some companies host formal dinners or receptions for employees (and their families) to unveil the new name and logo, others have more informal affairs, and still others simply announce the changes in internal newsletters or letters to employees' homes. Whatever the means, it needs to convey some sense of the significance of the event.

Strategy #4: Implement a Transitional Bonus Program to Increase the Urgency Related to Achievement of the Synergy Goals and to Provide a Reward Mechanism for Positive Results

A bonus program focused on the achievement of the synergistic goals identified following the acquisition will add a sense of urgency to achieving the goals and will allow key employees to be rewarded for exceptional results.

You might consider installing a threshold financial goal that must be achieved prior to any awards being payable under the program. Gradations would be achieved though establishment of a scale of results that would dictate the actual payout of awards. Without any potential payoff for employees, however, it is doubtful that employees will share the management's sense of urgency on reaching these short-term goals.

Longer-term, you might also consider implementing a three- or four-year performance share program that will reward key players for the achievement of long-term results.

Strategy #5: Implement Some "Quick Hits" That Will Signal to Employees That the New Company Is Making Decisions and Moving in a Positive Direction

In order to expedite the change process and provide some quick signals to employees that this is a new company with a new (and perhaps better) approach, you might consider announcing some inexpensive, but very visible, "quick hits." Some possibilities include

Casual Dress Policy—A very quick and easy way to announce to your new organization that the company is changing is to announce a casual dress policy that will apply to each day of the week, not just Fridays. Companies across the United States have changed their policies in order to enhance teamwork and internal communications. The rationale for many of these companies is that a more relaxed dress policy reduces organizational formality, enhances the work environment, and helps to improve interactions among employees and their supervisors.

Implement an Employee Assistance Program—If you don't already have one in place, you might consider implementing an Employee Assistance Program (EAP) for your employees. In addition to the direct services provided, it signals to employees the company's concern about the stress and anxiety that they may be feeling about current changes and can even provide services tailored to transition issues. It is a fairly inexpensive and easy program to implement. Offering an EAP may also help employees deal with their family/stress problems before they turn into more expensive medical/health problems under your employee benefit plans.

Distribute Information to Employees Electronically and Via Voice Mail— While e-mail notes and mass-distributed voice mail messages may not always have the personal touch of face-to-face communication, they can be an extremely efficient means of providing short, up-to-the-minute updates about specific issues or breaking information. And while it seems that most persons in a modern workplace are as comfortable with these as they are chatting on a phone, be judicious in their use, as well. Remember that what they gain in efficiency, they also lose in nuance and inflection. They allow distribution of the same message to all parties at the same time, but are more subject to being misunderstood or misinterpreted than face-to-face exchanges. Keep messages brief, don't overload message boxes for employees who travel and can't check them frequently, and don't assume that they replace all other forms of communication. But do use them to get updates out in a timely fashion.

Implement Flexible Work Schedules for Salaried Employees—Consider implementing a flexible work schedule for employees if this is not already in place. Most organizations establish "core" hours to ensure that employees will be available during a specific band of time necessary to ensure that meetings can occur and business can be conducted with customers (e.g., establish the hours between 10:00 A.M. and 2:00 P.M. as your company's "core hours").

"Ask the Chairman" Program—Many companies have successfully installed an "Ask the Chairman" (or COO, etc.) program to deal with employee questions. In these, employees are invited to submit their questions electronically, or they can be submitted in writing anonymously. The commitment should be to provide an answer within three to four days and also to publish the questions and answers in the next company newsletter or a similar format for the benefit of all employees (and to help reduce the redundancy of questions).

Strategy #6: Aggressively Review Regularly Scheduled Meetings and Eliminate All But Those Meetings That Are Critical for Information Flow; Ensure That the Right People Are in Attendance, But Reduce the Requirement for Senior Management Participation as Much as Possible; and Ensure Accountability and Follow-up for Commitments Made during Meetings

Times of significant change provide an opportunity for organizations, as well as individuals, to reassess practices and priorities. For most companies, meetings are a giant double-edged sword—they tend to be incredibly inefficient, but there doesn't seem to be an adequate alternative if multiple people need to be involved. During change as significant as the merging into or with another company, both problems increase exponentially. A great many more decisions have to be made and information conveyed, but so much needs to be done that there is little time to waste.

Most companies have a number of regularly scheduled meetings designed to provide information to senior managers but which are not held for the purpose of actually making decisions or deciding strategy. It is recommended that you review all standing meetings to assure that the meeting is streamlined in content and includes the right participants and eliminate any meetings the sole purpose of which is to provide information upward and not actually make decisions. (The rationale for excluding senior managers as necessary participants is two-fold. First, their schedules tend to be overbooked, and their availability is often subject to last minute changes. Second, if they are present, others often reserve opinions or ideas that might need to be voiced.)

The participant roster for each meeting needs to be reviewed to assure that the right people—and *only* the right people—are included. Persons who have no stake in, or responsibility for, the decisions resulting from the meeting can be kept informed in other ways. Those who do have a stake need to be in attendance, not participate secondhand or after the fact. (Referring again to senior managers, this assumes a structure with minimal micromanagement or second-guessing by those at the top.)

Consider whether or not there are alternative ways to provide the information that is currently being provided through standing meetings (e.g., written reports, regular reporting of metrics, memos, etc.). A great deal of preparation time is likely required for many of those meetings which is excessive work time that might be better used for other purposes.

You might also consider conducting workshops for managers about "how to run an effective meeting." This is a skill that can be learned and one notably lacking in many companies. Effective meetings typically have a built-in process to ensure that follow-up and action items are noted and commitments made during meetings are tracked. This skill training would focus not just on how to conduct a good meeting but would also train managers about how to professionally debate issues and resolve conflict as well.

It is surely a valid argument that once into the process there is no time to add anything additional, such as another training program, regardless of how valuable it is. However, it is also true that people faced with real need are likely to learn the most. Having trainers or facilitators work with groups "on the fly" using real issues rather than scenarios could offer a chance for significant learning and change (*if* you're confident enough in the skills of the trainer or facilitator).

Implementation within 60 Days

Strategy #7: Conduct On-Site Employee "Orientation" Sessions to Enhance Management Visibility, to Outline the Future Vision and Strategic Goals for the Company, and to Answer Employee Questions

Once the vision and strategic goals are decided upon, it is recommended that each member of your senior management team conduct on-site sessions (or at least live video broadcasts) with employees to outline the following:

- The new direction of the company,
- The company's mission,
- Its strategic goals/objectives,
- Images of each operation, including maps and pictures of the operation, and its employees and equipment,
- The new management team, including their experience and backgrounds,
- The rationale supporting the acquisition or merger, including the synergies behind the deal,
- The company's values and expectations, including what is required in order to be successful within the new organization, and, most importantly,
- Candid and honest answers to employees' questions.

These "orientation" sessions will allow employees throughout the new organization to meet members of the new senior management team. These meetings will also ensure that all employees receive a common message about the background, history, and goals of the company and better understand the "big picture" and how they each fit into that framework.

Both the substantive content of the sessions and the opportunity to ask questions, as well as the increased management visibility, are sure to be much appreciated by employees. These face-to-face opportunities should serve as a strong beginning for the newly combined company.

Strategy #8: Establish Systemic Communication Vehicles for Distribution to Employees at Regular Intervals

Once you have your communication function up and running, it is recommended that systemic internal vehicles be established for communicating information to your employees on a regular schedule. These types of communications could include:

- Monthly "President's Letter,"
- Quarterly newsletter/company magazine,

- Weekly electronic news updates (for "quick and dirty" updates about breaking news of interest,
- Integration news (a short-term newsletter to provide updates about progress on the synergies and transitional goals/objectives), and
- Bulletin board postings (e.g., performance metrics, key goals achieved, promotions/transfers, etc.).

Strategy #9: Make Supervisors the Company's "Primary Front-Line Communicators" for Employee Communications

Employees consistently state that the most credible source of company information is information they get from their supervisor. Accordingly, it is recommended that supervisors and managers should be the primary "front line" communicators of company information.

To ensure accountability for this function, several additional strategies are suggested:

1. *Quarterly Meetings with "Talking Points"*—It is recommended that managers and supervisors hold quarterly meetings with employees in their departments or business units to cover financial results and strategy. In this regard, the corporate communications group would provide all department heads with a brief quarterly communications package of "Talking Points," essentially a script that would highlight the company's financial results and any other key information that needs to be delivered to all employees.

2. *Supervisory Skills Training*—Offer supervisory training to assure that each supervisor is trained in various communication skills. Training content should include skill building in the following areas:

- Listening skills,
- How to conduct an effective meeting,
- Resolving conflict and engaging in professional debate,
- Presentation skills,
- Selling your ideas internally, and
- Coping with change.

These training topics could be included in any "Introduction to Supervision" workshops offered to employees or could be offered as stand-alone training workshops.

3. *Performance Management*—The effectiveness of a supervisor in conducting these meetings should be factored into his/her performance rating as a way to assure management accountability for delivering cogent and timely information to employees.

4. *Bonus/Compensation Systems*—Design your bonus and compensation

systems to reflect accountability for how well a supervisor communicates with his/her employees.

Implementation within 90 Days

Strategy #10: Increase "Two-Way" Communication
Opportunities Throughout the Company

Companies that are known for their communication excellence are real believers in the increased use of "two-way" communication opportunities (e.g., face-to-face opportunities for employees and management to openly exchange ideas). They believe that the openness of such settings and information exchanged between management, supervisors, and employees leads to greater teamwork and employee confidence in management. Productivity and employee morale are notably improved as a result of these efforts. Many companies hold regular "town hall" meetings with their employees (e.g., most companies set up these meetings at least annually, and many host them on a quarterly basis).

While it can be argued with some justification that regular on-site sessions with employees are both time consuming and expensive, these meetings will increase employee understanding of the company's strategic objectives and how they personally can help to meet those goals. In addition, recent surveys have indicated a preference among employees for a two-way communication process and frequent face-to-face communications directly from their immediate supervisor.

In addition to the recommended quarterly meetings which would be held with employees (and would be conducted by supervisors throughout the company in small groups), some other methods for increasing 2-way communications within your new organization include the following:

1. *Host an Annual Key Manager's Meeting*—It is recommended that the company bring together its key officers and employees on an annual basis to announce the company's future direction and strategic goals, to hear speakers on topics of major importance, to discuss the business and changes occurring within the industry, and to answer questions.

This type of meeting would typically last two to two-and-a-half days. While some companies elect to base such management meetings on a single theme annually (e.g., safety, industry changes, etc.), others choose to have key employees actually work in small groups on real and current issues of major importance to the organization.

In order to maximize the impact of such a gathering, you might consider videotaping the proceedings for widespread viewing among general employees, as well as publishing all presentations delivered. Questions asked and answered during the session should also be included, so that the information delivered is given its widest scope of impact and so employees do not receive distorted second-hand information.

2. *Conduct an Annual "State of the Company" Video Teleconference*—To kick off the changing communications climate, you might also consider holding a "State of the Company" interactive video teleconference with all employees (worldwide) at year end. Topics and issues could include:

• Year-end financial results,
• The company's vision and strategic goals,
• An overview of the acquisition process,
• Changes that have been made to date and those expected in the future (or at least the process/timeline expected to be followed in determining future changes),
• An introduction of the management team,
• Any anticipated additional force reductions,
• The state of the industry, and
• Answers to employee questions.

Such a meeting could be staged with a minimum of out-of-pocket expense as videoconferencing technology is rapidly coming down in price. After this meeting, its effectiveness should be evaluated in order to determine whether or not future annual (or perhaps quarterly) meetings would be desirable going forward.

Strategy #11: Require That All Senior Management and Key Operations Personnel Go through a "360-Degree" Performance Evaluation (e.g., Feedback from Subordinates, Peers, and Supervisors)

While normally associated with performance management rather than communications, 360-degree feedback is really both. In organizations where there is no regular means of "upward communication," other than reporting of numerical results, this is one way to begin to open up channels of communication and to do so with individual assistance.

This provides a way for the company's senior officers and general managers to better understand themselves and the perspectives of others regarding their strengths and weaknesses. The information obtained through this type of review (e.g., feedback about performance and behaviors from subordinates, peers, and supervisors) can be very revealing and insightful. Particularly during times of major transition, this type of feedback can often provide real impetus for change within a company's management team.

Without some objective insights about his or her performance, an individual has no real reason to change behaviors that have caused the individual to be successful in the past. These reviews should be confidential and the results can be shared with your executives by a professionally trained "performance coach." This trained facilitator would not only provide the direct feedback to the individual about his or her performance strengths and weaknesses, but would also help the executive to develop a personal action plan for improvement.

Employees should be advised that all of the company's management is going through this type of self-assessment and total review in an effort to strengthen performance at all levels. This announcement would indicate that executives will be "piloting" the program, which the company intends to roll out to all employees by the end of your next calendar year.

Implementation within 6 Months

Strategy #12: Install Video Bulletin Boards at Major Employee Sites

The implementation of video bulletin boards should also be considered for each heavily populated employee work location throughout your company if a similar mechanism is not already in place. Such a system would consist of an internal network of video monitors placed in break areas or lobbies that would be used to communicate important company information to employees. It could also be used to provide real time information on benefit updates, changes to strategy, employee job transfers/promotions, the company's stock price, as well as other incidental company and/or industry news.

The actual implementation cost of a video bulletin board system is very low. Essentially, all that is required is a PC (which drives the system) and a small number of basic television monitors that would be installed in heavily trafficked employee lobbies or break areas.

Corporate information can be downloaded periodically during the day and intertwined with the local information being provided to employees. Such an approach would provide an effective and immediate method of communication, given that the full potential of both audio and video media could be utilized to convey information to employees.

Strategy #13: Host Monthly Employee Luncheons/ "Early Bird" Breakfasts at Rotating Company Sites

An excellent way to increase management visibility and enhance employee trust is to provide opportunities for employees to sign up to participate in lunches or breakfasts with members of the company's newly formed senior management team. These lunches/breakfasts could be offered on a regular basis with members of management rotating among various company sites. These types of opportunities should generally be limited to 8 to 10 employees during any one gathering. Limiting the size of the group will maximize the ability of employees to actually speak to the hosting executive and minimize typical employee fears about asking questions in front of a large group.

These informal settings can help employees to better understand the company's financial situation and its strategy, as well as to get more comfortable with various members of the key management team. By sharing food together, employees generally become more relaxed and are more inclined to ask the real questions that are on their minds.

Executives will also benefit by "keeping a pulse" on the concerns and questions that employees have, instead of becoming somewhat isolated (which is a fairly common occurrence among members of a company's management team). Executives can ask questions of employees as well during these sessions to generate discussion and to open up new areas for dialogue and debate.

Executives will need to keep in mind, however, that some employees might show up (possibly out of coercion) but remain silent for fear of making a bad or wrong impression. Accordingly, he or she will need to be prepared to help reduce employee apprehensions by having some prepared remarks and some ready ideas about how to keep the conversations going.

Strategy #14: Initiate a "360-Degree" Performance Management System for All Employees Company-Wide

In order to provide feedback from every major constituent group to your employees, it is recommended that you consider implementing a "360-degree" performance feedback system, just as suggested for executives in the first 90-day time frame. Employees would receive feedback from their supervisor, their peers, and their subordinates. By receiving this feedback, employees will better understand where they are most effective and where they need to do some additional work. Even more importantly, this kind of program can begin to change formerly hierarchical structures and communication patterns in immediate and very visible ways.

Strategy #15: Increase the Effectiveness of Your Employee Benefit Communications

Employee benefit communications is another area of future opportunity. In the past, the major goal of most companies has been to provide basic information about benefit plans/coverage and to meet legal requirements. Given the organizational changes and the attendant uncertainty among employees about the future benefit program, new goals should be considered. New strategic objectives for your new company's future benefit communications could include the following:

- To positively influence employee attitudes toward their benefit program.
- To communicate the real value of the plans to employees.
- To provide information which will help employees better understand their benefits and to utilize them more cost effectively.
- To enhance the message that employees are owners/stakeholders of the Company.
- To explain and "promote" benefit plan changes or new services.
- To better coordinate written information to avoid sending "mixed" messages.
- To consolidate and/or reduce the number of employee benefit mailings that employees receive.
- To better inform management audiences in advance of plan and service changes.

If your company is staffed like many other companies currently, demands to provide these kind of communications to employees may exceed your available internal resources. Accordingly, it might be necessary to either increase internal staff or to access external help through consultants. The alternative is to forego the increased effectiveness that would accrue to the company as a result of improved employee and benefit communications.

Implementation within 12 Months

Strategy #16: Conduct an Employee Satisfaction Survey 12 to 18 Months Following the Close of the Deal (and Annually Thereafter)

In order to assure the continuous improvement of your communications delivery to employees, it is recommended that you regularly conduct an employee satisfaction survey within 12 to 18 months following the close of your merger or acquisition and annually thereafter. The information obtained as a result of this annual survey will help you to strategically determine the message content that you need to target for the upcoming year and will alert you to the commencement of any negative trends so that the issues can be addressed early. (A sample survey is provided in Appendix 6.)

Strategy #17: Develop a Company-Wide Communications Strategy Annually

It is important to develop an integrated planning effort to ensure that key messages are consistently being developed and delivered to all employees. There is a real need to align the company's communications objectives with its business goals. If employees do not understand how they can support and contribute to the company's goals and objectives, they will be less likely to be committed to and work toward those objectives, reducing the potential for real success.

Through the establishment of an annual planning meeting (which would include the company's CEO, COO, primary HR/communications contact, and key operational managers), a list of broad guidelines and priority messages for the upcoming year would be generated. By including these key players and making employee communication part of their active duties, you and your HR team will increase the likelihood that the messages will be more consistently delivered to employees at all locations.

Strategy #18: Initiate an "Orientation Workshop" for New Hires to Ensure an Early Understanding by New Employees of the Company's Vision and Strategic Goals

It is recommended that all new hires be exposed to the company's vision and strategic goals as soon after their hire as possible. You might consider conducting quarterly orientation workshops for employees hired during the past quarter. This would have the effect of exposing employees to the company's strategy, vision, and values early in their career with your company and would also allow them to meet and get acquainted with other new hires.

Such a new hire workshop could introduce employees to the company's management team via videotape, or live and in person, depending on schedules. Depending on what types of documents and tapes are developed for the orientation workshops recommended earlier, much of this work could be used during these sessions as well.

OTHER STRATEGIES FOR FUTURE CONSIDERATION

Other strategies that you may want to consider for future implementation include the following:

- Distribution of a written annual "Employee Annual Report" to all employees which would recognize the significant contributions of various employees and provide a mechanism to profile and celebrate both individual and organizational successes.

- Implementation of an Employee Candidate Referral Program (e.g., pay your employees for referring job candidates). This will lower your recruiting costs and may improve existing employee morale and the quality of your new hires.

- Consider implementing a quarterly report to senior management that would review the key performance indicators of your employee relations environment (e.g., staffing levels, turnover, voluntary resignations, absenteeism, hiring costs, etc.).

- Consider implementation of a "spot" bonus program from a prebudgeted bonus pool which allows officers and department heads to provide "on the spot" bonuses of between $100 and $1,000 (contingent upon a positive result, significant effort, or a contribution considered "above and beyond"). (*Note*: This program would not replace your executive incentives, but would provide a mechanism to reward lower level employees in your organization for excellent results or significant effort.)

CONCLUSIONS

If you elect to implement any or all of these recommendations, a financial commitment will be required by your organization, and professional communicators should ideally be included in both planning and implementation.

Most importantly, however, your company and its senior management team will need to embrace the fact that frequent and candid employee communications are an essential element of your company's future success, not just through the integration period, but always. To this end, a summary of some of the most important messages and themes that should be considered for distribution to employees during the early months of your integration effort are included in Appendix 1.

A proactive and aggressive communications program will, over time, ensure that you have employees who are informed, motivated and working in concert to achieve the company's strategic goals and objectives. Without each of these ingredients, your company will never be able to fully capitalize on the potential for future success that a merger or acquisition can create.

Chapter 10

Legal Issues

Faced with economic and competitive pressure to reduce costs and improve work processes following a merger or acquisition, most U.S. companies have been compelled to reduce their workforces post-closing. Whether it is called a reduction in force (RIF), downsizing, or "rightsizing," any aggressive staffing decisions carry potentially problematic consequences—not only because of their impact on the people, but also in terms of the financial, organizational, and legal implications that can arise.

For these reasons—as well as to make the best, and most fair, decisions—you need to move cautiously when it comes to reducing jobs and affecting people. All decisions should be based on documented, objective facts, and legal counsel should be consulted early in the process in order to protect confidentiality and ensure that any required notices are properly made.[1] In addition, well-planned and well-executed communications are essential.

This chapter examines the alternatives to a force reduction, the practical and legal considerations involved once you decide that staffing levels must be reduced, the steps that should be followed both in the planning and implementation stages, and the considerations involved in dealing with the "survivors" of your workforce reduction.

ALTERNATIVES TO A WORKFORCE REDUCTION

If your company is contemplating a workforce reduction, you need to seriously consider whether there are realistic alternatives that have the potential to deliver the desired outcomes. By critically examining your needs and alternatives before drastic action is taken, you show that you did not cavalierly decide to terminate employees but, in fact, had no other reasonable options. This can serve as evidence of the company's good faith, making its decisions easier to explain and defend if later challenged.

Some alternatives to workforce reductions that may generate some financial improvement for your company (and the implications of each) are listed below:

- *Nonemployment cost reduction*—Employer-sponsored special events could be eliminated or severely restricted, as can other company subsidies and services (e.g., cafeteria services, service awards, and club activities).

  Implications: The events and services that make your company unique would be eliminated which, while reducing costs, could negatively affect employee morale.

- *Attrition combined with hiring freeze*—You could implement a hiring freeze and allow regular terminations and departures to naturally decrease the employee population over time.

  Implications: Depending on the economy and local job market, progress in reducing the staffing levels could be slow.

- *Pay freezes, pay reductions, and benefit cuts*—Merit pay increases could be suspended indefinitely, employees could be required to "give back" a percentage of their current salary (e.g., 10–20%), or various employee benefits could be suspended, terminated, or simply reduced.

  Implications: Employee morale is likely to suffer, potentially causing reductions in productivity, increased absenteeism, and undesired turnover.

- *Voluntary separations*—You could elect to open a voluntary retirement program to all employees who wish to voluntarily separate from your company in exchange for severance and/or enhanced retirement benefits.

  Implications: You might be "oversubscribed" and lose more employees than you actually desire (including key people) thereby increasing recruiting expenses and training costs while reducing productivity and efficiency during the transition period.

- *Reduced workweek*—Designated employees could be reclassified from full-time to part-time and begin to work a reduced workweek schedule with corresponding salary and benefit reductions.

  Implications: Most employees need a full-time salary and might seek employment elsewhere if their schedule (and pay) is reduced. Morale and productivity could also be affected, not only for the reclassified employee, but also for their coworkers who would likely be required to assume more responsibilities.

- *Elimination of services*—The services of your company's consultants, independent contractors, part-timers, summer help, temporaries, and co-op students could be eliminated prior to affecting your full-time employees.

  Implications: People who perform necessary but low-skilled functions would no longer be available to work, thereby requiring higher paid employees to do projects that perhaps a less experienced person could perform more economically and enthusiastically.

- *Reduction in vacation/sick pay policies*—These policies could be significantly cut back or temporarily suspended.

  Implications: The reduction or elimination of these policies could potentially put your company at a competitive hiring disadvantage, could increase turnover, and could negatively affect morale.

If these actions do not lead to your company's desired results, a workforce reduction program should be considered. A listing of potential issues you may wish to consider before deciding on a program design is included in Appendix 7.

VOLUNTARY REDUCTIONS

Voluntary separations have significant advantages over those that are involuntary. The greatest of these is the "win-win" nature of a truly voluntary program, particularly if the program eliminates the need for an involuntary reduction in force (RIF). The employee gets to elect whether or not to leave the company based on his or her personal needs, and the employer is not forced to make (and often defend) the difficult decisions about who to cut and who to keep.

These programs do have their downsides, however, which include the fact that they are (1) expensive in the short run and (2) potentially impossible for employers with little available cash. Even more troubling in the long run, the employer lacks control over who will leave the company if the program is truly voluntary. Although the employer may limit its incentive offer to specified classes of employees, such distinctions must be based on objective, verifiable business needs.[2]

Employers must also recognize that some employees may accept their offer, but then sue for constructive discharge (e.g., allege that they were coerced into resigning or retiring). You can best protect against such litigation in the following two ways: (1) design an incentive program that strongly communicates its voluntary nature; and (2) incorporate severance agreements and releases into your program(s).

A company's decision to implement a voluntary incentive program requires the consideration of a variety of factors. Intended results, program costs, and the potential impact on business operations all should be evaluated assuming various levels of participation. Educated guesses generally can be made as to which groups will find the offer "too good to pass up," allowing you to identify potential problems that might result from the loss of key personnel. Such projections also allow for an analysis of the company on a before-and-after (hypothetical) basis, which may reveal the potential impact of a proposed plan on the company's race, age, and gender demographics. Such studies are usually discoverable in litigation, but they will not be considered evidence of unlawful discrimination if properly linked to objective business needs.[3]

Given that these documents are discoverable, all records of studies should reflect the unbiased goals of the program. Documents that imply that the company wants only older people to retire could be used to support allegations that improper age bias motivated the company's plan.

As far as possible, calculations should be made using only average statistics to avoid the impression that a particular age group was targeted for cuts. Keep in mind that your company may be sued for implementing a plan that has an unnecessarily detrimental impact on a protected group.[4] See Appendix 9 for a checklist of potential pitfalls that you will need to consider prior to restructuring your workforce.

On balance, although some analysis is obviously necessary and can be beneficial, this is an area in which you should not attempt to study exhaustively every possible (if unlikely) outcome. Rather, brief studies of costs, alternatives, and potential impacts should be undertaken, including preparation to demonstrate that, based on those studies, you designed a plan that contained the most justifiable combination of factors with the least detrimental impact on a selected group. Of course, so long as the plan is truly voluntary and is not accompanied with "a wink and a nod"-type communications about which employees should stay or leave, arguments about adverse impact should have little weight with a court.[5]

Before implementing any kind of incentive plan, you and your HR team should consider whether employees affected by the offer are covered by express employment agreements or handbooks. Similarly, existing benefit plans, collective bargaining agreements, and human resource policies may need to be modified before a program can be implemented.

In particular, you, your legal team, and management will need to consider whether or not to seek an agreement or general release from each employee as part of the program. Some elements of strategy in making this decision include the following:

• Requesting the release is likely to expose those employees who are considering, or are likely to consider, a lawsuit in response to their termination. A refusal to sign may identify not only troubled employees, but also problem areas in the workplace. Early disclosure of these potential plaintiffs and their areas of concern may enable the employer to prepare an early defense. On the other hand, seeking the release may arouse employee concerns and suspicions where there previously had been none and may alert employees to claims that they may never have realized were available.

• The release itself may have certain psychological value in deterring later litigation. Some employees may feel compelled to live with the choice they made in signing the release.

• Although an employee who signs a release may later choose to disavow it and sue, the existence of a release enables the employer to insist that the primary issue of any litigation must be the validity of the release.

The Older Workers Benefit Protection Act ("OWBPA" or "the Act") contains several provisions of special interest to employers designing incentive programs. First, the Act expressly allows employers to set minimum ages for eligibility in early retirement benefit plans. The Act also heavily regulates the terms under which an employee's voluntary waiver may be enforced.

Specifically, waivers will not be valid unless they are made knowingly and voluntarily. This standard requires the employer, among other things, to provide for a 21-day (for individual agreements) or 45-day (for group incentives) waiting period *before* acceptance and seven days after acceptance of the plan before severance payments are made. The Act also requires employers to (1) advise employees of the names of other employees covered by the incentive plan; and (2) urge the employees to consult with an attorney before signing the waiver.

As mentioned earlier, employees who accept incentive separation offers will sometimes turn around and sue their former employers, claiming that they were forced to resign involuntarily. The voluntary nature of any waiver signed will usually also be challenged.

To preserve the position it hopes to achieve through its program, the employer should take all available steps to ensure that its plan is truly voluntary and document those efforts fully. If possible to do so truthfully, you and your team should attempt to squelch rumors that those who do not leave voluntarily will be fired later. This avoids the "gun to the head" argument if constructive discharge is alleged afterwards. However, if further reductions are anticipated, you should be frank in presenting the company's prospects and future plans.[6]

As the program is being communicated, great care should be taken to instruct managers not to attempt to coerce the decisions of employees. Employers must avoid giving employees the impression that they have to leave now or be fired later or, just as importantly, the impression that some employees are "untouchable." Either situation could create significant problems in subsequent litigation.[7]

At the outset, you must decide whether the contemplated action is truly a RIF or something else entirely. For example, too often employees are notified that their "positions are being eliminated" when that is not really the case.

To the average person, "position elimination" means that the job the person was performing has been eliminated from the company's workforce. This can lead to dissatisfaction and mistrust, resulting in legal action if the person later discovers that another employee is performing the job they once held. On the other hand, when employees are advised that a RIF is occurring, they will understand that because a reduced number of people will continue to perform the same functions, they may well be replaced.

This type of communication may seem rather elementary, but incredibly enough, employers are frequently careless and cavalier in their use of the terms "reduction in force," "layoff," and "position elimination." Careful and accurate use of the appropriate term will go a long way toward minimizing the types of employee misunderstandings that often result in a legal challenge.

Once the plan has been publicized, the employer should encourage interested individuals to bring questions to designated HR or legal personnel who have been thoroughly instructed on the applicable laws. Another option is to hire an outside financial consultant or accountant to advise employees about the plan. The consultant should be instructed that the company has no interest in obtaining anything other than a truly voluntary decision to leave or stay. This approach can be good for employee morale and foster confidence in both the program and the company. Moreover, an employee who is advised by an outside consultant that a program is "too good to refuse" will have a hard time proving coercion or that the separation was really a constructive discharge.

In publicizing the plan, expiration dates must be clearly stated. OWBPA imposes applicable time requirements, in particular the 45-day consideration for group incentives and early retirement agreements and 21-days for individual offers noted previously. But the plan cannot be allowed to hang on indefinitely. A reasonable deadline or "window" should be set, balancing the needs of the employees to deliberate over this major decision with the pressing financial or other structural needs experienced by the company. Without a firm deadline, employees may delay in hopes that a better deal will come along.

INVOLUNTARY REDUCTIONS

Unfortunately, even after all other voluntary means have been exhausted, involuntary reductions may still be required to meet the employer's business objectives. The potential for legal action by employees who are involuntarily terminated is, of course, much higher. Therefore, you and your company must be prepared to defend each individual nonretention decision as well as the overall impact of the reduction on various protected employee groups.

Following development of the RIF general plan, you and your team should undertake an intensive study of critical department or group tasks. Individual strengths and weaknesses of incumbent personnel should not be considered in reaching these decisions. Rather, factors that should be considered include types of duties performed and percentage of time spent on performance, overlaps among jobs or departments, availability of qualified personnel for such positions, and the like.[8]

Once the critical tasks have been determined, you can move to the next step—determining which individuals should be retained to fill what positions. Most often, the manager of each particular area conducts an initial evaluation. However, many companies have used committees to evaluate personnel or to sign off on initial recommendations and others have experimented with peer review systems.

Whether an evaluation is conducted by an individual or a committee, the standards of evaluation must be clear and documented in writing. Similarly, evaluations should be documented as well.

An important question to be faced is whether evaluators will consult previous performance evaluations or if a new system is to be developed for the RIF. It is a simple fact that because most managers are not completely candid in the yearly appraisals, "grade inflation" inevitably creeps into the system. There are many advantages to using existing appraisals, however, because they lend some historical perspective to the differences among employees.[9] Perhaps even more important, employees generally will have failed to contest past adverse comments. Additionally, failure to consult existing evaluations may be held against the company.[10]

Whether or not previous evaluations are consulted, you and your HR and legal teams should consider adopting a special RIF evaluation system. The goal of this system is to rank employees relative to one another—numerical rating systems are used frequently. Inconsistencies with previous performance evaluation ratings, however, may be difficult to explain.[11]

Instructions as to factors for consideration, and their relative weights, should be given to evaluators. These factors should include prior performance ratings, unique skills, and other objective criteria. Consideration of seniority will serve to negate any implication of discrimination.[12] Employers are cautioned, however, not to base decisions on the relative salaries paid to incumbent employees because courts have construed such considerations as a proxy for age discrimination.

Once the initial evaluator has finished ranking employees and made retention/nonretention recommendations, a review must be conducted to determine whether adverse impact or some other form of discrimination is operating. This review should be conducted by senior HR or legal personnel familiar with the definitions and implications of discrimination.

The reviewers' committee should be instructed, first, to evaluate the rankings by cross-checking evaluations against the instructions, job descriptions, and relevant performance documents.[13] Next, retention decisions should be evaluated against the pre-RIF workforce makeup to determine whether or not protected groups are adversely affected. If adverse impact is found, it may be necessary to check each individual decision and evaluator carefully for indications of age bias and to review job descriptions and evaluation criteria to ensure that they are nondiscriminatory.

Reconsideration of the process or of particular retention decisions may be necessary at this point. Be aware, though, that employers are under no requirements to create another job, or "bump" another employee, in deference to an employee from a protected age group.[14] Moreover, even a drop in the overall age of the remaining employees may not support an inference that a particular employee was discharged because of age.

After the analysis is complete, employers are then in a position to communicate the information to the affected employees. Recommendations about how managers should handle the actual termination meeting with employees are included in Appendix 8.

OTHER ISSUES TO CONSIDER

Companies contemplating reductions in their workforce, whether voluntary or involuntary, should consider the following issues as well:

Communication

Employers should continuously communicate with employees at all steps in the process. Although a proactive communications program contains the risk of communicating improper statements, a well-developed program can reduce employee anxiety and anger by demonstrating the program's necessity and basic fairness. When coupled with reasonably generous severance benefits, effective communication may reduce the chance of litigation by employees.

Documentation

Throughout the process the employer must take care to document thoroughly the investigations, studies, and evaluations it undertakes. Any judge or jury will expect an employer to be able to present a paper trail providing evidence that a legitimate business need was the incentive for a RIF. The goal of such documentation is to reflect the company's actual needs, its concern for its employees, and the objectivity of its plans. It should not, however, whitewash the facts. Rather, the documents should contain frank analyses of the size of reductions necessary to achieve the desired ends and, if applicable, the inability of other methods (short of an RIF) to attain them. Although the documents prepared

for these purposes will usually be discoverable in court, objective documentation will go a long way toward evidencing the employer's good
faith.

Post-RIF

Do NOT replace employees who are terminated during a RIF within
one year. The other employees will undoubtedly find out about such
replacements which will then act as a catalyst to lawsuits and enhance
an employee's claim that the RIF was a pretext for unlawful discrimination.[15]

Ideally, a tight hiring freeze should be imposed after a RIF. If additional employees are needed, consideration should be given first to employees terminated in the RIF. In particular, employers should not deny
a job opening to an employee 40 years or older on the sole basis that he
or she may be "overqualified" for the position, as courts may view that
as simply another "code word" for age bias.[16]

Dealing with the Survivors

The effects of downsizing do not end after the termination notices have
been issued. Simply expecting survivors to be grateful to "make the cut"
may ignore serious morale problems and can lead to productivity losses
(and even sabotage). No company would want to find the economic
health of the organization worse *after* a reorganization than before. The
difference may lie in the manner in which the survivors are prepared
for "life after downsizing."

To the degree that events are sudden, unexpected, and cause dramatic
change, they may be perceived as traumatic by employees. The degree
of trauma experienced and the time needed for recovery and adaptation
to the changes vary a good deal from one individual to another. In
downsizing efforts the shock of the event affects not only those employees who lose their jobs, but also those who remain.

Employees who perceive the changes and accompanying "losses" as
personal are more likely to experience a typical grief reaction to the
event. These may be employees who viewed their work as more than
"just a job" (e.g., employees who found personal fulfilment in their work,
whose social networks were primarily made up of coworkers, and whose
social status was derived primarily from identification with the company).[17]

The intellectual understanding by employees of changes may vary a
good deal from their emotional responses to them, especially at first.
Corporations need to acknowledge this and plan to deal with it, even if
employees do not raise the issues.

In reacting to traumatic events, people grasp for explanations and un-derstanding. They try to regain a sense of stability and predictability. Emotional reactions to natural disasters are often resolved, in part, through concluding that they were out of anyone's control and people must just "get on with it." But in the process of coping, people naturally attempt to link some cause and effect and may assume the worst about those in decision-making roles for lack of a better explanation.

Poorly managed downsizing efforts result in decreased productivity, absenteeism, employee turnover, increased emotional stress, and anxiety claims, as well as a decline in quality. Companies that fail to promote sensitivity to the separation syndrome are likely to experience some or all of these negative results.

SUGGESTIONS FOR ACTION FOLLOWING THE DOWNSIZING

A corporate restructuring that places a high priority on the morale of the survivors should include the following action steps:

- Communicate clear expectations. Clarify what has changed and what has not.
- Plan the process to achieve the desired outcome. Solicit input and alternatives from employees and allow them to take an ownership interest in the threats to the company and the need for aggressive action.
- Be as open, honest and direct as possible—both before, during, and after the announcement of the workforce reduction.
- If possible, make only one cut rather than a series of small reductions to avoid the "slow death" and negative impact on employee morale.
- Recognize that the organization has suffered a loss and everyone must share in the pain (e.g., no executive bonuses while people are losing their jobs).
- Demonstrate to survivors that the company is empathetic and is offering as-sistance to those affected (e.g., EAP programs, etc.).
- Show respect for those being separated through retirement dinners, receptions, or informal gathering that will allow employees to reminisce, weep, and begin the "healing process."
- Continue to communicate a clear vision for the future.
- Spend resources on training and team building to help survivors forge new work relationships and work skills.

A well-thought-out plan and an empathetic approach that treats em-ployees fairly and with respect will go a long way toward achieving the objective of the workforce reduction—not only for those individuals di-rectly affected, but also for those survivors who will make or break your company's future.

NOTES

1. The Worker's Adjustment and Retraining Notification Act (WARN) requires employers to give 60 days' advance notice of plant closings and mass layoffs.

2. See *Bodnar v. Synpol, Inc.*, 843 F.2d 190, 193 (5th Cir. 1987), cert. denied, 488 U.S. 908 (1988).

3. See *Stanojev v. Ebasco*, 643 F.2d 914 (2d Cir. 1981); *Marson v. Jones & Laughlin Steel Co.*, 523 F. Supp. 503 (E.D. Wis. 1981); and *Wilson v. Firestone Tire & Rubber Co.*, 932 F.2d 510, 514 (6th Cir. 1991).

4. See *EEOC v. Chrysler Corp.*, 733 F.2d 1183 (6th Cir. 1983); *Polstorff v. Fletcher*, 452 F. Supp. 17 (N.D. Ala. 1978).

5. See *Russell v. Teledyne Ohio Steel*, 892 F.2d 1044 (6th Cir. 1990), cert. denied, 495 U.S. 922 (1990) (statistics as to employees who voluntarily retired could not be used to prove adverse impact or treatment on basis of age).

6. Such honesty will not imply age bias unless the actual risks to the employee's job are caused by age bias. See *Harris v. Malinckrodt*, 886 F.2d 170 (8th Cir. 1989).

7. See *Herbert v. Mohawk Rubber Co.*, 872 F.2d 1104 (1st Cir. 1989); see also *Henn v. National Geographic Society*, 819 F.2d 824 (7th Cir. 1987), cert. denied, 484 U.S. 964 (1987). A number of problems and subsequent litigation inherent in a reduction in force arise not because of discrimination, but because of poor communication. In the absence of clear and candid explanations about the downsizing plan, employees begin to believe that a sinister (and undoubtedly illegal) motive must lurk in the background.

8. A caveat is necessary here because an analysis of cost considerations may be used to suggest age discrimination, as more highly paid employees generally are older and more senior.

9. See *Conkwright v. Westinghouse Electric Co.*, 739 F.2d Supp. 1006 (D. Md. 1990). But note that primary weight should be given to evaluations of the employees in his or her most current position, if at all possible. *Connell v. Bank of Boston*, 924 F.2d 1169 (1st Cir. 1991), cert. denied, 501 U.S. 1218 (1991).

10. See *Duffy v. Wheeling Pittsburgh Steel Corp.*, 738 F.2d 1393 (3d Cir. 1984), cert. denied, 469 U.S. 1087 (1984).

11. See *EEOC v. Consol. Edison*, 25 FEB Cases 537 (S.D.N.Y. 1981).

12. This is not to say that decisions based on seniority are, in reality, based on age. See *Ludovicy v. Dunkirk Radiator Corp.*, 922 F.2d 109, 111 (2d Cir. 1990).

13. See *Stendebach v. CPC International*, 691 F.2d 735 (5th Cir. 1982), cert. denied, 461 U.S. 944 (1983).

14. See *Grubb v. Bendix Corp*, 666 F. Supp. 1223 (N.D. Ind. 1986). Although information regarding such a review is generally discoverable, it will not have a negative impact on the employer's case if conducted properly.

15. *Tice v. Lampert Yards, Inc.*, 761 F.2d 1210 (7th Cir. 1985); *Ridenour v. Lawson Co.*, 791 F.2d 52 (6th Cir. 1986).

16. The continuing performance of some of the terminated employee's duties does not necessarily show that the person was actually replaced. See *Barnes v. Gencorp, Inc.*, 896 F.2d 1457 (6th Cir. 1990), cert. denied, 498 U.S. 878 (1990).

17. Work is an intellectual, not an emotional, setting. Employees have long been expected to "check their emotions at the door." But issues such as creativity and dedication are deeply connected to emotions, and productivity may suffer if these issues are not addressed.

Chapter 11

Dealing with Employee Benefits in Mergers and Acquisitions

One of the most complex areas of merger and acquisition work is the handling of employee benefit issues. These plans can be a source of major off–balance sheet liabilities that must be dealt with by the parties to the transaction. In some situations, employee benefit plans will dictate whether the transaction will be structured as a sale of stock or a sale of assets. In more extreme cases, employee benefit plans (and their corresponding liabilities) may be the reason that a deal falls through. In still other situations employee benefit plans can be used as a major tool to accomplish the transaction.

TYPES OF BENEFIT PLANS

There are four major types of employee benefit plans. Each of these categories of plans will be discussed in more detail as follows:

Defined-Contribution Plans

You are probably most familiar with defined-contribution plans, which are referred to as profit sharing plans, thrift, or savings plans, money purchase pension plans, stock bonus plans, employee stock ownership plans, and cash or deferred profit sharing plans. Each of these plans is considered to be a "qualifed" plan under the provisions of Section 401 (a) of the Internal Revenue Code of 1954, as amended (the "IRC" or "Code").

These plans are characterized by the fact that each participant has an individual account that records his or her total interest in the plan assets.

As contributions are made to the plan, they are allocated among the participants in accordance with plan rules and credited to the bookkeeping accounts in the name of the individual participants. When an employee retires or terminates his or her employment, the amount of his or her benefits under the plan are determined solely on the basis of amounts then credited to his or her account.

Because the accounts of participants only reflect amounts actually held on their behalf by the plan's trustees, defined-contribution plans do not involve the possibility of unfunded past service liabilities. The most significant liability involved with these plans will generally be the liability for the contribution to the plan for the current year and, if it has not yet been made, the prior year.

Defined-Benefit Plans

Defined-benefit plans are pension plans that base the benefits payable to plan participants upon a formula contained in the plan. The formula will usually involve factors such as the age and service of the employee at the time he or she retires, as well as salary. The benefits under the plan are normally payable as a joint and survivor annuity to a married participant or a single life annuity to an unmarried one.

These types of plans are not funded using individual accounts, due to the nature of the promised benefit. Instead, the plan is funded on a group basis as a result of the calculations of an actuary. While there are minimum standards for the funding of this type of plan, they do not guarantee that the plan will have enough assets to cover the accrued benefits to date. In fact, defined-benefit plans can have large amounts of unfunded accrued benefits or can have large surpluses in funding.

Welfare Benefit Plans

Welfare benefit plans cover such plan types as hospitalization, surgical and major medical, life insurance plans, short- and long-term disability benefits, salary continuation plans, medical reimbursement plans, severance policies, group legal services, cafeteria (multiple-option) plans, and the like. If a plan covers a broad group of employees and is not a defined-contribution or defined-benefit plan, then it is probably a welfare benefit plan.

These plans are often funded through the purchase of insurance. However, many employers (especially large corporations) self-insure or self-fund some or all of these benefits and handle the payment of benefits on a "pay-as-you-go" basis. Other employers fund the benefits through the use of a trust fund established under Section 501(c) (9) of the IRC. These trusts may be overfunded or underfunded depending on the strategy of the employer and the benefits promised under the plan. As a consequence, there can be major hidden assets or liabilities that must be carefully reviewed before your merger or acquisition is finalized.

If the target company has post-retirement benefits (such as retiree medical, dental, or group life insurance plans), it is common for these benefits to be unfunded. They can represent a huge liability of the business to be acquired and must be carefully understood as well.

Another welfare-type plan that can have a substantial unfunded liability is a company's severance pay plan or policy. It is important to scrutinize the severance pay plan or policy of the target company to ensure that the simple fact of the sale of assets or stock does not automatically trigger the payment of severance to all employees.

Executive Compensation Plans

Executive compensation programs typically include deferred compensation plans, "top hat" plans, supplemental pension arrangements, extra life insurance, split-dollar life insurance and post-retirement life and medical/dental insurance. They also include various types of stock plans (e.g., stock options, restricted stock, stock appreciation rights, phantom stock, and executive stock purchase programs). Executives also typically have employment contracts that provide for specified benefits and payments upon a "change in control." These plans and programs need to be explored and understood during the due diligence phase of your transactions so that you fully understand the liabilities and substantial enhancements to pay and benefits that may be triggered as a result of the transaction.

TECHNIQUES FOR DEALING WITH TARGET COMPANY PLANS

In order to achieve your company's objectives for the merger or acquisition, you will want to consider the options available for dealing with employee benefit plans following the finalization of the transaction. Following is a summary of the chief techniques available:

Adoption of the Target Company's Plan "As Is"

It is possible for the purchaser to adopt the target company's plan "as is." The seller should represent and warrant the funding status of the plan and the price should be adjusted for any unfunded accrued liabilities. The parties should be precise as to what liabilities and responsibilities are being assumed so that prior legal violations remain the responsibility of the seller. The parties should also agree as to the division of responsibilities between the buyer and the seller with respect to the current plan year and the preceding plan year to the extent that they remain to be done (e.g., filing of Form 5500's, plan audits, etc.).

Even if the transaction is a sale of assets, the buyer cannot refuse to accept the responsibility for prior COBRA violations if it assumes the buyer's plan. If there were any violations, the buyer has until the end of the year following the acquisition to cure them. If it does not, the purchaser becomes liable for them. In order to avoid responsibility for unknown COBRA violations, the purchaser should consider not adopting the medical plans of the seller in an asset transaction.

If, however, the deal is structured as a stock purchase or statutory merger, the buyer cannot avoid responsibility for the prior operation of the plan. Accordingly, the purchase agreement should contain the necessary representations and warranties that the operations of the plan have conformed to all requirements of law. In addition, the purchaser must be careful to ensure that current contributions to the plan are reflected in the financial statements of the target company or that there is a special adjustment in the price for them.

Adoption of the Plan with Modifications

The plan's benefit formula can be changed to reflect the purchaser's ideas as to plan design or strategy, or the definition of eligible employees can be revised to reflect changes as well. Some sellers will request that a plan become fully vested on the sale to protect plan participants from possible forfeiture if the new owner terminates them. Some companies will even add or expand plan features prior to the sale in order to protect the employees of the selling company.

Plan Spin-off or Split-up

It is often the case that employees of the acquired business are covered by a plan that covers other company employees who are not part of the sale. In that event, the parties can divide the plan into two distinct plans, with the plan for the acquired company being adopted by the buyer while the plan for the rest of the seller's operations remaining the seller's responsibility.

Spin-offs of plans with individual accounts are relatively simple. The accounts of the seller are transferred to the spun-off plan. However, plans without individual accounts are more complex and will require actuarial calculations to accomplish a spin-off.

Plan Merger

If a merger involves two defined-contribution plans, the rules simply require that the account balances of each participant in the new plan be the same as their respective account balances in the two predecessor plans immediately prior to the merger. If the merger involves two defined-benefit pension plans, the participants must be protected from getting less, should the new plan terminate within the next five years, than they would have received if the two prior plans had terminated immediately prior to the merger. There are no such rules that apply to the merger of two welfare plans.

Plan Freezes

The target company's plans can also be "frozen" either as to future eligibility or future accruals, or both. If frozen as to eligibility, no new employees are permitted to enter the plan. If accruals are frozen, participants must be given prior notice of at least 15 days and will not earn future benefits under the plan.

Nonadoption of the Plan

When a plan is not transferred to a buyer, the sale normally causes a termination of employment of the employees of the acquired company under the plan. To avoid premature forfeiture problems, the buyer and seller usually agree on one of two major approaches: (1) the employees who are transferred to the buyer become fully vested under the seller's plan regardless of length of service; or (2) the seller's plan counts service with the buyer for purposes of vesting.

If a purchaser fails to adopt the seller's medical plan, a COBRA event will generally occur and require the seller to provide notices to employees and their beneficiaries to allow them to elect COBRA continuation coverage. This is a wasted effort since most buyers will be providing their own plan coverage to employees after the sale. It is therefore important that the purchase agreement assure no gap of coverage so that COBRA notice and continuation coverage is not required.

Severance pay plans are another source of potential problems. Some courts have ruled that if the purchaser does not adopt the severance plan, the rights of employees to severance pay will be forever lost if the sale of the business does not trigger the payout. As a result, sellers may want to require that buyers adopt the seller's severance plan or at least an equivalent plan.

Clone-Offset Plan

The purchaser may want to adopt a similar plan for employees so employees continue to be covered by equivalent benefit formulas. The new plan generally is identical to the seller's plan and gives employees credit for service with the seller for benefits and vesting purposes. So that there is no duplication of benefits, the buyer's plan offsets its benefit by any vested benefits payable under the seller's plan. These types of plans are eligible for a "safe harbor" design under Section 401(a) (4).

Plan Termination

A purchaser may not want to adopt a defined-benefit pension plan or a retiree medical plan because of large unfunded liabilities or simply because it does not fit with the buyer's benefits strategy.

If a seller terminates a qualified retirement plan, the employees will be fully vested in their accrued benefits to the extent that they are funded. If a plan is terminated after the sale is finalized, problems can result. For example, if the seller has transferred an overfunded plan to the buyer with the expectation that it will be continued, the termination of the plan could result in a windfall to the buyer. In contrast, if the seller has not transferred the plan to the buyer but has agreed to give employees credit for service with the buyer for purposes of vesting and eligibility, the termination of the plan by the seller could result in employees receiving reduced benefits under the seller's plan. To avoid these problems, it is recommended that the purchaser require the seller not to terminate the plan as to the buyer's employees unless their fully accrued benefits are funded.

Plan terminations can also be partial in nature because of the sale of a division or subsidiary. If the division or subsidiary being sold represents 20% or more of the covered employees under the plan, then the sale will be deemed a partial termination.

OTHER CONSIDERATIONS

Structure of the Deal

Most employee benefit plan considerations will not dictate the structure of a merger or acquisition. However, if a seller faces a potentially large withdrawal liability with respect to a multiemployer pension plan, then the seller may insist on the sale of stock rather than assets. In contrast, if a buyer does not want to inherit a burdensome plan from the seller, the buyer may require a sale of assets. Uncertainty of the taxation of employee benefits plans in asset transactions may cause both parties to prefer a stock deal.

Impact on Purchase Price

To the extent that an employee benefit plan involves a liability of the business, it should decrease the purchase price. To the extent that the plan represents a hidden asset, the purchase price should be adjusted upward.

The accounting rules for pension plans are contained in Statements 87 and 88 of the Financial Accounting Standards Board. FAS 87 and 88 require all or part of the unfunded liabilities of a defined-benefit pension plan to be reflected on the financial statements of the employer. However, this is reflected as an intangible asset on the balance sheet in an amount equal to the initial unfunded liaiblity. Do not be misled though—this is a "bogus" number and does not represent any true asset of the company.

Buyers should also look for off–balance sheet liabilities, as these can represent a hidden asset, particularly when a plan is overfunded. A new way to utilize surplus pension assets is to transfer a portion of the surplus to pay retiree medical benefits on a completely tax free basis. This may be an attractive option to those employers with large unfunded retiree medical liabilities and an overfunded pension plan.

Letter of Intent

Any letter of intent to purchase a target company should be prepared with extreme caution. If the buyer has not reviewed the target company's plans yet, it should condition any agreement to assume employee benefit plans on them being sufficiently well funded. There should be enough assets to both cover the projected benefit obligations of the plan under FAS 87 and 88 and to maintain the current levels of employer contributions.

Due Diligence

The investigative phase of the transaction is an important one. From a strict financial standpoint no area deserves more attention than employee benefits and their corresponding liabilities. All relevant plan documents should be reviewed as well as the summary plan descriptions, any plan audit reports, actuarial reports, collective bargaining agreements, summary annual reports, financial statements, Form 5500s, non-discrimination testing reports, COBRA compliance, and the like.

Purchase Agreement

The purchase agreement should contain detailed and explicit provisions with respect to the handling of employee benefits. If responsibility for a benefit program has been divided between the purchaser and the seller, it is far easier to have a fair division of the responsibility if it is negotiated in advance. Buyers rarely get significant concessions from a seller after the deal has closed.

CONCLUSIONS

Liabilities with respect to employee benefit plans have become less and less contingent and can no longer be erased simply by a plan termination. Accordingly, the treatment of employee benefit plans in mergers and acquisitions has become even more important than ever before. Both purchasers and sellers should take special precautions to carefully understand the potential pitfalls and problems associated with the employee benefit plans during a deal. And, through the negotiation process, each side should work to carefully craft the division of responsibilities and liabilities so that there are no future misunderstandings or problems for either company or their employees.

Chapter 12

Compensation Alternatives (Linking Pay to the New Business Strategy)

One of the best indicators of an organization's values, beliefs, and operating philosophy is how it rewards its employees. An early review of a company's compensation programs—everything from its base pay system to its strategy for bonus or profit sharing to its performance management process—can provide early warning signals of potential cultural conflict in a contemplated merger or acquisition. And immediate changes to these systems can set the tone for the future of the newly merged organization.

EMPLOYEE COMPENSATION

At the outset of a merger or acquisition, it will be necessary for the HR team to review the basic components of the other company's pay and bonus system. Components of the system include a review of things such as

- base pay,
- profit sharing, bonus, or gain-sharing programs,
- stock option grants, and
- retention bonus practices.

Once the "current state" of the organization has been analyzed and is understood, a discussion about the behaviors that your company wishes to promote and encourage needs to occur. This high level discussion will include a "blue sky" overview of the type of culture and organizational dynamics that the new company wants to create. For example, what characteristics do you want to promote?

- risk-taking/risk-averse
- flexible and informal/inflexible and formal
- decentralized/centralized
- results-oriented/people-oriented

How do these characteristics come into play? Let's take risk tolerance. If you want to create a risk-taking environment, your bonus system will have significant upside and downside risk, your variable pay program will be a high percentage of your total compensation package, and your executive pay program will be tied to shareholder value. Contrast that to a risk-averse environment in which bonuses have little upside and downside risk (e.g., not much focus on this aspect of the pay package, there is a low percentage of total compensation tied to variable pay, and executive compensation is not tied to shareholder value).

If you want to create a flexible and informal pay system, you would likely see

- many ad hoc programs,
- many exceptions,
- few job descriptions,
- general policy guidelines, but no handbooks,
- few signoffs required to approve changes, and
- a market pricing job evaluation system.

To create a decentralized organizational environment, authority would likely be found in the divisions (as opposed to the corporate center), there would be a small corporate staff, few corporate-wide policies, salary budget and pay levels controlled by the divisions, and bonus payouts based on division results.

If your goal is to create a people-oriented pay system, you would likely create many "entitlements", there would be narrow variations between employees in terms of merit increases and bonus payouts, retirement contributions would not be based on company results, there would be many seniority benefits, and you would likely see fairness defined as "consistent" application of policies and practices.

PAY SYSTEM ALTERNATIVES

Compensation is a real key to understanding an organization's hidden personality and, more importantly, is the best predictor of whether two organizations involved in a merger or acquisition will be compatible. When considering the type of new pay and bonus system to implement following a transaction, you will need to explore the various alternatives that exist. These include

- *Broadbanding*—a flexible and wide range of pay that involves a high degree of management subjectivity in determining the appropriate pay level for a specific job. This type of system eliminates a great deal of administrative detail and allows managers to be very flexible in paying for skills and abilities through a broad salary range.
- *Hybrid Broadbanding*—involves a pay range that is not quite so broad and flexible as a true broadbanding system, but which is similar in terms of management flexibility.
- *Market-Based System*—a system of pay which involves frequent assessments of the competitive marketplace to determine appropriate pay levels.
- *Skill-Based Pay*—involves a creative system of paying employees for their specific or unique skills and is particularly useful in an environment where employees move from one assignment to another (e.g., software development companies, consulting and other advisory environments, engineering and architectural firms, etc.).
- *Whole Job Ranking Analysis*—involves reviewing each job and ranking it in terms of the organizational whole to determine its relative worth.
- *"Hay Point" Evaluation*—involves ranking each job based on a series of points determined by an assessment of the position's requirements relative to knowledge, skills, and abilities required.
- *Job Slotting to Market*—a system which includes a subjective assessment of a position and a slotting of the job into a predetermined pay range.
- *Job Grades*—involves making an independent decision as to the grade into which each job should fall based on the importance to the organization.

The compensation system and philosophy selected will have a major impact on the type of environment that is created at the outset of the transaction. The pay system is of great concern to most employees, particularly if the systems of the two combining organizations are very different. There will be cries of "foul" and "inequity" if the systems are not merged quickly and if compensation levels are not evened out early.

If economics do not allow pay levels to be normalized quickly, there should be a two- to three-year plan to do so that is announced to employees soon after the transaction is completed. An early announcement of the plan to "equalize" and "unify" pay levels so that similar jobs are paid at roughly equivalent levels across the new organization will greatly reduce the dissatisfaction that is commonly experienced by employees when no information is made public about the company's intent in this regard. An early decision and announcement will also have the helpful effect of reducing employee apprehension and mistrust about the very personal and emotional issue of pay.

PROFIT SHARING AND BONUS PROGRAMS

In addition to pay levels and systems, you will also need to review the current state of your bonus or profit-sharing plans and programs. Questions will need to be asked about your future philosophy. For example, do you want to be decentralized or centralized? Are you trying to drive a "one-company" concept or are the business units intended to be stand-alone operations? The answers to these questions will significantly impact the type of bonus programs that you will design going forward.

In our experience, we have seen a "transitional" bonus plan be installed with great success. This is typically a "one-time" special program that is implemented to achieve and further the synergies and "value drivers" of the transaction. It is a program that rewards the quick success and achievement of the merger synergies and that helps to galvanize employees to quickly integrate the companies where possible.

Program metrics can include a specific listing of the key synergies with a percentage payout based upon a subjective (or quantifiable) level of achievement at year-end. This type of program sends a signal to employees that rewards are tied to the success of the new organization, not the company from which they came. It focuses employee efforts on the "drivers" of the transaction and can create a feeling of success and positive momentum throughout the organization.

Another type of bonus program that can be effective immediately post-transaction is what is commonly known as a "spot" bonus program. This is a program that allocates a total budget pool to department heads for their distribution to employees throughout the year. Actual allocations typically range from $100 to $5,000, with most awards falling in the $500 to $1,000 range.

Spot bonuses are based on key behaviors that the new organization wishes to reinforce. These key reward components can include such things as

- teamwork,
- collaboration among departments or workgroups,
- positive contribution to the new culture,
- significant business results (e.g., cost reduction, revenue enhancement, etc.),
- development of new products/practices that further the strategy of the new company,
- innovation and creativity,

- results that are "above and beyond" what might reasonably be expected from an employee, and
- other key characteristics and behaviors that reinforce the new company's goals and objectives.

These "spot" bonuses give the department managers who are closest to the action the ability to reward employee behavior "on the spot" and immediately. This type of bonus plan can serve as a strong reinforcement of the type of behaviors and results that the new company wants to reward. It also sends a strong message that the new company is in touch and interested in employee results and willing to spend the time, effort, and money to say so. Given that early impressions are critical, this type of program can initiate the new relationship with employees from the other firm with some positive momentum and a show of caring.

EXECUTIVE COMPENSATION

The issues relevant to executive compensation are very similar to those discussed above but should be expanded to include a review of several other issues including

- *Employment Contracts*—Is it typical for executives and key managers to have an employment agreement that provides for some security and stability among the senior management team?
- *Restricted Stock*—Many companies offer senior executives restricted stock grants that have restrictions that fall away upon the meeting of certain performance or financial objectives.
- *Performance Shares*—Is it appropriate to consider a grant of performance shares to top level management which have targeted financial objectives over a three- to four-year period?
- *Retention Bonus*—Are there certain key positions that warrant the implementation of a special retention package that pays off if an executive stays with the company for a specific period of time? Is such a bonus necessary to rerecruit key people and let them know of their value to the new company and its management? Are there certain positions that, if the individual officer or executive should exit, would leave the company extremely vulnerable and/or would negatively impact the company's strategy or the achievement of the synergies of the deal? If so, then a retention bonus should be carefully considered.
- *Stock Options*—Is an additional grant of stock options necessary to align the objectives of the new management team with the focus and strategy of the combined company? Should a "mega-grant" be considered which would provide for a significant financial gain to the affected individuals if the company meets its goals and objectives in short order?

ALTERNATIVES TO COMPENSATION

In addition to the standard pay and bonus review that most companies typically consider, there are other nontraditional ways to compensate people as well. To meet the changing needs of your workplace, you might appeal to their personal needs for both time and development. Among the most successful programs in this regard are

- *Employee Training*—Employees are generally hungry for a career path and development of their skills and abilities so that they do not get stale. Through the use of both in-house and external training programs, employers can offer a significant addition to an employee's pay without the unacceptable fixed-cost entitlement programs of the past.

- *Tuition Reimbursement*—Employers gain through the increased skills and education of their employees while employees gain more knowledge, remain marketable, and increase their loyalty and career commitment to the company sponsoring their education.

- *Flexible Work Arrangements*—Many companies have peak work hours that coincide better with split shift, part-time and flextime work hours. Employees have personal needs as well that militate toward offering nontraditional hours.

- *Worker-Friendly/Family-Friendly Work Environments*—Programs that attract and help to retain employees center around the growing diversity of workers and lifestyle requirements. Included in these worker/family-friendly programs are family leave programs, well-baby programs, lactation rooms, day care centers, elder care referral programs, child referral programs, financial counseling, and wellness programs, including fitness centers and company-sponsored physicals each year.

- *Perquisites, Amenities, and Conveniences*—Many family-friendly conveniences are being offered at work to improve employee productivity, assist in recruiting, and lessen turnover for logistical reasons. These include convenience services on location (shoe repair, dry cleaning, meal purchasing, film development, etc), laptop computers, computers, phones, fax, software for home computers, car services for off-hour travel, financial planning seminars, investment education and scholarship referral services.

COMMUNICATION OF THE NEW PROGRAM

With both employees and executives, it is important to communicate the philosophy of the new company's pay system as well as the components (e.g., the "nuts and bolts" of how it operates) early in the game. A quick decision about the emotional issue of pay will reduce employee anxiety and fear and give employees a sense that the new company is focused on internal equity and the equalization of pay levels quickly.

Developing a common compensation strategy also promotes a sense of unity: "We are truly in this together." Despite the best of intents, however, it is unlikely that most companies can "normalize" very different pay strategies overnight. More common is the development of a two- to three-year strategy to address the pay issues and to develop a common range of pay levels for jobs across the organization.

Early communication of both the philosophy and strategic plan for compensation is advisable. Communication can come through letters to employees, face-to-face employee meetings, intranet updates, cosponsored HR and supervisory sessions where employees can ask questions both of their immediate supervisor as well as the HR representative, and the like.

A multitude of various methodologies is recommended for the delivery of your communications, though. People hear a message in different ways. Some of us are more visual, some more auditory, and some need to get information in a combination of forms to really understand. A combination of the written word, meetings, and one-on-one discussions with supervisors is generally the course that leads to the most positive outcome: *employees who really understand why the system is changing and what's in it for them.*

Chapter 13

Methods to Measure HR Success

In order to know whether or not HR is delivering on the strategies outlined in the previous chapters, practitioners need measures and metrics to make the business case as to effectiveness. Metrics are essential to demonstrate the value of an organization's human capital and HR practices to internal stakeholders; however, many HR practitioners are reluctant to use such measures.

Senior management lives or dies "by the numbers" after the completion of a merger or acquisition. Jobs are won and lost as a result of key financial measures post-deal. Increasingly, the feeling expressed among executives is that if human resources really wants to be a business partner, then it too must be judged by similar standards.

Why are HR professionals so reluctant to quantify their results? Because the idea of quantifying what is in the hearts and minds of people runs counter to the basic values of many. Some people feel that measuring people and their feelings as if they were products is distasteful or even wrong. Unlike financial data and analysis, HR data is generally derived from softer, qualitative sources such as employee surveys or focus groups. Some would argue that this data is less exacting and less precise, and therefore less reliable than other "hard" information.

Oftentimes, people who fill HR positions are people who *like* people and who are not particularly interested in learning how the business operates or supporting the company's business strategy. They were moved into the job for the wrong reasons and sometimes lack the skills necessary to add the "science" to the HR function—so they resist quantification, arguing that the organization should make decisions based on "what's right" or "based on instinct" or "gut reactions."

While this approach may have been viewed as sufficient in the past, a less than proactive approach will not, however, cut it for the future. Concern about whether or not HR programs or practices will measure up is no reason to avoid finding out whether or not, in fact, they do. Knowledge of measurements, formulas and ratios can give HR practitioners added credibility with line managers and can help HR personnel be perceived as part of the business, not just "staff" or "overhead."

Metrics are a tangible way of demonstrating the value of the HR function to non-HR people in your organization. Developing measurements can also help you justify the good business sense of focusing on the people in your new organization.

If you can demonstrate a bottom-line benefit for training and development initiatives, for developing the culture, for soliciting employee input, and the like, you will be better able to obtain the necessary resources—not just capital, but human talent as well. A sound strategy to measure your success in dealing with the post-deal people side of any merger or acquisition includes three key components:

EFFICIENCY METRICS

Efficiency measurements are the basic building block of any metrics program that you might consider adopting. These are the measures that allow you to consider how you are doing in the basic areas of people development: turnover, terminations (both voluntary and involuntary), average job tenure, average length of time to recruit new hires, costs per hire, absenteeism, employee productivity, and intellectual capital.

The Saratoga Institute is a leader in benchmarking and regularly conducts an annual survey of 25 industries, reviewing between 60 and 70 metrics. The results that they find are sorted by industry, company size and geographic region. In the United States, nearly 1,000 companies participate and the report is available for roughly $2,000 each year.[1]

STRATEGIC METRICS

Although efficiency metrics are useful and can indicate trends and issues that need to be further considered, sometimes such metrics can be used out of context without looking at the value creation side of things. For example, you cannot really tell if a turnover rate is good or bad. You can decrease your turnover rate by hiring people who will never leave, but that is not necessarily good.

It is important to focus on strategy before you decide what you will measure and before you target a need to beat your industry benchmarks. It makes good business sense to think about the logic of where the organization is going, not just the measurement.

The key is to develop unique metrics that assess strategic value and effectiveness, not just efficiency.[2] Sound measures center around quality, efficiency, and service. You might use five key factors that can be applied to anything you elect to measure: the cost, the time to do it, the quantity involved, the quality involved, and the human reaction.

Apply this five-factor framework to staffing. You can measure the costs, the time it takes to fill a position, the number of requisitions, the quality of the new hires, and the satisfaction of the hiring manager with the process.

RETURN ON INVESTMENT METRICS

In addition to efficiency and strategic metrics, human resources should look toward a variations on the typical financial metrics. Return on Investment (or "ROI") is becoming a widely used measurement to demonstrate the financial viability of many critical HR initiatives. This ratio is calculated by assigning monetary value to an HR program and dividing the value by the program's costs.

10 KEY HUMAN CAPITAL METRICS

While there is no "magic bullet" or set of metrics that is appropriate for every company, there are several generally accepted HR metrics that should be considered as tools for quantifying how you are actually using your human resources and how you rate at implementing your HR responsibilities.

These common HR metrics include the following:

1. Revenue Factor $= \dfrac{\text{Revenue}}{\text{Total FTE}}$

(FTE = full-time equivalents: regular employees plus contingent labor)

This is the basic measure understood by managers.

2. Human Capital Value Added =

Revenue − (Operating Expense − $\dfrac{[\text{Compensation Cost} + \text{Benefit Cost}])}{\text{Total FTE}}$

This is the prime measure of people's contributions to an organization. It answers the question: What are people worth?

3. Voluntary Separation Rate $= \dfrac{\text{Voluntary Separations}}{\text{Headcount}}$

This represents potential lost opportunity, lost revenue, and more highly stressed employees who have to fill in for departed colleagues.

4. Human Capital ROI =

$$\text{Revenue} - (\text{Operating Expense} - \frac{[\text{Compensation Cost} + \text{Benefit Cost}])}{(\text{Compensation Cost} - \text{Benefit Cost})}$$

This is a ratio of dollars spent on pay and benefits to an adjusted profit figure.

5. Total Compensation Revenue Percent =

$$\frac{\text{Compensation Cost} + \text{Benefit Cost}}{\text{Revenue}}$$

If you monitor pay and benefits in comparison to revenue per employee, you can see the return on your investment.

6. Total Labor Cost Revenue Percent =

$$\frac{\text{Compensation Cost} + \text{Benefit Cost} + \text{Other Labor Cost}}{\text{Revenue}}$$

This allows you to see the complete cost of human capital.

7. Training Investment Factor = $\frac{\text{Total training cost}}{\text{Headcount}}$

8. Cost Per Hire = (Advertising + Agency Fees + Employee Referrals + Travel Cost + Relocation Costs + Recruiter Pay/Benefits) / Operating Expenses

9. Health Care Costs per Employee = $\frac{\text{Total Cost of Health Care Benefits}}{\text{Total Employees}}$

10. Turnover Costs = (Costs to Terminate + Cost per Hire + Vacancy Cost + Learning Curve Loss)

The downside of using metrics is that it can lead to a focus on measurement to the detriment of the people side of the business. Too much financial focus can snuff out creativity and innovation. However, the drive for financial accountability and quantitative assessment is a critical issue with companies and their boards. We in human resources need to be the experts in valuing human capital, and metrics are a way to demonstrate how we are doing in this regard.[3]

NOTES

1. See www.saratogainstitute.com.

2. For an exhaustive new study of the metrics that appear to have the most potential for ongoing use, see Brian E. Becker, Mark A. Huselid, and David Ulrich, *The HR Scorecard: Linking People, Strategy, and Performance* (Harvard Business School Press, 2001).

3. M. G. Singer and M. J. Fleming (eds.), *Effective Human Resource Measurement Techniques: A Handbook for Practitioners* (Society for Human Resources Management, 1997).

Chapter 14

Why Some Mergers Succeed
(And How Yours Can Too)

It is easy to criticize and find fault with M&A situations that have not gone well, but much harder to determine why some companies succeed in integrating two previously separate companies where most fail.

PRIMARY REASONS FOR INTEGRATION SUCCESS

In a nutshell, the primary reasons for integration success include:

Knowledge of the Target Company and Its Business

You need to know what you're buying—and what you're buying into—from every perspective that's pertinent to the deal. The CEO, CFO, financial analysts, and investment bankers will all undoubtedly have perspectives about the value and potential synergies from a business strategy and financial standpoint. But in order for the value to be realized, the package as a whole is going to have to work—people, systems, technology, and all the rest.

In any complex situation there are *multiple valid realities*, that is, different ways of seeing and understanding the same information accurately. Problems arise, in part, because people tend to see things from only their own perspective and to assume that there perception represents all that is valid or important. Making a deal really work requires getting beyond this to address all of the issues on which the creation or realization of value actually rest—every leverage point that could undermine things, all the way through the finalization of integration.

There needs to be clarity about the characteristics that have driven and shaped the organization—products, technology, or markets (or other useful descriptions of the business drivers). There also needs to be an understanding about how these characteristics have been supported through the structure and culture of the organization. What kinds of backgrounds and experience have most of the senior managers had (i.e., what spells out career success in this organization) and how have decisions been made? For each of these issues (and many more) there will be varying perspectives by people in your own organization. How, for instance, do the operations managers in your organization view the target company and what are their expectations about the integration process? How different is this from the views of finance, accounting, or law about the requirements and complexities involved?

Through thorough prescreening and extensive due diligence, you can carefully evaluate and understand the key drivers of potential merger success (or failure). Some of what needs to be accomplished is simply verification of information. Is what you been told about the cost factors for HR systems, such as benefits and pension plans, readily backed up by available data? At the other end of the spectrum lies an understanding of the human factors of the organization. Is this an organization with significant human capital potential? If so, what would it take to unleash it? By better understanding the processes, systems, and procedures in place in the target company, you will be better able to anticipate potential problem areas and establish plans for a successful integration.

Clarity of Acquisition Purpose/Vision for the Future

From within the many perspectives outlined above, there will be specific priorities around which a particular deal is framed—most typically those that justify the monetary value of it. When the strategic rationale supporting the decision to merge or acquire another entity is clearly articulated, employees will understand the key reasons for the deal and can more quickly "get on board" and support the transaction. (This may also help clarify those aspects of the deal that are seen from other perspectives, but possibly *not* by the decision makers of the deal.)

To the extent that the future vision and strategic direction of the deal is clear and straightforward, employees can more quickly adjust and start moving to support the underlying goals and objectives of the transaction. Clarity about the "larger picture" of the deal can also be very useful in providing guidance to resolve conflicts about specific decisions regarding change, within a given department, for instance (rather than leave these to be determined through "petty politics," as sometimes happens).

A Clear Understanding of "Value Drivers"

If you base your transactions on the idea that 20% of the actions will drive 80% of the value with the greatest probability of success in the shortest time frame, then you have the potential to be vastly more successful in your integration effort. Despite what may seem to be an overwhelming number of details that *should* be covered in a merger or transaction, as outlined in this book, we do understand that there will almost always be more work in shorter timelines than there are hands to do it. By focusing on the *organization's* goals for each deal, and the value drivers most necessary to accomplish them, you can better identify the leverage points that will create the most return for the energy invested. (There will always be many urgent demands, and everyone will assume that theirs is the most crucial, but some issues will penetrate to the heart of what is likely to make or break a deal down the road and addressing those may resolve a host of others.) Quick "wins" generate positive momentum among employees that can generate enthusiasm and optimism for the deal. Such energy can translate into additional synergies and productivity that was not even anticipated at the outset of the transaction.

Along with the key "value drivers" of the deal, you need to communicate the key actions and accountabilities and a timeline for achieving these actions. This will build a commitment to the plan and will help spark a sense of urgency among employees to "get it done" now.

Ensuring a Good Cultural "Fit"

The due diligence effort should include a great deal of focus on the cultural compatibility of the two entities. This includes a look at such issues as management style, operating philosophy, policies, practices, processes, communication style, employee relations climate, and the like. The question of "fit," of course, necessitates understanding the culture of your own organization as well as that of the other. Anticipating compliments and conflicts between these requires attempting an objective look at both, and the ways in which they might affect each other—for good and for ill.

Initially, this information about cultural fit can simply "play in the background" as you move through the early details of the deal, sensitizing you to specific questions or concerns. As your impressions are verified or changed along the way, this information becomes critical to the integration processes, and programs to assist in transitions.

Detailed Post-Acquisition Plans

Prior to the close of the transaction, well-developed post-acquisition plans should be created so that you have a clear strategy and action plan for the critical first 100 days after the ink dries. Employees expect and anticipate a great deal of decision making and change to occur during this period and are most receptive to adapting during this time. A well-developed plan indicates to employees that the acquiring company has its "act together," and such a plan can generate some confidence by employees in the new management team.

Rapid Integration

Companies with the best histories of merger success are those who succeed in rapid integration. They ensure sufficient financial and human resources are devoted to the integration process and that all key players are focused on short-term "value drivers" that have the best potential for big payoffs. They also make sure that everyone involved has a sense of urgency about the need for a quick integration in order to be successful. In our experience, no executive has ever looked back on a deal and wished to do it slower—speed is of the essence. *The faster you go, the better your chances of success.*

Early "Re-Recruitment" and Appointment of Key Executives

All employees need to be "re-recruited" to the new team following the closing of the deal, and none any more than members of the senior management team. The acquiring firm should conduct a variety of one-on-one visits with key employees to talk about their future role with the company and the company's confidence in their abilities, and to address the "me" issues early on (e.g., relocation, pay, benefits, bonuses, etc.) Without these types of conversations, key players can wrongly assume that they are not considered important to the new company and can quickly jump ship.

Expedited and Focused Decision Making

There is never a more important time than the post-closure period to make decisions quickly and get the word out. Employees are anxious and looking for all the information that they can learn about the new company. The more decisions that are made early in the process, the more confidence and enthusiasm employees will have in the new management structure.

Frequent and Candid Employee Communications

Frequent two-way communication with employees is critical to ensure merger success. Employees are generally starved for information post-closure and will read or listen to any and all information about the new company, especially regarding long-term direction and strategic goals. Employees also want to assess for themselves the candor and credibility of the new management team, which can best happen through face-to-face meetings in small groups throughout the company.

Focused Transition Teams and Integration Process

Transition teams that have specific goals and a short timetable are critical. The process of integrating two companies needs to be well thought through and organized with a principal integration leader who has real decision-making power.

Fair and Impartial Employee Selection Process

Employees will be highly skeptical of any new transfers or appointments. The process of selecting who stays, who goes, and who "wins" is very important in establishing credibility among employees. If the process appears politicized or one-sided, employees will be turned off very early, and it will be hard for management to regain a firm basis of trust.

Celebration of Early Wins

In order to generate maximum momentum, onging results need to be announced regularly and employee and company successes celebrated. If the rationale for the deal has been made clear, the value drivers most critical to its success outlined, and plans for their implementation put into action, then celebrating results only acknowledges and reinforces each of these.

Move Cautiously on Cost Cutting and People Reductions

It takes some time to learn who the key players are, so don't move too quickly to reduce the workforce. If reductions are made too early, based entirely on cost estimates, there is no flexibility for adjustments as new opportunities may emerge in the midst of the deal. (And at the current pace of such deals, new opportunities might emerge from successive deals that are already in the works.) Also, first choices of employees to fill key positions don't always work out as hoped (e.g., some opting for alternative opportunities), and these can create domino effects, necessitating additional changes and decisions. Understand the strengths and weaknesses of key employees, learn the organization and how it works, and then make decisions.

The need for caution and conservatism does not, by the way, negate suggestions about the need for speed. Once decisions *are* clear, key people in place, and staffing needs determined, people will be ready to move on—both those who will stay and those who will not.

Reward Key People for Results

Successes should be recognized through bonuses, stock options, and other reward mechanisms. Visible rewards signal a sense of urgency for achieving results and give people a personal reason to want to achieve the organizational goals.

It is important that recognition *not* stop at the organizational levels usually entitled to company perks unless the desired message is that these are the only persons expected to achieve results and contribute to making the deal work. Times of transition are often opportunities for new faces to emerge, and the efforts and activities that merit recognition are often noted widely throughout an organization.

Sensitivity to Acquired Employees

Acquiring companies need to show respect, compassion, and fairness to the employees of the acquired company. If you fail to show respect for their heritage and history, you will quickly lose any hope of building a solid relationship for the future.

Institutionalize New Processes/Methodologies

Act quickly to implement new policies, processes, and procedures to begin the integration process and start the change process. Employees are more adaptive early after the close of the deal than they will be months after it is growing more familiar.

It is very difficult to be creative and maintain enthusiasm during the intensity and pressures of a merger or acquisition. Too many demands keep us from exploring unfamiliar solutions or from studying the mistakes of the past that could, if perceived, help us to avoid them.

Consider the opening lines in A. A. Milne's classic, *Winnie-the-Pooh*:

Here is Edward Bear, coming downstairs now: bump, bump, bump, on the back of his head, behind Christopher Robin. It is, as far as he knows, the only way of coming downstairs, but sometimes he feels that there really is another way, if only he could stop bumping for a moment and think of it.

It is our hope that the information provided in this book will provide you an opportunity for a broader perspective, an alternative to simply being driven by immediate and unfocused demands, and a chance to avoid the fate of Edward Bear. Both you and your company's employees deserve better.

Chapter 15

Some Stories of Mergers
and Acquisitions

In this final chapter, we'd like to present some stories from our own experiences with mergers and acquisitions, as well as some of the thoughts and ideas that others have reported about these same companies. Rather than trying to cover the whole spectrum of possible transaction types, though, we've decided to focus on a few examples that include a range of issues and numerous decades of history. The thought is to go somewhat further in depth than breadth, with the idea that in human experiences, what is *most* specific is often what is also *most* generic.

As will be noted, not only is the practice of mergers and acquisitions not a new occurrence, neither are the issues that tend to come with them. In fact, as noted in a CEO speech as far back as 1956:

Every organization has in it much that is good and desirable, but each organization also has its weaknesses and peculiarities. A merger of two companies is far more than a financial transaction. . . . There are many problems inherent in the methods of expansion which we have used so extensively. . . . The feeling of personal insecurity often associated with mergers must be overcome. It must be replaced with the confidence that there will be greater opportunities and that every employee will be advanced without favoritism. Mergers must not result in stepchildren.

Mergers frequently require the reconciling of different philosophies of business. Planning and patience are necessary in order to avoid inequities to individuals and to protect personal pride. It is not easy to bring people who have been trained differently into a smoothly functioning team under a consolidated leadership. The acceptance of a certain amount of entrenched inefficiency must be necessary: likewise new talent must be recognized and rewarded. A period of months may be required in which to locate people into positions where their abilities may be utilized and their shortcomings minimized.[1]

PETROCO

Petroco (a pseudonym) began as one of many small independent oil refining operations of the early 1900s. By the end of the twentieth century, Petroco was the product of over 100 mergers, acquisitions, and joint ventures. This was in the context, though, of an industry that had been in existence since the mid-nineteenth century and that had already been through periods of significant consolidation and diversification.

The value of oil as a fuel was only discovered at the end of the 1850s, but this set off an "oil rush," which produced 25 active wells and 21 refineries in Pennsylvania alone by 1860.[2] John D. Rockefeller got into the oil business in the mid-1860s. By 1880, Standard Oil refined 90 to 95% of all the oil produced in the United States. It continued to gain strength in all aspects of the industry for several decades, buying up small independents or forcing them out of business. In 1911, Rockefeller's monopoly was finally dissolved, breaking the company into seven separate entities (to become known in the oil industry as the "seven sisters").

Petroco began with the purchase of a small refinery in need of much upgrade and repair by a young entrepreneur who learned the business as he went. The early days involved a great deal of turmoil, including periods of significant financial insecurity and competition with former allies who at one point hired about half of the young founder's best employees out from under him. According to the company's own history, the business survived primarily through the extremely hard work and dedication of the founder who was notorious for working long into the night and through weekends as well. He was also involved in the intricacies of the operations, spending a great deal of time with workers in the plant itself whom he came to trust and to treat as something of a large family. It was through these experiences of struggle and survival that the culture of Petroco was formed. (According to stories told by employees who remembered him, in addition to having no other interests or hobbies outside work, the founder also suffered from insomnia and would not infrequently call an operator at 2:00 or 3:00 A.M. to ask about the pressure or temperature on a certain piece of equipment and recommend an adjustment he thought necessary.)

The espoused values of Petroco's culture included extreme dedication and loyalty. These were exhibited through the "artifacts" of what might well today be considered workaholism. The driving forces behind such behavior could have been fear of failure, or personal ambition, or greed. But according to speeches given by the founder, his motivation was something more like the passion or intensity that drives a scientific researcher. In his mind, what drove a businessman were things like pride in his workmanship or the need to provide security to employees and their families or obligations to those who had invested their savings in the company.

The first note of any major cultural differences came as a result of a proposed merger between Petroco and a larger competitor in the late 1940s. Though larger, the competitor actually had lower net profits. And whereas Petroco was now a publicly traded company with many ties to the financial community, the competitor, though technically a public company, operated essentially as a partnership of the cofounders. But the differences appeared in many subtle ways, apparently, such that Petroco's founder noted that there was little resemblance in the character or the psychology of the two companies.

The differences were manifested in a dinner conversation in which Petroco's founder reacted to the enthusiasm of a member of the other company regarding vacations. Reportedly, Petroco's founder remarked that for Petroco, work was their "vocation, avocation, and vacation." Despite all the differences, the two companies completed the merger, apparently with Petroco's culture dominating.

The early 1950s marked significant milestones in Petroco's history. Acquisitions continued at a rapid pace bringing Petroco into a nationally prominent position. At the same time, doctors informed Petroco's founder that there were problems with his health, and the future leadership of the company was, for the first time, in question.

Despite the very directive style, typical of founding entrepreneurs, Petroco's management was based on a collaborative approach without distinct divisions of labor. (Everyone was expected to be fully devoted to work, was all.) A number of young executives had worked their way up through the ranks, including relatives of the founder. The commonality and experience helped to firmly fix the company's culture. Also typical of a founding entrepreneur, Petroco's founder continued to be actively involved in running the company despite his health issues, if more from a distance—spending more time at home, but apparently just as much time on the phone talking with employees about operational issues.

Loyalty appeared to work both ways, with the founder and managers taking a personal interest in the welfare of both employees and their families. Lavish celebrations were held at holidays and to recognize significant accomplishments. Social clubs were sponsored for both employees and spouses. And for many years, individual gifts were purchased and wrapped for each child of every employee in attendance at the annual Christmas party. It was a culture of complete involvement—and one very difficult to maintain *ad infinitum*.

According to other interviews, the younger executives carried on the legacies much as they had received them. Twelve- to eighteen-hour workdays were common, and work continued through the weekends. Growth continued primarily through acquisitions, expanding current operations, acquiring larger means of transportation and distribution, and reaching into new, but related, industries.

By the early 1960s, the volatility of oil refining and the price fluctuations for petroleum products caused Petroco to look for ways to expand into new markets. Profits in refining and sales were flattening, and there did not appear to be any simple way to improve profitability through increasing efficiencies. Petroco began by expanding its own operations beyond the fuels produced by most refineries to produce petrochemicals. It continued this expansion through its largest acquisition to that point, which formed the foundation of a new division focused on the chemicals industry.

By 1966, Petroco as a whole had merged with or acquired more than 75 other companies. By 1967, the chemical division alone was made up of 63 facilities covering manufacturing, research, service, and distribution facilities and was located in 22 states and 14 foreign countries.

Another new direction was also launched in the late 1960s with the purchase of a relatively large construction company. The connection here was an outlet for the use of asphalt, another byproduct of petroleum refining for which new markets were being sought.

With the death of Petroco's founder in the late 1960s, a major milestone in the company's history and culture was set. The company had grown and expanded tremendously from its initial roots in the early part of the century and now included many executives and managers, all of whom had come up in the company under the watchful eye of the founder. Leadership now fell, collectively, to two very different individuals, but ones who were seemingly able to complement each other's differences. The older was a nephew of the founder and the younger a law school graduate who had only joined the company in the early 1950s. Though they had fairly distinct roles—the elder working at the policy level and the younger more in charge of operations—they reportedly were able to continue the legacy of shared responsibility and overlapping efforts established by the founder.

Acquisitions continued at a frenetic pace through the end of the 1960s and into the early 1970s with as many as three per month being completed at times. This was especially true in the chemical division which both acquired and divested companies and divisions rapidly, as profits dictated.

As is also not unusual, the true change of power to a new executive management team also brought a change in focus from the entrepreneurial style of the founder to a more formal management style. A new headquarters was built, company operations formalized into new divisions, and even the company name changed to reflect the more diversified operations in which it was involved.

Within only a couple of years of the founder's death, his nephew began experiencing his own health problems, and management of the company seemed to fall rather directly to the younger of the team (whom we'll refer to, for ease of reading, as Adams.) Change in the larger environment of the world and of markets continued, as it always had, providing new challenges to be faced. The late 1960s and early 1970s produced not only social turmoil as a result of the Vietnam War and political crises, this period also created significant dependence on foreign oil by the United States and saw the formation of OPEC, as well as the social and political rise of the environmental movement.

Not only were there new external threats to Petroco, the changes in management style and philosophy that had occurred internally created new ways by which the company now responded. Petroco had never been successful in petroleum exploration, despite a number of attempts, and had set up its operations around acquiring the raw materials it needed through external sources. Adams apparently had a view that Petroco needed now to act like the larger organization that it was and to respond to the new threats by securing its own direct access to crude oil, especially. A new division was established for this purpose with agreements for exploration and access to supplies in numerous countries around the world.

At the same time, profits in existing operations took fairly dramatic drops through a variety of circumstances (strikes in customer companies, etc.), and several large and key mergers and acquisitions fell through. Complaints began to be voiced by citizens groups about possible health damage from the emissions of various company operations, and government requirements were developed requiring the production of unleaded gasoline—requiring significant change to existing equipment and operations. For the first time, major austerity measures were undertaken in the company to reduce costs, including a reduction of executive salaries, elimination of the traditional Christmas parties, and scrutiny of even business-related travel and expenses. Many of the original employees who had started in Petroco with the founder were now reaching retirement age and leaving, as well. The face of the company was changing.

The 1970s was a period of fluctuation and turmoil for Petroco. Profitability returned and continued throughout the decade, though erratically. Mergers and acquisitions continued at a record pace. Younger executives were placed in senior positions creating a new generation of management in the company.

It was also a time of both internal and external political turmoil and intrigue, much of it around the very tenuous relationships with foreign governments involved in the crude oil supply chain. By the beginning of the 1980s, the next major transitions were underway. Two major acquisitions outside the realm of Petroco's experience were completed— one involving an experimental energy production process and the other an insurance concern. And soon after these were done, Adams was forced into retirement due to allegations of political wrongdoing and to growing dissatisfaction with his direction for the company. Petroco was faced with a crisis of confidence in a way that it had never experienced.

Adams was replaced as CEO by the chief operating officer at the time, a chemical engineer who had distinguished himself through his expertise in economic analysis, whom we'll call Calvert. As opposed to Adam's style of analyzing issues and selling ideas, Calvert was a consensus builder. He was also an operations manager, familiar with the core technologies of the business both by background and experience.

Calvert quickly began to reset the course for the company. He instituted another major effort at cost cutting to address stalled profits and carried the formalization of the structure a step further by decentralizing operating authority to each of the company's divisions and establishing a corporate body for setting overall strategy and reviewing results. Each of the divisions would be responsible for proving its worth through its own profitability.

Where the 1970s had been a period of great profits and expansion, the 1980s became primarily a time of focus and consolidation—as well as new challenges. One of the first decisions Calvert faced was divesting the company of the two large acquisitions that had just been made when Adams departed. While the strategies for these may have had their own logic, the requirements for making them successful were never implemented and the skills for doing so seemed to lie outside the expertise of the executives and managers at the time. The two companies were sold at a significant loss and a strategic decision made that future acquisitions would only be related to the core businesses of Petroco.

The 1980s also brought significant external threats to Petroco in the form of a threatened hostile takeover and of environmental litigation. While the company was able to survive both of these challenges successfully, they seem to have created yet more levels of complexity to its world. The company had long faced a combination of business and political forces with which it had to compete and negotiate, but now threats seemed to arise from previously benign sources. Investors were no longer just passive partners, they were becoming more active in their demands. And local communities were no longer just neighbors and customers, in some cases they were very active adversaries.

The back-to-basics strategy championed by Calvert, along with a more favorable economic climate, reestablished the company's profitability. Even more crucial at this time, his very open and forthright approach in acknowledging the company's responsibility in the case of a large environmental spill helped to clean up what had become a rather tarnished company image—but did not resolve relationships with environmental activists, as a whole.

As in all large-scale change, there were questions about the magnitude of the changes the company faced. Were they industry cycles of basic supply and demand, or were they larger changes to the industry itself? And if larger changes, would the values on which the company was founded, and the strategies by which it had survived historically, continue to be successful?

In general, the historical culture and values seemed to succeed. But the 1980s were also a time of increasing efficiencies in which the basic corporate mantra was "downsizing." Anything and anyone not directly linked to a profit stream was put under scrutiny for being extraneous. Some companies in the oil industry faced this early on and others only later after pressure for profitability increased.

Increased efficiencies in the industry, overall, and a corresponding increase in supply of products over demand, drove down profit margins. For the first time, the refining and marketing portion of Petroco, which had always generated the majority of profits as well as cash flow for investments in the other divisions, was losing its place of preeminence in the company. Profits in the other divisions, especially in the chemicals area, were becoming major factors in Petroco's well-being.

Between 1988 and 1995, the chemical division completed some 50 or more additional acquisitions. Most of these were simply additions to existing operations and expansions within known markets. Others expanded the realm of the businesses somewhat. But as noted earlier, business lines were divested just as quickly as they were bought if they did not remain profitable.

The early 1990s also saw the first of a series of efforts aimed at increasing efficiencies within Petroco. Each brought in a new management consulting firm, each with a slightly different approach, but all with the same basic goal—to reduce inefficiencies and to improve profitability. With Calvert having shifted much of the administrative, as well as the operational, decision making and responsibility to the divisions, the first effort was aimed primarily at the central corporate functions. The largest effect of this effort was the early retirement of a few hundred employees.

Problems with profitability continued to plague the refining and marketing division of the company, though, and the next efforts were aimed specifically at it. A new group of external consultants was brought in, again with the aim of increasing efficiencies. It was clear that the ultimate goal was a return to profitability, but how to achieve that, or just what efficiency actually meant, was not clear. Tensions between the company divisions increased, as well, including questions about how products were priced between them in order to reflect profits or losses, and no small amount of resentment by the refining division about its role in supporting the growth of the other divisions through decades of lean profits.

Changes in the larger industry continued, and a new period of consolidation actually began, though the extent of it was not apparent at the time. A third group of consultants was brought in, again focused on the refining and marketing division. But before the latest round of recommendations could be implemented, change of a previously unprecedented level was announced.

In the mid-1990s, the office of chief executive once again changed hands. The new CEO had, as did previous executives, rather long experience with the corporation, but was primarily a financial, rather than an operations, person. And immediately on the heels of his installment came a visit by a person claiming to represent a voting majority of the institutional investors, demanding changes to improve the stock price and returns to shareholders. Recommendations, apparently, were for a breakup of the company with the thought that each division, if sold, would represent a greater value than would the entire organization.

The company managed to put the investors at bay, for a time, but then announced a deal that had apparently been in contemplation for some time. The refining and marketing division, which had been the heart of both the culture and the operations of the company since its founding, was to be merged with the similar operations of a competitor. In this case, the competitor was not only the larger company, it was also the larger investor. And while the deal was announced as a "merger of equals," it became clear early on that Petroco's culture was not to remain.

It took approximately 18 months to complete the merger from the time that it was announced. It was a period of great consternation for those affected and involved. The top view from both sides was apparently that the business approaches were very similar and that this created very similar cultures. But from the first due diligence visits by Petroco's managers to the other company's headquarters it became clear that the corporate cultures, in terms of assumptions, expectations, and underlying values, were radically different.

Through all the change efforts, Petroco had tried to establish a much more flexible style of management with more open communication. The other company maintained its efficiency through a very top-down hierarchy—essentially a very command-and-control environment according to the reports brought back. And the differences came to light in some interesting ways through the process.

Many of the final details of the deal were still in discussion at the time that the merger was announced. Key executive positions were decided in advance, but all other positions were held in limbo. Importantly, the differences in both the ownership structure and the cultures created additional tensions. An initial agreement had apparently been reached about a process for employee selection in which employees would be allowed to apply for open positions, with the intent that the most qualified persons (regardless of company affiliation) would be selected. In the absence of being able to give employees definitive information about their specific jobs, Petroco wanted to at least inform employees about what the process was to be. But through much discussion and debate it became clear that the other company, first, felt no similar level of concern about loss of jobs, and second, was opposed to communicating anything in advance to employees lest it just "stir up trouble." And because of the nature of the deal, Petroco was virtually forbidden from communicating even with its own employees, so that unwanted information would not be transmitted back to the other company.

In the end all administrative jobs were transferred to the other company's headquarters. Where there were redundancies in departments, or in cases where the other company did not even have similar internal functions, whole departments were eliminated. Virtually no clerical staff was even considered for the move to the new location in spite of many of them having decades of experience with the company and being quite qualified and competent. Despite months of work on various alternatives, there was no application process in the end. Each company simply got a certain number of positions, according to its share of ownership in the venture, and was allowed to place individuals into these roles—but the selection and announcement process happened within about a three-week window of time, with no real chance for preparation or discussion.

One of the authors of this book was involved in the design and delivery of a series of change management programs for the employees who were to be most affected. These were delivered over a process of several months. The initial proposal had been a three-stage process. The first would simply help to prepare employees for the magnitude of the changes that were being faced. The second would occur at the time that transitions of employees actually began and would be tailored to the varying needs of different groups: those who were terminated, those taking early retirement, and those who would be moving to the new company.

In the end, only one round of programs was approved, and these were extremely difficult in that employees came to the sessions expecting or hoping to hear additional information about the changes that were to happen and no such information was available. By the time that decisions were announced, it was only a matter of weeks before the changes were implemented.

While many of Petroco's employees were placed into the new company, they were generally put into positions as subordinates to persons who had previously been their peers, professionally. As one senior manager put it, it felt like he was treated as a new hire with no knowledge of the business despite his two decades of experience. Needless to say, there was a great deal of bitterness by employees about the process. In the end, since there were virtually no equivalent alternatives in nearby locations, most employees who were offered jobs took them.

Since that time, most employees seem to have made the best of things. But even in those cases, there is still a sense of loss for the history and camaraderie that had once been shared within Petroco. And while many employees still work in the same locations with many of the same co-workers as before, the feeling of loyalty and caring about the company that had once prevailed is gone. The value of something like loyalty is not typically seen in day-to-day operations. It is what appears in a time of threat or crisis. It is what caused employees to literally move into the refinery decades ago to protect it from a devastating flood. It is one of the things that provides a sense of meaning beyond just the financial rewards for work done. It provides a reason for showing some concern about customers' concerns. And it is a primary force behind an employee proactively working to initiate new ideas or resolve problems early versus simply waiting for directions.

This is not to say that the merger between the companies has been a failure or that it is doomed to be so in the future. There are appearances that relationships are beginning to form and that progress is being made, at least in some cases. But in the midst of this particular merger, a great deal was lost that will not easily, if ever, be regained. Whether what was lost was of any real value is at least partly a matter of opinion and perspective. If so, it is not something that will show up easily on a balance sheet. But it may be a loss that could have been avoided, and the results could have very subtle and long-term consequences. If a company only needs employees to carry out directions, that can be monitored and measured. But capturing initiative or creativity, or a willingness to forego other opportunities, is more than just a matter of ownership or monetary exchange. How the merger might have affected these "softer" issues and how the new company deals with them will be seen over time.

The merger is not the end of the story for Petroco either. Some months later it was announced that the company would move its headquarters from the rural location it had occupied for some 75 years to a larger city. There was a sense that the company needed to make obvious and drastic changes in order to transform itself. (There were also many negative feelings in the rural community about the merger and the consequent loss of jobs, pride, etc.)

A downsizing of the corporate staff and a reorganization of the corporate functions accompanied the move. Following the typical corporate trend, the emphasis was on reducing headcount as much as possible although there was a real effort to retain as many jobs as possible in the community in which Petroco was formerly headquartered, and a planned transitional strategy for continuing some community support.

But the real effect of the merger on Petroco seems to have had much more to do with the culture and identity of what is left. While Petroco had always been something of an anomaly in terms of the mix of its operations, separating the original core of the company left only what had been acquired for diversification. There were now three primary operating divisions: chemicals, lubricants, and construction. And though each of these was growing in its own right, including expansion into Europe, Latin America, and the Far East, it was difficult to identify any common thread between them.

The primary customer driving the company was now clearly the financial community. The goal of the company was return to shareholders. The general concept seemed to be to replicate something of a "GE model," excelling in each of the business areas in which it operated.

The lubricants division had the only widely recognized name brand and was heavily driven by a marketing culture. The construction division had shown the highest return on investments and was continuing to grow rapidly through acquisitions. The chemical division, which had taken on the "dominant sibling" role during all the transition, continued to grow and expand, but as of last report still only provided half the actual operating income to Petroco as compared to the equity income from the merged refining division. At last report, there was still no unifying vision spelling out what Petroco actually was, or was to become.

SUMMARY AND ANALYSIS

While the recent pace of mergers and acquisitions may seem unprecedented, Petroco is an example of a company with a long history of growth and development in that arena. And if longevity counts, it would have to be considered successful, by at least some measures.

A key question is why it worked when it did and whether what was successful is continuing to work at this point. From our perspective, in this case, the question is probably best answered in terms of organizational culture and its effect on many other aspects of the business.

As is the case for most companies, Petroco's culture was formed around the personal beliefs and values of a founding entrepreneur. In this case, the founder was someone whose foresight seemed to come from extremely detailed analysis and success through perseverance and dedication. He took only studied risks, and only after careful investigation. And he was apparently quite strong in his convictions about his approach.

He seemed to have a deep sense of purpose about his work, believing that it achieved a much greater good than just personal wealth. While extremely demanding of himself and those who worked with and for him, he also expressed a great sense of responsibility for the welfare of employees and their families. His vision seemed to go beyond the company, to the community in which it was embedded.

Interestingly, this founder might have felt quite at home in the current business climate of Internet startups. He certainly would have had no problem sharing the crazy hours and frenetic work pace. What his personal convictions might have been if he were a young person today, of course, could only be speculated.

The downside to the founder's approach, if it was such, was that the exploration side of the oil business could not be played from "safe" perspective. Not having its own direct access to a supply of crude oil confined Petroco to being a smaller player in the industry. But that, of course, is only hindsight and guesswork about what might have been otherwise—and further investment might just as well have made Petroco one of the long list of extinct companies early on. And if survival as an independent entity is seen as the goal, few of the original "seven sisters" of the oil industry were successful, despite their access to supplies, in those terms.

The success of so many acquisitions might be seen in terms of the values set down by the founder, as expressed in the quote at the beginning of this chapter. This CEO obviously understood the importance of incorporating people into the processes. And this was in the context of a very strong and explicit culture. Not only were the values of the company clearly stated, if the stories are true, but they were born out in the actions taken. There were strong underlying beliefs (basic values) that were clearly articulated in the stated ideas (espoused values) which were in concert with what could be visibly seen of the company and its actions (the artifacts). The close alignment of these three factors creates what we would call *organizational integrity* (a concept to be explored much further by these authors in other contexts).

Assuming that Petroco did exhibit *organizational integrity* in the ways described, and did make a concerted effort to incorporate newcomers into its ways of doing things, it would seem to explain its successes in mergers and acquisitions. To bring employees in through such a process, in which the assumptions and expectations were fairly clear and in line with what was experienced, would create a much easier transition than a "conquer and enslave" mentality that sometimes seems to occur.

But to *maintain* a state of organizational integrity is something of a different matter. As the environment changes, so do the requirements for survival. In most business situations, having the time to analyze all the factors to one's satisfaction is a luxury, if not an impossibility. Most situations seem to demand a response, lest the opportunity is lost.

In the case of Petroco, there might be an interesting lesson to be seen at the time of the transition to Adams as the CEO. While he apparently continued to exhibit the same work ethic as the founder (with whom he had worked as an assistant earlier), it is not clear that he did so from the same underlying values. He apparently sought to transition the company into a larger arena than it had ever been a part of—an environment that seemed to require a different set of skills than were readily available in Petroco. While this was not necessarily a wrong strategy, it seems to have overreached the capacity of the organization, and to have done so without attempting to create the necessary capacity internally.

Just as importantly, if not more so, Adams' frenetic work pace seemed to have come from something other than the founder's passion and sense of a larger purpose. What drove Adams is not clear, but following his departure he was consistently described as having been bored or distracted in his final years. Interpreted, it would seem that he had lost connection between his actions and the underlying values that drove them.

By the time an organization has reached a more formalized stage, the process of mergers and acquisitions is typically handled as a functional and strategic process rather than a cultural one. Concerns are centered around functional alignment and how to achieve efficiency as quickly as possible. And as long as all that is required is applying current skills to familiar situations, functional alignment should usually be achieved.

It is likely that by the 1980s, with the "back to basics" approach, keeping acquisitions targeted to only those that were already in closely aligned businesses may have simplified the transitions. But based on our experiences, business similarities do not necessarily reflect similarities in organizational culture, and therefore do not predict successful M&A transactions in and of themselves.

The merger of the refining and marketing division of Petroco was clearly a different process than had ever been experienced by the company. Not only was it tremendously symbolic in terms of the "invasion" of the original plant sites on which the company was founded, by "outsiders," it also left a void for which there was no obvious remedy in terms of a common identity for the company.

This is not to say that this was a dramatic shift away from what was otherwise occurring. Since the time that the divisions had begun decentralizing, each had continued to develop a more autonomous identity. The chemical division, especially, seemed to want out from under the aura of being in an "old" and "dirty" industry (a perception sought by the chemical industry as a whole). But rather than instituting a new direction toward which the company would move, the changes simply removed the vestiges of what had been.

Organizational culture helps first to establish a sense of identity (e.g., what the organization is versus what it is not; how those who are a part of it are similar, and how they differ from those outside, etc.). The loss of the refining division seemed also to be a loss of connection with the company's history and therefore with the culture as it had been established.

Culture creates a sense of what is important to survival through a history of what are experienced or understood as successes. In this way it also helps an organization to filter information from its environment—what might be relevant or important and what can be ignored. Though there was contact between the various divisions of Petroco, and even some small amount of personnel movement between them, there was no real shared history of commonality directly between each of the three remaining divisions.

Each, it seems, will continue to develop in its own direction, as part of its own industry, and in response to what is in its own best interest—despite attempts to overcome the differences. Each has essentially a different knowledge base from which it works—a different sense of what intellectual capital is needed and valued. Each, in itself, might represent a good potential partner for mergers or acquisitions—but in order to do so successfully, each will need to understand its own unique culture and characteristics that form the assumptions from which the organization works and the mechanisms by which it anticipates its environment. (The alternative, of course, would be some unforeseen circumstances that would draw the entities together and begin to form bonds of common successes.)

What is creating success in mergers and acquisitions today for the Cisco's of the world seems to be much the same as that which created success for Petroco historically. The culture was clear, the transitions were planned and purposeful, and the people mattered. Whether the same strategies for success can be continued as companies age may be yet another question.

Petroco's founder lived in an age when corporate paternalism was an accepted practice, and he seemed to have exemplified the better side of such, if reports are true. But the rules and the relationships in business have changed. Ambitious entrepreneurs still work "manic-like" hours, but most seem to count on moving quickly to the next project or opportunity. Stability, it would seem, comes not from organizational structure but from self-development and marketability, and undoubtedly from much more ephemeral "community of practice" connections than company identity. If true, then what will be needed to attract the best talent will be the lure of the opportunity to fulfill one's *own* dreams, not the promise of being taken care of. So are there lessons that carry over?

Petroco's founder seems to have seen the value of people to an organization. So, it would appear, does a company like Cisco—even if the issues and the ways of demonstrating value are somewhat different. M&A deals aimed solely at market share and growth to satisfy investment analysts seem not to see the relevance of those same success factors. In an age and environment in which key talent is not only at a premium, but the focus of virtual battles, human capital may become a key link in both valuing and structuring future deals.[3]

There will undoubtedly continue to be organizations that rise to dominance in their industries and maintain some longevity, with a core of key executives in place. But how the total organization achieves a sense of stability in a rapidly changing environment, while meeting the needs of a workforce with different expectations, will be an ongoing challenge for a while. The greater the opportunities available in the larger environment for individuals, the greater will be the need for focusing on the human side of these transactions.

NOTES

1. From a speech by Paul Blazer to the Newcomen Society of Lexington, Kentucky in 1956.

2. Daniel Yergin and Joseph Stanislaw, *The Prize: The Epic Quest for Oil, Money, and Power* (Touchstone Books, 1993).

3. Devin Leonard, "They're Coming to Take You Away," *Fortune*, May 29, 2000.

Appendix 1

HR Due Diligence Issues Guide

MANAGEMENT ISSUES

A. Organization charts
B. Appointment of key employees and succession plans
C. Senior management committees (membership and structures)
D. Company policies
   1. Codes of ethics
   2. Communication documentation
E. Employment contracts
F. Change of control agreements
G. Consulting agreements
H. Key personnel files
 I. Indemnification agreements
 J. Non-compete and/or confidentiality agreements
K. Employee loans
L. Executive physical exams
M. Special agreements, perks, and other fringe benefits

POLICY AND COMPENSATION ISSUES

A. Employee handbooks
B. Vacation plans
C. Severance plans
   1. Written
   2. Unwritten

D. Sick pay programs

E. Diversity programs

F. Special early retirement plans

G. Stock options

H. Employee and executive compensation plans
   1. Base salaries
   2. Deferral plans
      a. Employees
      b. Directors
   3. Incentive programs
      a. Short-term
      b. Long-term
   4. Details of stock grants and bonus payments
      a. Current
      b. Last five years
   5. Recent changes to plans
   6. Proposed changes to plans
   7. Communications to employees about these plans
   8. Financial counseling or planning agreements

I. General compensation
   1. Base salary increases
      a. Merit increases and promotions
      b. Bonuses and other increases
   2. Incentive and bonus arrangements
      a. Short-term
      b. Long-term

J. Selection and placement
   1. Employment documents
      a. Applications
      b. Confidentiality agreements
      c. Citizenship compliance (Form I-9)
      d. Testing procedures
      e. Correspondence templates
   2. Affirmative action plans
   3. EEO compliance
   4. Veteran 100 reports
   5. Job posting procedures
   6. Temporary employment and co-op procedures

K. Performance management systems
   1. Selection of system type
   2. Forms

L. Job descriptions and evaluations

M. Human resources policies

N. Communications policies and procedures

O. Drug and alcohol testing

    1. Programs and procedures
    2. Five-year history of problems and complaints

P. Postings and notifications (e.g., FMLA, ADA, EEO, etc.)

Q. Employment records
    1. Content
    2. Retention
    3. Terminations
    4. Access policies and procedures

R. Training records
    1. Programs
    2. Procedures

S. Service award programs

T. Credit union issues

U. Community service involvement (e.g., United Way, Red Cross, etc.)

EMPLOYEE CENSUS DATA

A. Date of birth

B. Age

C. Date of hire

D. Salary

E. Gender

F. Location

G. Position

H. Benefits plan coverage elections

I. Categorization by class (e.g., exempt vs. nonexempt, seasonal, casual, part-time, retirees, etc.)

J. Regional wage and benefit information (data, surveys, etc.)

LABOR

A. Workers' compensation
    1. Plan (insured or self-insured)
    2. Claim files
    3. Loss experience
    4. Pending or potential large claims
    5. Vendors and third-party administrators

B. Unemployment compensation
    1. State rates
    2. Claim files
    3. Loss experience
    4. Vendors and third-party administrators

C. Safety and health compliance (OSHA, MSHA, etc.)
    1. Inspection reports

      2. Company filings
      3. Compliance issues
      4. Safety award programs

D. Fair Labor Standards Act
      1. Wage and hour compliance
      2. Payroll records
      3. Policies
      4. Inspection reports

E. NLRB issues
      1. Union drives
      2. Union contracts
         a. Grievance records
         b. Contract history
         c. Current labor-management relations
      3. Unfair labor practice charges
      4. Current or pending union issues

F. Collective bargaining agreements

LITIGATION AND CLAIMS

A. Policies and postings

B. Internal investigations
      1. Current
      2. Prior five years

C. External investigations (e.g., OFCCP, DOL)
      1. Current
      2. Prior five years

D. Lawsuits
      1. Current
      2. Prior five years
      3. Potential threats

EMPLOYEE BENEFITS

A. Qualified plans
      1. Summary plan descriptions
      2. Summary of material modifications
      3. Plan documents and all amendments
      4. Trust documents
      5. Latest Form 5500 reports (plus Forms 5300-5301)
      6. Summary annual reports
      7. Most recent IRS determination letters and pending filings
      8. Pension valuation reports
      9. 401(k) valuation
     10. Administration and recordkeeping agreements
     11. Accounting statements of plan assets
     12. Trustee reports

13. Discrimination testing reports
14. Recent communications to employees
15. Recent plan audits (internal and external)

B. Welfare plans
   1. Summary plan descriptions
   2. Summary of material modifications
   3. Plan documents and all amendments
   4. Insurance contracts and policies
   5. Latest Form 5500 reports and summary annual reports
   6. Administrative and third-party agreements
   7. Accounting statements of plan assets
   8. Recent communications to employees
   9. Recent plan audits (internal and external)
   10. Premiums and contribution rates
   11. Employee eligibility criteria
   12. Termination clauses
   13. Waivers of premiums in life insurance and medical plans
   14. Special arrangements made with any employees
   15. Funding levels for self-insured plans

C. Other plans
   1. Benefit restoration
   2. ERISA forfeiture plan
   3. Salary continuation plans
   4. Nonqualified excess benefit pension plan

D. General benefit plan information
   1. Plan year
   2. Eligibility periods
   3. Contribution rates
   4. Funding of plans
   5. Actuaries
   6. Actuarial assumptions
   7. Carriers and third-party administrators
   8. Plan assets
   9. Investment performance
   10. Employee premiums
   11. Employer premiums
   12. Claims data for past three years
   13. Past COBRA compliance
   14. Number of retirees
   15. Commitments to retirees (including special arrangements for executives, etc.)
   16. Reportable events over the past three years
   17. Staff reductions due to past mergers or acquisitions
   18. Disposition of plans
   19. Payment of benefits

E. Active employee information
   1. Enrollment election forms

      2. Beneficiary designations
      3. QDROs
      4. Proof of legal guardianship or adoption papers, as needed, for dependents
      5. LTD and LOA history files
      6. Previous employer plans
        a. Pension
        b. Savings
        c. Rollovers
      7. Credited service information

F. Retiree information
      1. Enrollment election forms
      2. Beneficiary designations
      3. Life insurance amounts
      4. Pension information
        a. Benefit withholdings
        b. Tax withholdings

INTEGRATION OF HR DATA SYSTEMS, RECORDS, AND INFORMATION

A. HR data, benefits, and payroll
      1. System provider(s)
      2. Employee data format and compatibility with new systems
      3. Employee history data
      4. Exception identification and processing
      5. Electronic data transmissions and communications
        a. Savings plans
        b. Credit union
        c. Actuarial
        d. Third-party administrators (e.g., employee benefits, payroll, EAP, etc.)

B. Compensation
      1. Stock option administration
      2. Salary administration
        a. Budgeting
        b. Incentive compensation

C. Affirmative action plans

D. Data system/database access

Appendix 2

Post-Deal Integration Checklist

1. Decide the overall strategic approach for combining the organizations using the following guidelines:

   • Announce large-scale changes in one major announcement as early as possible.
   • Combine the best features of both organizations.
   • Design a new HR organizational structure with compensation, incentives, and benefit programs tailored to fit the new workforce.

2. Select the total compensation objectives of the new entity, considering the following:

   • Cash compensation vs. employee benefits
   • Fixed vs. variable compensation
   • Competitive market position
   • Performance measures

3. Determine how cultures should be integrated, identifying the elements of each organization's culture and keeping the "best of the best."

4. Identify the core values of the merged organization, considering the following:

   • Being "best"
   • Being the fastest to reach the market; superior responsiveness
   • Importance of people as individuals

- Superior quality
- Superior service
- Encouragement for risk taking
- Importance of profits, cash flow, or growth

5. Decide how the new organization will be staffed, and address the following issues:

    - Key roles
    - Organizational structure
    - "Keepers" in the new organization
    - Selection and retention processes
    - Use of job titles
    - Clearly define responsibility/reporting relationships

6. Determine how the HR function should be structured.

7. Develop policies on severance, outplacement, and retention.

8. Determine the emphasis that will be placed on communication, addressing the following issues:

    - What should be communicated to various stakeholders (employees, shareholders, customers, media)
    - What information should be communicated, and when
    - How to get customer/employee feedback at various stages

9. Determine how to meet training and development needs, addressing the following issues:

    - What training is needed by management and by HR?
    - What training/communications are needed for new policies and procedures?
    - What training is needed to integrate certain functions and practices?

10. Identify HR policies and procedures that need to be addressed, including, but not limited to, the following:

    - Compliance (e.g., benefits, overtime policy, etc.)
    - Disciplinary processes
    - Dress code
    - Employee records
    - Employee services

- Employment of relatives
- Flexible hours
- Hours in a week
- Overtime/shift differentials
- Sick days
- Vacation

11. Decide how and when governance and authority structures should change and how to communicate these changes.

12. Integrate HRIS, records and information, and outline retention guidelines.

13. Identify organizational initiatives, such as the following, to focus employees and promote new values and behaviors:

- Orientation meetings
- One-on-one meetings with management
- Focus groups
- Employee surveys

Appendix 3

Model "100-Day" Strategic Plan

ASSUMPTIONS

- Agreement is reached on key terms of the transaction by the parties.
- Finalization of the merger agreement.

ACTIONS

- New CEO will meet individually with key officers of both companies (all officers ideally, but top five officers at a minimum) to assess strengths, weaknesses, and attitudes and to respond to individual questions and concerns.
- Officers who will not be a part of the new company are notified by new CEO (including a discussion about the timing of their departure).
- New officers are notified by CEO of their assignments/duties and sign retention agreements.
- Form S-4 is signed by the boards of both companies.
- Meetings with employees are held at both company locations to accomplish the following:

  1. Announce the merger terms (e.g., headquarters location, severance program, management team, name of new company, etc.);
  2. Outline early performance expectations;
  3. Explain the expected timeline for future events and key decisions (e.g., date of special meeting to approve the merger, job reductions, moves, transfers, etc.);
  4. Answer employee questions.

- Press release is issued detailing the terms of the merger and a general timetable of future events.

- Press conference is held to address media concerns and answer questions.

- Letter is sent from new CEO to all employees reiterating key points made at employee meetings (with additional question-and-answer piece addressing any follow-up issues, including responses to media inquiries at the press conference) and telling employees that everyone is responsible for and will be measured for the year on their contribution to the success of the merger integration effort.

- Off-site meeting is held with small and select key officer group to accomplish the following:

  1. Get acquainted and begin the team-building process;
  2. Explain the new CEO vision/philosophy for the company (including a focus on organizational structure/governance changes, anticipated restructuring and expected force reductions, plus operating philosophy and short-term strategic goals);
  3. Discuss the timeline for expected events and decisions;
  4. Lay out early performance expectations; and
  5. Outline the post-merger bonus performance parameters.

- A "merger team" is created, consisting of key individuals from both companies who will have responsibility for merger-related integration activities.

- Employees are sent information about what to expect (both personally and professionally) as the merger progresses.

- Decisions are made regarding the frequency and format of transition communications to employees (e.g., monthly meetings, letters, electronic mail notes, special issue of an integration update newsletter, etc.) and responsibility is assigned to a specified group.

- An off-site working meeting is held with all new officers to begin the process of creating a vision/values statement and to outline the key short-term goals.

- Merger management training is offered to educate managers and officers on what to expect, what happens and why during a merger, and how to avoid the most common management mistakes.

Note: Also refer to Appendix 4 for actions during the first 100 days related specifically to employee communications.

Appendix 4

Employee Communications Implementation Plan

WITHIN 30 DAYS

1. Conduct a vision/strategy meeting with all members of the senior management team (including key operations personnel) to outline the future direction and strategic goals for the new company.

2. Finalize and announce the new company name to employees and aggressively work on the development of the new corporate identity (e.g., by changing signs, stationery, and business cards immediately and potentially celebrating the new name/logo through employee receptions/gatherings).

3. Establish a communications function and dedicate the resources necessary to make it successful, including a professional staff and adequate budget.

4. Enter into retention agreements with senior management and key operations personnel to ensure continuity of management.

5. Implement an interim transitional bonus program to increase the urgency related to the achievement of the synergy goals by providing employees with the opportunity to be financially rewarded for positive and timely results.

6. Implement some "quick hits" that will signal to employees that the new company is making decisions and moving in a positive direction:

   - casual dress policy—every day
   - inclusion of new and former employees in the EAP
   - distribution of information electronically and via voice mail
   - implement flexible work schedules for salaried employees
   - "Ask the Chairman" program

- review and modify organizational structure/reporting relationships/job-levels, as appropriate

7. Examine all regularly scheduled meetings, eliminate all noncritical gatherings, and consider other alternatives for exchanging important information. Consider the meeting roster to be sure that the right mix of people is invited to attend and reduce senior management participation in lower-level meetings. Ensure accountability and follow-up for commitments made during meetings.

WITHIN 60 DAYS

1. Conduct on-site "employee orientation" sessions to enhance management visibility and explain each officer's background and experience. Outline the rationale for the purchase of [acquired company]. Explain the rationale for the early retirement program and provide status update. Outline the future vision and strategic goals for the company. Explain the company's expectations and governance/decision-making processes and answer employee questions.

2. Establish systemic communication vehicles for distribution of company-related information to employees at regular intervals. Some examples of periodic and ongoing communications include the following:

- monthly "President's Letter"
- quarterly newsletter/company magazine
- weekly electronic news updates
- integration progress updates
- bulletin board postings

3. Acknowledge supervisors as the company's "front-line communicators" and make them primarily responsible/accountable for delivering company information to employees.

- Provide supervisors with "talking points" (developed by the corporate group) for delivery to employees each quarter during face-to-face meetings.
- Ensure accountability via changes to the performance management, bonus and compensation systems.
- Provide supervisory skills training workshops to give supervisors the tools needed to effectively communicate with employees.

WITHIN 90 DAYS

1. Hold a key manager's meeting for the company's top 50 to 75 employees initially (and thereafter on an annual basis) to explain the company's vision and strategic goals in advance of widespread distribution to the workforce.

2. Conduct a "State of the Company" video teleconference—world-wide—initially (and annually thereafter) to update employees on the company's financial performance for the year; progress on the integration effort; any new policies, ben-

efit, or incentive programs; the status of any key projects; and any other major decisions. Consider using the teleconference as a time to recognize employees who have been key contributors during the year.

3. Offer communication skills training to supervisors to ensure their effectiveness as the company's front-line communicators. Possible skills training topics include the following:

- how to conduct an effective meeting
- debating issues/resolving conflict in a professional manner
- selling your ideas internally
- coping with change
- listening skills
- good presentation skills

4. Require that all senior management and key operating personnel go through a "360-degree" performance evaluation (e.g., feedback from subordinates, peers, and supervisor).

WITHIN 6 MONTHS

1. Host monthly employee luncheons/"early bird" breakfasts for small groups of employees at rotating sites.

2. Install video bulletin boards at major work locations to provide updates and news of interest to employees.

3. Initiate a "360-degree" performance management system for employees company-wide.

4. Increase the effectiveness of employee benefit communications through an enhanced HR partnership with the company's professional communication specialists.

WITHIN 12 MONTHS

1. Conduct an employee satisfaction survey during [appropriate date] (and annually thereafter).

2. Develop a company-wide communications strategy annually to ensure consistent message delivery.

3. Conduct quarterly new hire "orientation" workshops so that employees are indoctrinated early with an understanding of the company's vision, values, and strategic goals, including what it takes to be professionally successful in this organization.

OTHER STRATEGIES FOR FUTURE CONSIDERATION

1. Develop an annual "Employee Annual Report" which would celebrate significant employee contributions and company successes and would serve as an

annual recognition forum for employees. Following the distribution of the report to all employees, you might consider inviting all employees (and their spouses) recognized in the report for a reception/dinner honoring their contribution.

2. Implementation of an employee referral program (e.g., the company pays its employees for referring job candidates—this lowers your recruiting costs and may improve the quality of your new hires. It also may generate some enthusiasm and pride among your employees).

3. Develop a quarterly report to senior management which provides a review of the key performance indicators of your employee relations environment (e.g., turnover, staffing levels, absenteeism, hiring costs, benefit costs, etc.) so that trends and issues can be identified and addressed early.

4. Consider implementation of a "spot" bonus program (e.g., a prebudgeted pool of funds which would be available to each officer/department head) to provide "on the spot" contemporaneous bonuses to employees for performance excellence, in amounts ranging from $100 to $1,000.

Appendix 5

Key Post-Merger Employee Messages

MISSION

To communicate information and develop plans/programs that will help stimulate employees to work toward an expedited, smooth, and successful transition; and to ensure that employees understand the company's vision and strategic goals for the future so that they can make better decisions within that established framework.

Reaching these objectives will help ensure that the newly combined ABC organization is ready to compete as a single, well-integrated unit as soon as the integration effort is complete.

OBJECTIVES AND KEY MESSAGES

1. Provide employees with the business-related information that they need during this time of uncertainty and tumultuous change.

   - Provide employees with an understanding of the future direction of the company, as well as the key strategic goals and objectives.
   - Attempt to provide a general timetable for the on-going decision-making process, including who will be involved in making key determinations.
   - Explain the company's expectations for how employees should handle their day-to-day activities during this period of uncertainty.
   - Help employees to understand the new ownership and the background/experience of the company's new leaders (those who have been named to key roles in the past six to nine months).
   - Explain the company's rationale for offering the voluntary retirement program and discuss whether or not it is likely that additional force reductions

will follow. If so, explain the process for deciding which jobs and people will be terminated.

- Continue to express appreciation to employees who will retire under the early retirement program for all that they have done and all that they are doing for the company.

- Express appreciation and provide recognition and financial rewards for the significant efforts of employees during [insert key developments].

- Acknowledge the anxiety and stress that employees have been living with over the past [number] of years and indicate that decisions are now being made to resolve many of the issues of concern. Commit that these decisions will be announced to employees as quickly as reasonably possible as decisions are reached.

- Continue to update employees about potential staffing changes (e.g., promotions, transfers, voluntary retirements or resignations, upcoming force reductions, etc.).

- Provide employees with information about how the governance and/or decision-making process has or will change.

2. Explain why the purchase of [name of acquired company] by ABC Corporation makes good business sense and establish it as an important cause behind which employees can and should rally.

- Communicate about the external forces that are impacting the industry.

- Continue to explain how the purchase of [name of acquired company] can and will lead to the creation of value for both entities.

- Continue to highlight the exciting growth prospects for the newly combined company.

3. Outline the integration process, announce teams and team members, and explain how/when decisions will be made.

- Explain how the transition teams will function.

- Announce the teams and team members, explaining why they were selected and what their roles will be.

- Outline the timeline for major decision areas and who will make the decisions.

- Reiterate that representatives from both companies will have a voice in the decision-making process.

- Explain that the company will do everything possible to be objective and fair, but admit in advance that the process will not be perfect.

- Attempt to dispel any unwarranted fears or concerns among not only employees, but also officers and key management.

- Stress the need for urgency about making decisions and showing progress toward meeting the company's synergy objectives.

4. Communicate about the opportunities for advancement, reward, and personal development for employees who remain with the combined company.

   • Highlight the opportunities that the newly combined company can provide for personal growth and development.

   • Communicate about the highly competitive compensation, bonus, and benefits package that is being created for the new company.

   • Underscore the company's commitment to helping employees enhance their skills and create opportunities for advancement.

   • Announce the adoption of an interim transitional bonus program as quickly as possible, if approved. Highlight the fact that the bonus program is being implemented to provide employees who significantly contribute to the integration goals with a financial opportunity to be rewarded for that effort.

   • Stress that the timelines established for the integration goals are very important and that those employees who enthusiastically meet the objectives on schedule will have the best potential for rewards under this bonus program.

5. Lay the groundwork for a single, positive, "one company" culture for the newly combined entity.

   • Share the governing philosophy of the new senior management team, including any differences to be expected from the previous culture and operating philosophy.

   • Define the characteristics and qualities that the new company will value and reward.

   • Urge employees to begin to view the organization as a single company with a single set of objectives, owners, and customers.

   • Encourage employees to look for opportunities that will advance the integration process and benefit the combined company.

   • Reiterate the message that the new organization is committed to communicating fully and often with employees and that the company wants to hear what employees think.

6. Provide employees with the company's vision/strategic goals and also share the "value drivers" of the transaction.

   • Outline the company's vision for the future and its key strategic goals and provide some guidance as to how employees can contribute to reaching those objectives.

   • Provide employees with general direction/philosophical guidelines for how to make the integration process a success.

   • Communicate the "value drivers"/synergies of the deal and discuss how employees who are not part of the teams can also contribute.

   • Provide an outline of the key deadlines for major accomplishments and milestones.

- Celebrate the achievement of key objectives, both with written recognition to employees (e.g., letters from the president, announcements in newsletters, and employee/spouse gatherings, etc.) as well as financial rewards under the transitional bonus program.

7. Motivate employees to put forth their best efforts during this period of transition.

   - Explain why a quick and well-coordinated transition is important.
   - Continuously reinforce the importance of a high level of performance during this critical integration period.
   - Acknowledge that this is and will continue to be a period of stress for the next several months. Also acknowledge that this has been a great period of uncertainty for employees, but commit the company to resolving key issues quickly and communicating those decisions as they are made in an effort to decrease stress and employee concerns.
   - Reiterate that the transition period offers an opportunity for recognition and reward for employees who perform at a very high level.
   - Share information about current and future incentives (e.g., the stock option awards, the transitional bonus plan, if approved, etc.) for accomplishing this transition quickly and well.

8. Give employees all the information that is available as soon as it is available so that they can turn their attentions to "the business of doing business."

   - Develop and announce what the new HR policies and practices will be as soon as possible for expedited implementation.
   - Provide information about financial authority and decision-making scope (e.g., through a "delegation of authority" or some similar mechanism).
   - Attempt to dispel unnecessary or groundless concerns and fears, not only among employees, but also within the management ranks as well (e.g., retention agreements, etc.).
   - Anticipate and answer as many questions as possible, in advance of the issues being raised or misinterpreted by employees.

9. Increase management's visibility and availability in order to enhance employee confidence and understanding of significant organizational issues and direction and to reduce employee frustrations and uncertainty.

   - Significantly increase management's availability and visibility by walking around and talking to employees more frequently.
   - Indicate a willingness to answer employee questions.
   - Follow up and provide answers quickly.

Appendix 6

Sample Employee Survey Questions

1. Overall, how would you rate ABC Corporation as a place to work compared with other companies you know about?

   A. One of the best
   B. Above average
   C. Average
   D. Below average
   E. One of the worst

2. How do you rate ABC Corporation as a company to work for now compared with when you first started working here?

   A. It's better now.
   B. It's about the same.
   C. It's not as good now.

3. How do you feel about your job (i.e., the kind of work that you do)?

   A. I like my job a great deal.
   B. I am somewhat satisfied with my job.
   C. I don't strongly like or dislike my job.
   D. I am somewhat dissatisfied with my job.
   E. I don't like my job at all.

4. How would you rate ABC Corporation on each of the following, considering your experience here as well as what you know about other companies?

	Great	Good	Average	Poor
Your employee benefits				
Your pay				
Your opportunity for advancement				
Working for a supervisor you respect				
The people you work with				
Your job security				

5. How would you rate ABC Corporation on each of the following, considering your experience here as well as what you know about other companies?

	Great	Good	Average	Poor
Listening to your problems/complaints				
Providing you with timely/accurate information				
Encouraging suggestions for improvement from you				
Providing you with authority to make decisions about how to do your job				
Providing training so that you can learn new skills and develop your talents				
Having enough qualified people to do the work in your area				
Doing something about your problems/ complaints				
Treating employees fairly and consistently				
The ability of ABC Corporation's senior management				
The ability of top management in your department				
Treating employees with respect as individuals				

6. In your opinion, what issues need to be addressed by ABC Corporation management that have not yet been considered or acted upon?

A. Communications

B. Policy issues

C. Employee morale

D. Compensation

E. Employee benefits
F. Training/performance management
G. Professionalism/respect

7. Any other comments/suggestions?

Appendix 7

Workforce Reduction Considerations

REDUCTIONS

- How many jobs will be affected?
- Who will decide which jobs will be eliminated?
- What process will be used to decide which jobs to eliminate?

ORDER OF REDUCTIONS

- Should temporaries and co-ops be affected first?
- Should full-time employees be affected last?

BASIS FOR SELECTION

- How will reductions be determined?
- Factors to be considered:
  —Seniority?
  —Performance?
  —Special skills?
  —Experience?
  —Attendance?
  —A combination of all of these?

JOB RIGHTS

- Should more senior employees be allowed to "bump" those employees with less service, even though they may be "overqualified" for the less senior position?

- Should the philosophy be one that requires retraining of employees rather than allowing for separations?

- Should affected employees have preferential rights to transfer or apply for open jobs for which they are qualified?

- Should a hiring freeze be implemented?

SEVERANCE/RELOCATION BENEFITS

- What amount of severance will be granted?

- Will outplacement be provided?

- Will medical, dental, and life insurance coverage be continued? If so, for how long? Will this constitute the first months of COBRA?

- Will educational assistance be continued so that the affected employees can go for "retraining" at company expense?

- Will employees be reimbursed for all expenses associated with their relocation? If not, what will not be covered?

- Will the purchase of the employee's home be provided for by the relocation policy?

- Will employee assistance coverage be continued for a period of time following termination to help affected employees deal with the trauma of job loss?

- Will a reemployment pool be instituted for affected employees? For how long?

COMMUNICATION ISSUES

- How should notices to employees about the upcoming reduction in force be delivered?

- Forms to consider:
  —Video
  —Company newsletter
  —Bulletin boards
  —Letter to home
  —Electronic message
  —Face-to-face meetings with supervisors

- How will the news of an individual's termination be delivered? By his or her supervisor? By a representative from human resources? Or through a combination?

- Should there be a notice to civic/community leaders?

- Is the WARN Act implicated by the force reduction? Are additional legal notices required?

- How should senior management/key managers be updated?

REMAINING EMPLOYEES

- How often and in what form will updates on company changes be made?

- Will there be counseling sessions or training on dealing with the stress of change for those employees who remain with the company?

Appendix 8

Guidelines for Handling Employee Termination Meetings

One of the most difficult and stressful tasks for a manager is actually telling an employee that his or her job is being eliminated. Even if the process has been well communicated, it will be important to reconfirm to affected employees that "our organization, necessitated by financial and business conditions, requires a corresponding reduction in staff."

Following are some general guidelines about how to handle the actual termination interview with an employee:

1. Review in advance what should be said to each employee. Think about how you can keep the interview focused on the business need for the termination and the benefits in the separation package. Do not let the meeting last any longer than 15 to 20 minutes. Here are some suggestions:

DON'T:

- Don't argue with the employee.
- Don't react to any accusations aimed at you personally.
- Don't refer to any negative performance factors unless you have reviewed the situation in advance with human resources.
- Don't promise or commit to any deals beyond the severance package.
- Don't indicate to the employee that you do not agree with the decision.
- Don't reveal the names of other employees being terminated.
- Don't get defensive and think you have to justify your decision. (This type of reaction will encourage the employee to think that there is a chance of changing your mind.)
- Don't imply that there is the possibility of a job elsewhere within the company or give false assurances.

- Don't imply that the employee can possibly "hold out" to get a better offer.
- Don't answer questions when you are not sure of the answer.
- Don't discuss severance decisions with anyone outside of the company (e.g., media, local business people, etc.)
- Don't call the person to relay the news. Do it in person.

DO:

- Do use a private meeting room or office.
- Do deliver the news in person.
- Do have another person in the meeting as a witness.
- Do make sure that you will not be interrupted.
- Do be as positive as circumstances will allow.
- Do stick to the facts and explain the severance package.
- Do be patient.
- Do have empathy, but be firm.
- Do allow for reaction by the employee, but keep yourself under control and bring the employee back to the reality of the situation.
- Do make sure that the employee understands that the decision is final.
- Do refer employees to human resources for specific individual questions that you cannot answer.
- Do make arrangements with internal or external security personnel (as appropriate) if there are any advance concerns or indications that the employee has a bad temper or may be violent.

2. During the interview, you should treat employees with respect and compassion. If employees are terminated in a manner that leaves their self-respect intact, one of the primary causes for lawsuits will have been eliminated—vengeance.

3. Be sure not to make any promises to any affected employee that he or she will be transferred to a job within a division or otherwise placed within the company. Resist the natural urge to give assurances or provide false hope.

4. Do not negotiate with an employee about his termination or his or her severance benefits. Most of all, do not offer a more generous severance package than the program provides.

5. When the employee enters the office, skip the small talk and get right to the meeting's purpose in the first two minutes. Describe the company's situation, and state the reason for termination. For example:

"I've asked you here today to tell you about an important decision that we've reached. Through our recent cost reduction program, we've taken a hard look at how we are doing our work and have decided we need to make some changes.

I'm sorry to say, [name], that your position is being eliminated as of [date]. This decision has been reviewed by senior management and is final. Now, let's talk about your severance package."

Caution: Do not use the word "layoff" in your termination meeting. This implies an anticipated future return to work, which is not the case in a job elimination.

6. Hand the separation agreement and general release to the employee. Next, explain that signing the document will entitle the employee to the specified separation benefits noted in the agreement. Explain the benefits. Tell the employee that the agreement does not have to be signed right away but must be signed and returned within 21 days (or 45 days if it is a group incentive) or the employee will not receive any severance benefits. Also let the employee know that the separation payments will not be made until the agreement has been signed and the seven-day revocation period has expired.

Note: The 21- or 45-day review period is required by law and gives the employee the opportunity to review the agreement with a legal advisor if he or she so chooses.

7. With some employees these steps can be accomplished without serious interruption. With others there may be a strong emotional reaction to the news. No matter how well the delivery of the information is handled, some employees will react by expressing disbelief, shock, or anger, or by crying or withdrawing. If the employee is visibly upset, say something like this:

"[Name], I can see that you are upset and I can understand that. I want to be sure that you understand the separation package and what you are entitled to at the time of your separation from the company. Do you have any questions about the package or the timing of your departure?"

If the employee withdraws in silence, wait patiently until he or she starts to talk. Or you can help the employee return to the reality of the situation by saying something along these lines:

"[Name], do you understand the benefits that the company is providing in the severance package? Do you have any questions about them? If not, here's what we'll do next."

8. Request that the employee gather any personal belongings in his or her office or work station and leave to consider the agreement. Set a time for the employee to contact you (usually one to two days) to advise whether or not he or she desires to return to work out the remaining period of time prior to the termination date—generally two weeks—or whether he or she desires to be paid two weeks in lieu of notice. Indicate that you will provide a box for his or her personal effects to be picked up at a mutually agreeable time (if the employee does not elect to return to work). Advise the employee to make contact with the outplacement program. The employee should then be asked to leave the building.

Appendix 9

Checklist of Potential Legal Pitfalls in Workforce Reductions

FEDERAL LAWS

Title VII of the Civil Rights Act of 1964

- Prohibits discrimination on the basis of gender, color, race, or religious or national origin.

Age Discrimination in Employment Act (ADEA)

- Prohibits age bias against individuals 40 years of age or older with no cap on age (exceptions: bona fide executives or high-level policy makers can be forced to retire, but they must be at least 65 years old, have worked in their position no less than two years, and be eligible to receive a pension of at least $44,000 annually).

Americans with Disabilities Act (ADA)

- Prohibits discrimination based on a person's disability if, with or without reasonable accommodation, the person is qualified to do the job.

Uniformed Services Employment and Re-Employment Rights Act of 1994

- Prohibits discrimination against military personnel.

Older Workers Benefit Protection Act (OWBPA)

- Employers seeking releases from employees concerning ADEA rights must make sure that the release meets the "knowing and voluntary" standard. To do this, the employer must fulfill the following requirements:

  —The waiver must be part of an agreement between the employer and the em-

ployee, which can be understood by the average individual eligible to participate (e.g., written in plain English).

—It must state the ADEA rights or claims that are being waived.

—The employee cannot waive any rights or claims that may occur after the date
the waiver is executed.

—The waiver must give the older worker consideration above that to which he
or she is already entitled to receive.

—The older worker has to be directed in writing to consult with an attorney
before signing the agreement.

—The individual has to be given at least 21 days to consider the offer. However,
if the waiver is part of an exit incentive program offered to a group or class of
employees, the individual must then be given 45 days to consider the offer.

—After the agreement is executed, the individual has seven days to revoke the
agreement, after which it becomes final.

—If the waiver is part of an exit incentive program, then the employer must
also (1) provide information about the class, unit, or group of individuals
affected and the eligibility factors of the program and the time limits; and (2)
give the individual the job titles and ages of all individuals who are eligible,
as well as those who are not eligible for the program.

Voluntary Early Retirement Incentive Plans

* The OWBPA gives the following examples of voluntary retirement programs or
window plans that are lawful:

—flat dollar amounts

—service-based benefits

—a percentage of salary to all employees above a certain age

—flat dollar increases in pension benefits

—percentage increases in pension benefits

—incentives that credit years of service and/or age

Rehabilitation Act of 1973

* Prohibits discrimination against people with disabilities by government contractors.

* The definition of disabled under this law includes "any person who (1) has a
physical or mental impairment which substantially limits one or more of such
person's major life activities; (2) has a record of such an impairment; or (3) is
regarded as having such an impairment."

Worker Adjustment and Retraining Notification Act (WARN)

* Requires employers to give advance notice of plant closings and mass layoffs,
not only to employees, but also to community leaders and other government
officials.

- WARN defines plant closings as "a permanent or temporary shutdown of a single employment site. . . . Provided that the shutdown results in an employment loss during any 30-day period for 50 or more full-time employees."

- Employment loss is an employment termination, a layoff in excess of six months, or a reduction in hours of work of more than 50% during each month in any six-month period.

- Mass layoff is a reduction in force at a single employment site resulting in an employment loss during any 30-day period for: (1) at least 33% of the full-time employees and at least 50 full-time employees; or (2) at least 500 full-time employees.

- Covers employers of more than 100 employees, excluding part-time employees, or of 100 or more employees who, in the aggregate, work at least 4,000 hours per week, not including overtime.

Advance notice of 60 days must be given to: (1) the union representing employees or, where there is no union, to all affected employees; (2) the state dislocated worker unit; and (3) the chief elected official of the unit or local government within which the plant closing or layoff is to occur.

Employee Retirement Income Security Act (ERISA)

- Prohibits employers from discharging employees who have exercised any right under an employee benefit plan or testified in any inquiry or proceeding relative to ERISA or to the Welfare and Pension Plans Disclosure Act.

- Prohibits employers from discharging workers in order to stop them from getting their vested pension rights. This means that employee terminations based on an attempt to prevent vesting or pension rights violates ERISA.

Consolidated Omnibus Budget Reconciliation Act (COBRA)

- Requires employers to continue group health insurance coverage for terminated employees, their spouses, and dependents for up to 18 months after the employee's termination; for up to 29 months for employees disabled at the time of layoff or termination; and for 18 months for employees who have new jobs but whose new plans do not cover preexisting conditions. Employers pay nothing for the insurance but can charge employees up to 102% for the first 18 months and up to 150% for the last 11 months.

STATE LAWS

Many states and localities have their own laws forbidding employment discrimination. Several states also have laws on termination benefits and timing of payment, as well as insurance provisions.

COMMON LAW

Most of the federal laws do not apply unless the employer meets certain minimum requirements on the number of employees. Most state antidiscrimination statutes and common law claims by employees have no such requirements. Employees also have the right to jury trials and compensatory and punitive damages under state and common law.

The common law includes the following problem areas:

- *Written employment contracts*—provide that the individual can be discharged only for limited and specific reasons.

- *Covenants not to compete*—can be held invalid because of their excessive geographic or time limitations or because they prohibit the employee from using general knowledge gained on the job or because they are not supported by valid consideration.

- *Employment manuals or application forms*—that contain provisions stating that discharge will be for "just cause" only or giving employees implied contractual rights.

- *Employment for a specific term*—cases in which the employee was fired before the end of the term can give rise to a breach of contract lawsuit.

- *Employer misconduct*—in which the employer mishandles the termination process, leaving it open to claims for such wrongs as defamation, fraud, or intentional infliction of emotional distress.

OTHER POTENTIAL EXPOSURES

Other areas ripe for legal exposure include union contracts, policy manuals, benefit plan books, and severance pay policies.

Selected Bibliography

Argyris, C. "Tacit Knowledge and Management." In R. J. Sternberg and J. A. Horvath (eds.), *Tacit Knowledge in Professional Practice: Researcher and Practitioner Perspectives*. Lawrence Erlbaum Associates, 1999, pp. 123–140.

Argyris, C., and R. Putnam et al. *Action Science: Concepts, Methods, and Skills for Research and Intervention*. Jossey-Bass, 1985.

Augustine, N. R. "Reshaping an Industry: Lockheed Martin's Survival Story." *Harvard Business Review* (May–June 1997).

Becker, Brian E., Mark A. Huselid, and David Ulrich. *The HR Scorecard: Linking People, Strategy, and Performance*. Harvard Business School Press, 2001.

Bohm, D. *On Dialogue*. Routledge, 1996.

Bridges, W. *Managing Transitions: Making the Most of Change*. Addison-Wesley, 1991.

Cantoni, C. J. "Mergers and Acquisitions: The Critical Role of Compensation and Culture." *ACA Journal* (Summer 1996).

Cartwright, S., and C. L. Cooper. *Managing Mergers, Acquisitions and Strategic Alliances: Integrating People and Cultures*. Butterworth-Heinemann, 1996.

Childress, J. R., and L. E. Senn. *In the Eye of the Storm: Reengineering Corporate Culture*. The Leadership Press, 1995.

Clemente, M. N., and D. S. Greenspan. *Winning at Mergers and Acquisitions: The Guide to Market-Focused Planning and Integration*. John Wiley & Sons, 1998.

Clemente, M. N., and D. S. Greenspan. *Empowering Human Resources in the Merger and Acquisition Process: Guidance for HR Professionals in the Key Areas of M&A Planning and Integration*. Clemente, Greenspan & Co., 1999.

Davenport, T. O. "The Integration Challenge." *American Management Association International* (January 1998).

De Geus, A. *The Living Company*. Harvard Business School Press, 1997.

Deal, T. E., and A. A. Kennedy. *Corporate Cultures: The Rites and Rituals of Corporate Life*. Perseus Books, 1982.

Drucker, P. *The Effective Executive.* HarperBusiness, 1966/1993.

Drucker, P. F. *Management Challenges for the 21st Century.* HarperCollins, 1999.

Feldman, M. L., and M. F. Spratt. *Five Frogs on a Log: A CEO's Field Guide to Accelerating the Transition Mergers, Acquisitions, and Gut Wrenching Change.* HarperCollins, 1999.

Galpin, T. J. *The Complete Guide to Mergers and Acquisitions: Process Tools to Support M&A Integration.* Jossey-Bass, 2000.

Goffee, R., and G. Jones. "What Holds the Modern Company Together?" *Harvard Business Review* (November 1996).

Heifetz, R. A., and D. L. Laurie. "The Work of Leadership." *Harvard Business Review* (January–February 1997).

Jaffe, D., C. Scott et al. *Rekindling Commitment: How to Revitalize Yourself, Your Work, and Your Organization.* Jossey-Bass, 1994.

Katzenbach, J., and T. R. Team. *Real Change Leaders: How You Can Create Growth and High Performance at Your Company.* Times Books/Random House, 1995.

Katzenbach, J. R. *Teams at the Top.* Harvard Business School Press, 1998.

Kotter, J. P. "Leading Change: Why Transformation Efforts Fail." *Harvard Business Review* (March–April 1995).

Marks, M. L., and P. H. Mirvis. "Rebuilding after the Merger: Dealing with 'Survivor Sickness.' " *Organizational Dynamics* (Autumn 1992).

Marks, M. L., and P. H. Mirvis. *Joining Forces: Making One Plus One Equal Three in Mergers, Acquisitions, and Alliances.* Jossey-Bass, 1998.

Mirvis, P. H., and M. L. Marks. *Managing the Merger: Making It Work.* Prentice Hall, 1992.

Polyani, M. *The Tacit Dimension.* Peter Smith, 1966/1983.

Pritchett, P. *Resistance: Moving beyond the Barriers to Change.* Pritchett & Associates, 1996.

Pritchett, P. *After the Merger: The Authoritative Guide for Integration Success.* McGraw-Hill, 1997.

Right Management Consultants, Inc. (RMA). *Lessons Learned from Mergers & Acquisitions: Best Practices in Workforce Integration—A Research Report.* RMA, 1999.

Schein, E. H. *The Corporate Culture Survival Guide: Sense and Nonsense about Culture Change.* Jossey-Bass, 1999.

Scott, C., and D. Jaffe. *Managing People at Work: Leading People through Organizational Transitions.* Crisp Publications, 1995.

Singer, M. G., and M. J. Fleming (eds.). *Effective Human Resource Measurement Techniques: A Handbook for Practitioners.* Society for Human Resource Management, 1997.

Teal, T. "The Human Side of Management." *Harvard Business Review* (November 1996).

Index

About the Authors

TERESA A. DANIEL is Vice President and Chief Human Resources Officer of Special Metals Corporation in Huntington, West Virginia. She began her career as a corporate transactional attorney, then moved to HR management, where she now specializes in employment law, employee benefits, corporate communications, corporate strategy and policy development, and executive/director compensation. Experienced in the public as well as the private sector, she is the author of numerous journal articles and is an active teacher and lecturer to professional civic groups.

GARY S. METCALF is Senior Manager, InterConnections, LLC, a consultancy in Ashland, Kentucky, specializing in organizational change, particularly those that arise during the course of mergers and acquisitions. He has published a number of journal articles. Formerly a manager and internal consultant in several *Fortune* 200 corporations, he has also been a counselor and family therapist for non-profit community agencies. His most recent work focuses on the theoretical aspects of organizational change and development and their impact on people.